Cycling into Saigon

David R. Cameron and Graham White

Cycling into Saigon:
The Conservative Transition
in Ontario

UBCPress · Vancouver · Toronto

© UBC Press 2000

All rights reserved. No part of this publication may be reproduced, stored in a retrieval system, or transmitted, in any form or by any means, without prior written permission of the publisher, or, in Canada, in the case of photocopying or other reprographic copying, a licence from CANCOPY (Canadian Copyright Licensing Agency), 900 – 6 Adelaide Street East, Toronto, ON M5C 1H6.

Printed in Canada on acid-free paper ∞

ISBN 0-7748-0813-6 (hardcover)
ISBN 0-7748-0814-4 (paperback)

Canadian Cataloguing in Publication Data

Includes bibliographical references and index.
ISBN 0-7748-0813-6 (bound); ISBN 0-7748-0814-4 (pbk)

1. Ontario – Politics and government – 1995- * 2. Ontario – Politics and government – 1990-1995.* 3. Ontario – Politics and government – 1985-1990.* I. White, Graham, 1948- II. Title.
FC3077.2.C35 2000   320.9713'09'049   C00-910734-7
F1058.C35 2000

This book has been published with the help of a grant from the Humanities and Social Sciences Federation of Canada, using funds provided by the Social Sciences and Humanities Research Council of Canada.

UBC Press acknowledges the financial support of the Government of Canada through the Book Publishing Industry Development Program (BPIDP) for our publishing activities.
Canada

We also gratefully acknowledge the support of the Canada Council for the Arts for our publishing program, as well as the support of the British Columbia Arts Council.

Set in Stone by Brenda and Neil West, BN Typographics West
Printed and bound in Canada by Friesens
Copy editor: Susan Broadhurst
Proofreader: Darlene Money
Indexer: Annette Lorek

UBC Press
University of British Columbia
6344 Memorial Road
Vancouver, BC V6T 1Z2
(604) 822-5959
Fax: (604) 822-6083
E-mail: info@ubcpress.ubc.ca
www.ubcpress.ubc.ca

Contents

Preface / vii

1 Transitions / 3

2 The 1985 and 1990 Transitions / 17

3 Transition Building Blocks: Bureaucrats, Politicians, and Mandates / 41

4 Bureaucratic Preparations / 60

5 The Parties Prepare for Power / 76

6 Cycling into Saigon: The Common Sense Revolutionaries Take Over / 102

7 Not Politics but Good Government: Making Transitions Better / 139

Appendices
A Two Public Policy Forum Documents Given to Opposition Parties / 161
B Excerpts from *Mission '97* / 167
C The Liberal Approach to Organization, Management, and Decision-Making in the Government of Ontario / 169
D The Conservative Transition Team / 180
E Political Briefing Material Given to Conservative Ministers / 181
F Speech by Premier Harris to Deputy Ministers, 27 June 1995 / 183
G On the Record. Ensuring a Place in History / 187
Peter DeLottinville and Ian E. Wilson

Notes / 196

Bibliography / 202

Index / 205

Preface

The Conservative Party's decisive victory in the June 1995 Ontario general election stunned the pundits, the other parties, large segments of the Ontario populace, and not a few Conservatives. Here was a party mired in the political doldrums for a decade – light-years behind the Liberal Party in the polls at the campaign's outset – espousing hard-right nostrums widely dismissed as too radical for moderate, mainstream Ontario. Yet it garnered a larger share of the vote – 45 percent – than the Tories had attracted since 1963.

Within a remarkably short period, the new Conservative government, led by Premier Mike Harris, had embarked on unquestionably the most sweeping program of political change in Ontario history. The Harris Conservatives were able to launch these diverse and far-reaching changes so quickly in large measure because the transition from the outgoing NDP government to the incoming government had been so successful. Conservative hands had taken control of the levers of power smoothly and effectively. It had been a singular performance. Indeed, in many ways it had been a textbook transition, although in the light of the number of deputy ministers who lost their jobs in it, one senior official likened some of its elements to a drive-by shooting.

In this book we chronicle and analyze the 1995 Ontario transition. Our account is largely concerned with detailing the efforts by the political parties, the Ontario public service, and the outgoing government to prepare for and implement a transfer of power, and is based on interviews with bureaucrats and politicians directly involved in the transition. We think that those potentially or actually enmeshed in other transition exercises have much to learn from the Ontario case. We also believe, however, that the 1995 transition merits attention for its highlighting of some very basic yet often overlooked facets of our political system.

The peaceful and effective transfer of power from one set of political leaders to another is quite simply an essential feature of our democracy.

Yet how does it take place? Who should take responsibility for ensuring that it is carried out well? What is the proper role of the politicians and what is the proper role of the officials? At another level, questions about transitions are essentially questions about good and effective governance: How do elected political leaders position themselves to implement their policy agendas? What is the appropriate relationship between elected politicians and appointed bureaucrats? Must strongly ideological parties take special steps to realize their goals? What are the unspoken but crucial norms and processes that guide or constrain the actions of senior government figures – political and bureaucratic?

Such questions underpin our study of the 1995 Ontario transition. They make it clear that transitions are about far more than "plumbing" – essential but mundane, low-level administrative practices. Transitions are about the transfer of political authority and the legitimate exercise of political power. They are also about enabling politicians to transform their ideas into state action. These are central issues of democracy and modern governance.

In addressing these issues, we have organized the book as follows. Chapter 1 sets the context of the study by exploring the nature of transitions and their particular functions in democratic and parliamentary settings. This chapter also looks briefly at the Canadian experience with transitions. It concludes with some necessary background to the Ontario election of 1995.

Chapter 2 examines the two previous Ontario transitions, to the Liberals in 1985 and to the NDP in 1990. These exercises offer a useful counterpoint to the 1995 transition.

Chapter 3 looks at some of the key political and constitutional issues that must be considered in coming to grips with transitions. Issues such as the relation between the public servants and the politicians (in opposition and in government) and the nature of parliamentary government in Canada form the heart of this chapter.

The next two chapters set out the preparations made for the transition at the bureaucratic and political levels. In Chapter 4 we look at bureaucratic transition processes from the vantage points of both the central agencies and the line ministries. In Chapter 5 we review the transition activities of both the Conservative and the Liberal parties (although the Liberals never had the opportunity to put their transition plans into practice, their preparatory work was of high quality and warrants attention).

Chapter 6 analyzes how the actual transition unfolded, as the political and bureaucratic streams of preparation came together. It looks at transition both from the perspective of "the centre" and from the perspective of the line ministries.

The final chapter offers conclusions about the 1995 Ontario transition, touching on preparations for a possible transition in 1999, and considers what lessons may be drawn from this episode that may benefit those contemplating or experiencing future transitions.

Supplementing the main text, several useful and important documents are included in the appendices. This material is reproduced in part to flesh out points made in the text but also because – beyond the Ontario-specific details – it provides illustrations of approaches and ideas with wide applicability. Included in the appendices are papers developed by the Public Policy Forum and given to both opposition parties prior to the election, a Liberal paper that is a model of deriving concrete organizational design from abstract political principles, a key Conservative document provided to newly appointed ministers, and an examination by former Ontario Archivist Ian Wilson and Peter DeLottinville, both of the National Archives of Canada, of issues relating to the disposition of official documents in a transition.

An account of how we went about our work is in order at this point. A few weeks before the 1995 election was called, we were invited by Cabinet Secretary David Agnew to take a look at the planning already under way in the Ontario public service in preparation for the transition. While he offered his cooperation and that of his officials, our study had no official status: we were neither formally engaged by the Ontario Government nor offered any funding for the project. Accordingly, no government (or political) figures exercised any supervision or control over any phase of our work.

We were not privy to any transition-related meetings of government officials or of the political parties' transition teams, either before or after the election. However, we did interview a substantial number of bureaucrats, in both the central agencies and line ministries during the election campaign, as preparations were in train. We reinterviewed most of these bureaucrats several months later, both to follow up on how the plans and preparations worked out when the actual transition occurred and to tap into their retrospective assessments of the entire transition exercise. All told, we interviewed ten deputy ministers and another nine public servants who held less senior posts; several of the latter served as their ministries' representatives on Cabinet Office's transition contact team (see Chapter 4).

Most of the party officials involved in the transition were too busy or too leery of our project to agree to interviews until the smoke had cleared after the election and the transition. Once the government was in place, though, both Liberal and Conservative transition team members and other key party figures proved only too willing to share their experiences and insights with us. We interviewed eight members of the Conservative transition team and five who had worked on Liberal transition preparations.

Finally, we interviewed another six persons who fit into none of the categories listed above: these included persons experienced in transitions in other jurisdictions, ministers' political staff, knowledgeable outside observers, and three politicians. Former Liberal Leader Lyn McLeod graciously agreed to be interviewed on the record and allowed us to reproduce excerpts of the paper prepared for her, "The Liberal Approach to Organization, Management, and Decision-Making in the Government of Ontario" (Appendix C). Brenda Elliott and Bob Runciman, ministers in the Harris cabinet whose portfolios we examined in some detail, kindly agreed to be interviewed on the record.

Beyond this, our interviews were conducted on a not-for-attribution basis; all unattributed quotations in the text are taken from these interviews. About half of the interviews included both authors. Most of the interviews took place in 1995 and 1996; a small number were conducted in 1997.

In addition to these formal interviews, we made short phone calls to a number of political and bureaucratic figures involved in the transition to check facts or follow up leads. As well, our work on the transition came up in conversation with still others, who gave us the benefit of their perspectives and experiences. Information gleaned in these ways is treated in the same not-for-attribution manner as that gathered through the formal interviews.

Most of the material in Chapter 2 on the 1985 Liberal and 1990 NDP transitions was gathered in two dozen similar not-for-attribution interviews with political and bureaucratic figures conducted in 1991 and 1992. Much of that chapter was published as "Traffic Pile-ups at Queen's Park: Recent Ontario Transitions," in *Taking Power: Managing Government Transitions*, ed. Donald J. Savoie (Toronto: Institute of Public Administration of Canada and Canadian Centre for Management Development, 1993).

We were given access to documents prepared by the political transition teams and by Ontario Government officials, including briefing material developed by political staff for their party leader, briefing books prepared by Cabinet Office for the incoming cabinet and their advisors, and ministry briefing books given to specific ministers. Though enormously valuable to us, and doubtless to those for whom they were created, little of this material proved particularly sensitive in terms of advice or information of a confidential nature. Indeed, most of the material we saw that had been prepared by the public service was based on information available in public sources, albeit widely scattered and sometimes obscure public sources. In our view, the Ontario public as well as the parties and their leaders would be well served were such information to be made widely available, perhaps through the Ontario Government's Web site, as soon as it is collected and processed.

A preliminary version of our central findings was presented as a paper,

"Cycling into Saigon: The Tories Take Power in Ontario, 1995," at the June 1996 meeting of the Canadian Political Science Association (CPSA) held at Brock University, St. Catharines. The interest generated by this paper, not only among academics but also among journalists, party activists, and public servants, convinced us to proceed with this book. We circulated copies of the paper to many of those we had interviewed and solicited their comments and criticisms; a good many people responded with detailed and thoughtful comments that proved helpful in preparing this book.

A great many people helped us research and write this book. Most we cannot identify by name, since they were promised anonymity when they agreed to be interviewed. Bureaucrats (and former bureaucrats), politicians, political staff and transition team members, and others involved with the transition in some manner were very generous with their time and insights. All were busy; some, those who occupied very senior political and bureaucratic positions, were very busy indeed. It is a remarkable testament to their support for this project, their interest in good governance, and their trust in us that not one person we approached for interviews turned us down. As noted above, a number of people were interviewed twice; some not only were interviewed several times but also responded to follow-up phone calls and requests for additional information, clarification, and interpretation. Without the cooperation and candour of these respondents, the book quite simply would not have been possible. To them, our deep thanks.

At the suggestion of Richard Dicerni, then deputy minister of environment and energy, David Agnew, who was cabinet secretary under the Rae government in 1995, called us to propose the project. We are grateful to both for their sensitivity and support throughout. We trust it will not betray confidentiality if we single out two other individuals who were particularly helpful; anyone familiar with the transition will appreciate that we could not have written this book without their contributions. David Lindsay, Mike Harris's top political aide and big-picture thinker extraordinaire, and Karen Pitre, the heart of the Liberal transition team, submitted to lengthy interviews, provided documents and advice about additional potential interviewees, and reviewed draft chapters of the manuscript. Special thanks also to Lyn McLeod, Bob Runciman, and Brenda Elliott for consenting to on-the-record interviews.

We are very grateful to Ian Wilson, former archivist of Ontario, now national archivist, and Peter DeLottinville for contributing an important original paper on the disposition of governmental and political papers in a transition. Shelly Ehrenworth of the Public Policy Forum provided us with documents prepared for the party leaders and agreed to their publication as an appendix. Lyn McLeod agreed to let us publish the paper prepared for her by Karen Pitre, Michael Kirby, and Tom Zizys.

At UBC Press, it was Ken Carty who initially encouraged us to consider expanding our CPSA paper into a book. As the manuscript took form, Laura Macleod and Emily Andrew provided both advice and support, all the while exhibiting signal tolerance of our inability to meet our self-imposed deadlines. Two anonymous reviewers provided helpful and constructive criticism that led to a number of improvements in the book. So, too, our former colleague Evert Lindquist, now of the University of Victoria, took great interest in our project and made many helpful suggestions.

In the White household, Cathy, Kate, Heather, and Patrick proved well able to contain their excitement about yet another book project but nonetheless contributed essential support in untold intangible ways. Remarkably, the mood of the Cameron family was much the same, although Stevie's support and wise counsel, as always, were invaluable.

Finally, the title of the book? Readers unable to contain their curiosity should flip forward to the opening of Chapter 6.

Cycling into Saigon

1
Transitions

Taking Power

Let us begin with the basics. Politics is about power: who has it, how they got it, what they do with it, how they lose it. Politics is not *only* about power, of course, but no matter the issue, questions of power are never very far below the surface. People like having power; once they have it, they like to keep it, and they do not normally find it easy to give it up. Dictators typically rule for long periods, unless they are toppled, and many are the politicians in a democratic country who continue to run for public office until defeated, or until faced with certain defeat.

Constitutional governments fashion norms, rules, political practices, and institutions designed to tame and regulate the exercise of power and to provide for its orderly transfer. As much as possible, they seek to ensure that its exercise serves the interests of the bulk of the population who do *not* hold power. The trappings of constitutional government mediate the emergence of political authority, or the right to rule. We sometimes speak of power being "clothed" with authority, but in reality the relationship between power and authority is much more intimate and synthetic, for in clothing power with authority the nature of power itself is transformed and its exercise is profoundly altered. A tyrant or dictator may seize power but cannot seize legitimacy, for that is something that is granted, not grasped, and it depends on the recognition of others, not on the will or brute force of the political actor. Power without authority exists as long as the capacity to retain it continues; power *with* authority – the legitimate exercise of power – derives its force and its durability in part from the act of recognition itself. The sovereign is sustained not simply by the sword, but by the citizens' willing consent.

Conceptually, therefore, a transition, the taking of power, can be an act of one or two dimensions. An unconstitutional transition is an act of one dimension, in which power is taken, pure and simple. A constitutional transition is an act of two dimensions, in which power is taken by those recognized as having won the right to rule; power is taken as authority is granted. Constitutional transitions also entail the giving up of power by those who recognize and accept that they have lost the authority to rule. The event may be seamless and unitary in appearance, but analytically it is binary.

The distinction between these two kinds of acts – and, behind them, the distinction between unconstitutional and constitutional government – is in evidence throughout the contemporary political world, as new states are formed on the ruins of the old and unfree societies dismantle old regimes and seek to replace them with democratic systems based on popular consent. The transition from one regime to another – in which one kind of political system is supplanted by another that is qualitatively different – is a more fundamental matter than a transition in government power within a given regime. Regime change has proven to be a difficult course to navigate, and countries in the throes of such transformations can exhibit elements of both the old and the new systems operating awkwardly side by side for a time. In recognition of this fact, Freedom House, the American think tank that attempts to chart the progress of liberty in the world, places countries into three categories: free, unfree, and partially free. In Russia, several months prior to the 1996 presidential election, a constitutional lawyer at Moscow State University was asked by one of the authors if she thought that Boris Yeltsin would win the upcoming election. She replied, "Yes, I think he will. But if he thinks he won't, there probably won't be an election." Clearly, the roots of constitutional government have yet to take hold deeply in Russian soil.

Nestled within the transition from one regime to another, in such circumstances as these, is the process by which governments themselves are changed. One of the vital signs of the presence or absence of constitutional government is the way in which the political community handles the reassignment of government power. The capacity to effect an orderly shift of government power and authority presupposes a distinction between the political office and the officeholder – between the monarchy and the person who is king or queen, between the prime ministership and the politician who is holding the office, between the presidency and the sitting president. The office continues while the officeholders come and go. A transition from this perspective, then, is a change set within a framework of continuity: the transfer of the responsibilities and prerogatives of office from one person to another. A government may be understood as an interlocking set of offices, and a government transition transfers responsibility for this set of offices from one group of people to another. One of the most reliable indicators of constitutional political order is the capacity of the regime to manage changes of government in an orderly, peaceful, and routine fashion.

Behind the distinction between office and officeholder lies another: the distinction between the state and the government of the day. Unless the authority in question is charismatic, and therefore based directly on the personality of the leader, the right to rule derives from the structures of the state, from the offices and functions it creates, and from the processes it provides for the ordering and channelling of political power. Government itself is a concrete manifestation of the state, and is the principal means by which state sovereignty is activated. Governments come and go with the political tides; the state is more stable and enduring, if more abstract.

Government Transitions

The transfer of government power is one of the most delicate moments in the life of any political order. If politics is about power – getting it and keeping it – a transition is the moment when those who have power, give it up, and when those who seek it, take it. It is an occasion of high sensitivity, like the first handshake in the forest.

Transitions in constitutional regimes are concentrated points of light in the political system, exposing as few other moments or occasions do the deeper values of the political order, the first-order principles beneath the ideologies that even the fiercest political enemies hold in common. Sovereignty is in transit: the affairs of state are momentarily arrested as they are transferred from the care of one leader or set of politicians to the keeping of another.

Government transitions in a constitutional order may best be understood by reference to what they are not. They are not a species of coup d'état, in which one group takes power from another by violence or the threat of violence. Nor are they shifts in the political regime, involving the replacement of one set of political institutions with another, as in the conversion from presidential to parliamentary models, or from colonial to self-governing status. Still less are they revolutions, which in their fullest expression not only overturn the political order but also involve social and economic upheaval.

An essential requirement of a constitution is that it establish authoritatively the rules for government transition. Elaborate laws of succession, for example, regulate transitions in monarchies. The king is dead, long live the king; but who will be king? The rules of royal succession in the United Kingdom are worked out to the nth possible successor to the throne, which shows just how seriously the shift in the political power of kings and queens was taken to be when they still possessed active sovereignty. This seemingly excessive elaboration of transition arrangements grew out of the painful realization of what could happen to the realm if powerful contenders vied for the crown. A failed succession, a botched transition, was at times the prelude to civil war. All too often the death of an entrenched autocratic leader brings on a succession crisis and profound political problems.

In democratic countries, changes in government after general elections are the chief means by which political change is consciously effected. Clearly, major policy shifts may occur as a result of the pressure of external events or through re-evaluation of existing priorities and approaches, and as such may be introduced in these circumstances by a sitting government. But insofar as a political society has the capacity autonomously to consider and implement new policies and chart new directions in governance, the principal mechanism for doing so is the replacement of one government with another, the assumption of power by a new leader and/or a new political party that has emerged victorious in a general election. This is the device that injects new blood, new energy, and new direction into a democratic system of government. Similarly, declining to elect a new leader and party into office is the device by which an electorate supports continuity, rewards good management, and authorizes incremental change.

The transitions that concern us are thus the peaceful, institutionalized, constitutionally sanctioned transfers of power and authority within democratic regimes from one set of elected leaders to another. In highlighting these positive characteristics of transitions we do not mean to imply that all transitions are of a piece; clearly some are carried out much more effectively than others. Accordingly, as we prepare to evaluate particular transitions, it is useful to address more precisely what transitions entail in our democratic society.

What Is a Transition?

Something that is conceptually akin to a transition, as we have been employing the term, occurs when a government party changes leaders and a new premier takes over, or when a party is returned to office with a new electoral mandate and perhaps a new policy direction or a different cabinet line-up. We limit our attention, however, to instances of one political party supplanting another.

When do transitions begin and end? It is possible to think of transitions in a temporally restricted fashion; for example, as the period between the election and the swearing-in of the new government, or in an expansive fashion, as the period beginning with the preparation for government, which often occurs well before the election campaign begins, to the end of the incoming government's "settling-in" period, which often can extend up to the end of its first year in office.[1] It is probably a mistake to attempt to define government transitions too precisely in terms of time periods, rather than in terms of the nature of the activity and the process itself. In this book, we think of a government transition in fairly simple terms:

as the process by which a new government assumes responsibility for the levers of power. This means getting into a position to take and implement decisions, but not the decisions themselves. Thus we do not include everything that a new government does in its early days. The policy and political decisions of the new government are not, per se, part of the transition; getting into a position to take them, however, is.

Transitions are composed of two distinct stages and several streams of activity. The first stage, the preparation stage, occurs in the period prior to the election, when the various actors are readying themselves for a possible change of government. It is marked by several streams of activity that traditionally do not touch one another, or touch one another only slightly. The political party or parties that see themselves as having a shot at dislodging the government will typically engage in some planning and preparatory work; and the bureaucracy will ready itself, with a greater or lesser degree of sophistication, for whatever might result from the election. The second stage, the actual taking of power, starts after the election. At this point the activity of unsuccessful parties ceases, and the streams of activity of the successful party and the bureaucracy converge. Taking power is pre-eminently a matter of assuming control of the machinery of government; in a parliamentary democracy this means, for all practical purposes, creating a cabinet of responsible and effective ministers and gaining control of the bureaucracy. If, in an unconstitutional coup d'état, the first thing that the new regime wants to control is the means of public communication – the radio and television stations, the newspapers, the airports, and the train stations – in a constitutional coup, which is what a government transition after an election amounts to, the top priority is to secure the direction of the means of governing – the public service.

Transitions in Canada

Recognizing the importance of government transitions, researchers and analysts in the United States have devoted serious attention to this subject and have built a substantial literature on it. Much less work has been done on transitions in parliamentary systems.[2] The reasons for this discrepancy likely lie in the fundamental differences between the American congressional-presidential system and the Westminster cabinet-parliamentary system. The parliamentary system permits the voter to elect a government, not just a chief executive officer who will then create a government, as does the US president. The parliamentary party system normally makes it clear who the new governing team will be at the point that the election is won. If it is the party that has been the official opposition (as is typically the case), both the leader and the senior party politicians will probably be reasonably well known to the electorate, making the taking of power and the naming of the cabinet more predictable or routine events. Moreover, the scale and complexity of American transitions differ qualitatively from those of parliamentary transitions primarily by virtue of the hundreds of top-level bureaucrats who must be recruited to replace those dismissed because of their political links to the outgoing administration. In parliamentary transitions, the permanent officials are key players in making transitions work, whereas in the US, much of the transition is about replacing senior officials.

In addition, the informality and the practices of confidentiality that characterize most systems following the British parliamentary model may discourage intensive inquiry into the transition phenomenon. More speculatively, it may be that a constitutional monarchy, in which the principle of continuity is represented by the crown as head of state, makes shifts in who holds government power seem less remarkable. In the United States, the presidency combines the functions of both the head of state and the head of government, making the election of a new person to that office the British-parliamentary equivalent of the selection of a new prime minister and the accession to the throne of a new monarch combined.

In any event, when we turn our attention to Canada, the lack of writing by scholars and practitioners alike immediately becomes apparent. Considering the frequency and the importance of government transitions, surprisingly little is known about taking power in Canada. Canadians, at the federal, provincial, and territorial levels, have known over 100 transitions since Confederation.[3] Yet the only book about them is *Taking Power: Managing Government Transitions,* a 1993 collection of studies edited by Donald Savoie. This volume contains five analytical or comparative chapters, one on the 1993 federal transition and the rest on transitions in Quebec, Ontario, Manitoba, and British Columbia. Beyond this the published academic literature on Canadian transitions consists of a smattering of journal articles and book chapters. Michelmann and Steeves offer a detailed look at the Devine government's purge of the Saskatchewan civil service when it took office in 1982.[4] Former Saskatchewan Premier Allan Blakeney and academic Sandford Borins devote a chapter of their book, *Political Management in Canada,* to the question of transition.[5] Plasse examined the 1976 Quebec transition through a focus on the ministerial *chefs de cabinet*.[6] Bourgault and Dion have written a series of papers examining transitions in Ottawa and Quebec City from various theoretical perspectives, but primarily focusing on the roles of deputy ministers, ministers, and political staff.[7]

This literature covers a number of cases spanning the country – though not, significantly, over a long period: only in the 1980s did scholars turn their attention to transition – under a variety of circumstances. Common to all, however, is the attempt to sort out relations among a complex set of variables falling into three broad categories: party ideology/program, government structures, and people. Transition efforts attempt to bring all three into balance, but inevitably the most problematic and important aspects of transitions are those involving people: politicians (and their staff) and bureaucrats. Party ideology, as manifested in the agenda that the incoming government party wishes to implement, may be ill defined or crystal clear, and it may be moderate and incremental or sweeping in scope and speed. However, although political realities may over time bring about modifications to the agenda and the party's commitment to it, during transition they are little subject to change. As well, a striking feature evident from the literature is the infrequency of major structural change. Few incoming administrations do other than tacitly agree to work within the structural arrangements they have inherited from the previous government; almost all tinker with some features of government organization, but few attempt to reshape it to any substantial degree. In some cases this reflects lack of interest and understanding of government structure, while in other cases the new government knowingly leaves structures largely intact, calculating that the potential gains from extensive reorganization are outweighed by (or lack the priority of) other considerations, at least during the period of transition.

Thus the greatest practical opportunities for change involve the personnel of government. Opportunities, however, are not always seized effectively, nor are changes always positive. Bourgault and Dion, for example, examine the conflict that beset the first years of the Mulroney government as a result of the establishment during the transition of "chiefs of staff" in ministers' offices. The idea was to impose these high-powered political figures between ministers and their senior bureaucratic officials and thereby to alter their relations and the role of the permanent officials.[8] This illustration is provided not to draw attention to the experiment's failure, or to the cause of its failure, but to underline the centrality of the relationship between politicians and bureaucrats.

If the literature thus inclines us to highlight the interaction of key political and bureaucratic players, it also reminds us to do so within the context of party program and formal government structures. The 1995 Tory transition is best understood in terms of how the transition planners integrated these sets of concerns and in terms of the potential friction points between them.

Our Study

Savoie summarizes the situation aptly in his observation that "there exists very little literature on transitions in Canada. How they are planned, who participates, and how they are executed often appears to be shrouded in a veil of secrecy."[9]

Our volume contributes to the literature on Canadian transition by studying the 1995 Ontario transition when Mike Harris's Tories took power after the 8 June election and began to implement their "Common Sense Revolution." Unlike most previous transition studies, it is based on interviews and information gathering that occurred before and during, as well as after, the election. Typically, transition studies have had to content themselves with looking back at the event after it has occurred. Our methods and approach are described more fully in the Preface.

During much of Canada's history, planning for the taking of power appears to have been a rather casual matter for politicians and party activists, and readying the affairs of state for the possible arrival of a new government seems to have been a relatively informal process for senior public officials. When government was smaller and simpler, the need to engage in elaborate preparation was much reduced. In addition, when parties stayed in office for a generation or more – as has happened often over the course of Canadian history – the inclination to devote special attention to the process of transition was understandably reduced.

In recent years, however, the situation has been changing. For some time, major federal political parties and the federal public service have engaged in sophisticated transition planning, and this practice has been growing in several provincial jurisdictions. This is true not just of large provinces such as Ontario and Quebec but also of smaller jurisdictions such as New Brunswick.[10] Given the pressure on politicians to make good quickly on their promises, together with the expectation that the bureaucracy will deliver efficient, flexible public service, we see little reason to believe that this trend will wane in the foreseeable future.

A fuller understanding of transitions would be beneficial in three respects. First, as crucial and recurrent events in a democracy, transitions need to be examined and accounted for as integral to the process by which free people govern themselves. Simply put, effective transitions are about good government and are thus fitting and appropriate subjects for academic inquiry. The relation between politicians and bureaucrats, long a central concern of students of government and public administration, comes into particularly sharp focus during transitions. Second, practical benefits can be derived from improved understanding. Transitions can be done well or badly. The act of taking power is not in itself ideological or partisan. How it is done may well serve partisan purposes, but a successful transition has more to do with planning, organization, technical considerations, and sheer good luck than with ideological purity. To the extent that this is so, one jurisdiction can learn from another: a political party can draw advantage from understanding how another party handled the taking of power, regardless of partisan stripe; public servants in one part of the country can organize their transition work more effectively, knowing how it has been done elsewhere. Third, greater public discussion of the phenomenon may make it easier to introduce reforms to improve the quality of transitions without in any way undermining the principles of parliamentary government. Based on our analysis, we propose means of institutionalizing communication channels among the key transition players. In sum, our intention is to place a good deal of emphasis on the practical lessons that might be drawn from the Ontario experience; that will be the focus of the closing chapter.

Let us now set the context for our analysis of transitions in Ontario by sketching out briefly some of the salient features of the province's recent political experience.

The Ontario Context

On several counts the 1995 Ontario election proved a remarkable affair, not least because for the first time in living memory, virtually everyone – politicians as well as pundits and voters – expected it to bring about a change of government. While this elemental fact held obvious implications for transition planning, it is not the only feature of note that needs to be understood in order to place the Tory transition in context. By way of illustration, the 1995 election was the third in a decade in which a party entering the campaign with a seemingly insurmountable lead in the polls failed to register a victory. The following thumbnail sketch of recent Ontario politics highlights the developments and events most germane to our treatment of recent transitions.

For many years, of course, transitions were unknown in Ontario for the very good reason that the government did not change. From 1943 to 1985, the Progressive Conservative Party governed the province without interruption; wags dubbed Ontario "the longest surviving one-party state this side of Albania." The long Tory hegemony depended on a complex confluence of factors: politically astute leadership; competent, moderate, responsive government that embodied the apparently contradictory principles suggested by the party's curious appellation, "progressive conservative"; a formidable political organization; the benefits of having a party of a different political stripe hold power in Ottawa for much of that time; a perennially divided opposition (which produced that political *rara avis*, a stable three-party system); the well-known distorting effects of the first-past-the-post electoral system, which routinely converted a minority electoral following (usually below 45 percent of the vote) into comfortable legislative majorities; and a prolonged period of prosperity in which Canada's richest province "shared all the booms and only some of the busts" of Canada's post-war economic history.[11]

Thus during this era, despite brave words come election time, "the opposition, in their heart, never really imagined they would one day be the government," as one long-time Liberal MPP put it.[12] In consequence, when newly chosen Tory Leader Frank Miller called an election for 2 May 1985 with his party cruising at over 50 percent in the polls, the conventional wisdom was that the only outcome in doubt was the contest for second place. Yet it soon became evident that the Conservatives' magic had deserted them. Miller and his supporters had pushed the party too far to the right, effectively abandoning the middle of the political spectrum to David Peterson's Liberals. The Tory political machine, which had not been maintained in top running order during the later years of Bill Davis's premiership (1971-85), was perceptibly weakened by bitter internal division over Davis's stunning decision to overturn decades of Tory dogma by granting full public funding to Roman Catholic separate schools. And the usually sure-footed Conservatives ran an ineffective, at times inept, campaign.[13]

When the election dust had settled, the Conservatives held a slim margin in seats – fifty-two to the Liberals' forty-eight – but were unable to hold on to power when, after protracted negotiations, the NDP threw their twenty-five seats behind the Liberals, making David Peterson premier. The Liberals and the New Democrats signed a unique "Accord," in which the NDP undertook to support the Liberals for two years in return for the Liberals' public commitment to a detailed policy agenda and a guarantee not to call an election for two years. The Accord period of Liberal minority rule – it was not, as it was often described, a coalition since the NDP held no cabinet seats – witnessed extensive policy innovation and government activism that proved popular with the voters. Thus, when Peterson pulled the electoral plug just weeks after the two-year deal with the NDP had expired, the only real issue was how handsomely the people would reward the Liberals. Quite handsomely indeed, as it turned out: with 47 percent of the popular vote the Liberals took ninety-five seats to the NDP's nineteen and the Tories' sixteen.

The second Liberal mandate (1987-90) unfolded rather differently from the first. A senior public servant seconded into Peterson's office summed it up aptly in remarking, "I've never seen a government age so quickly."[14] Though the province continued to enjoy remarkable prosperity, with annual growth rates of 5, 6, and 7 percent, the Liberals seemed to have shot their reformist bolt during the Accord years, so that the government lacked a clear policy agenda.[15] Peterson's preoccupation with matters constitutional in the latter stages of his mandate contributed to the drift. A series of mini-scandals sapped the government's energy; though none was very serious by itself, they all contributed to an image of impropriety and unsavoury ties to powerful interests. Still, the opposition parties seemed in no position to capitalize on the Liberals' vulnerability; the Conservatives were dispirited and disorganized, and the NDP had not captured public support to any significant degree. Indeed, NDP Leader Bob Rae had privately made plans to quit provincial politics following what he fully expected to be his third disappointing defeat. The Liberals thus began their 1990 campaign with a commanding lead in the polls.[16]

In the phrase that would tellingly reappear with respect to the Liberals in 1995, their support in 1990 proved "a mile wide but an inch deep." The Liberals ran a weak campaign and suffered not only from attacks on their integrity (reinforced by a widespread public perception that their early election call, after barely three years of a five-year mandate, was nothing more than a cynical power grab) but also from Peterson's close association with the disastrous implosion of the Meech Lake Accord a few weeks before they headed to the hustings. The NDP ran a strong, largely error-free campaign but won as much by default – for many electors, the Liberals and the Conservatives were discredited, while the NDP had never been given the opportunity to govern – as by converting voters to its policies and programs. As well, for once the New Democrats were extraordinarily blessed by the electoral system, which transformed their vote share of just under 38 percent into a comfortable legislative majority (74 of 130 seats).[17]

If Bob Rae and his New Democrats swept to power through good fortune, their luck deserted them almost immediately. By the time they took office, Ontario had already entered the worst prolonged economic downturn since the Depression, leaving the NDP with declining revenues, soaring social welfare costs (exacerbated by a federal policy on transfer payments that singled out Ontario for especially punitive treatment), and precious little fiscal room to manoeuvre. The severity of the recession might not have necessarily sealed the NDP's fate, but the range of adverse political circumstances they faced – some of their own making, some not – virtually assured that Bob Rae would be a one-term premier. The NDP made a series of decisions that cut into their traditional base of support, most notably an embarrassing reversal of their commitment to introduce a comprehensive public auto insurance scheme and the well-intentioned but politically disastrous "social contract" exercise, which cut public spending in part by abrogating collective agreements with powerful public sector unions. The unrealistic expectations held by the party's social activist allies as to what an NDP government could and should do led inevitably to disappointment and disillusion. At the same time, the NDP had to contend with some of the most virulent anti-government interest group campaigns ever mounted in Ontario politics.[18]

Even aside from these pervasive problems, it was scarcely imaginable that the NDP could repeat its rich harvest of seats with so few voters as had favoured them in 1990. Nor was it at all likely that the essentially urban NDP could hold the dozen rural or semi-rural seats that had secured its victory the last time around. Finally, the NDP, which had come to power in no small measure on its reputation for integrity, found itself enmeshed in a debilitating series of minor scandals. Where the Liberals' peccadilloes had mostly involved dubious fundraising practices, NDP ministers proved clean financially but subject to repeated lapses of judgment that called into question both their probity and their competence. As much as anything in politics is preordained, the NDP were certain to be defeated when they went to the people. But who would replace them?

For many, the answer was so obvious that the question was hardly worth posing. The NDP's decline in the polls from mid-1991 on was matched by Liberal gains. Most of Peterson's best ministers had been re-elected in 1990, giving the Liberals a strong and experienced front bench. Moreover, the Liberals could reasonably expect most voters to associate their recent time in office not with petty scandals but with unbridled good times. Even the omens from Ottawa were promising: having vanquished the reviled Mulroney Conservatives (albeit under new leader Kim Campbell) in the 1993 general election, Jean Chrétien's Liberal government continued to enjoy strong popularity among Ontario voters. The Ontario Liberal Party was well financed and well organized.

Two areas did concern some Liberals: leadership and policy. In 1992 the Liberals had become the first major Ontario party to choose a woman as its leader. In a toughly fought, extremely close battle, Thunder Bay MPP Lyn McLeod, who had been first elected in 1987 and who had held mid-range portfolios in the Peterson cabinet, defeated veteran MPP Murray Elston, one of the most senior and respected of Peterson's ministers. McLeod proclaimed herself a proponent of a "new" non-confrontational politics of inclusion and consensus building, but – as is typical of Ontario opposition leaders – made little impact on the public; shortly before the election, half of those who planned to vote Liberal were unable to identify the party's leader.[19] As journalist John Ibbitson wrote, "Most people who had met Lyn McLeod found her intelligent, warm, committed and capable. The problem was, most people in Ontario hadn't met Lyn McLeod."[20] On the policy front, although party committees were at work churning out earnest policy papers, the popular impression was that the Liberals didn't particularly stand for anything and were waiting to assume power by default as the NDP government self-destructed.

And why not? The Tories posed no threat. They had managed to stave off annihilation in the 1990 election, but only just. Millions of dollars in debt, the party had closed its provincial office and laid off its permanent staff as economy measures. Leader Mike Harris was dismissed by opponents and pundits as a former golf pro who had made little mark in his time in the legislature; his wooden speaking style and unfashionably right-wing views also told against him. The Tory caucus was a largely rural rump short on experience and profile – all of the senior ministers of the Davis era were long departed. Throughout the entire NDP term, the Conservatives languished at or below 25 percent in the polls. The Tories apparently hammered the final nail into their own coffin when they released their political manifesto, *The Common Sense Revolution,* in May 1994. Bad enough that they had defied conventional wisdom by exposing their platform to scrutiny and attack far in advance of the election, but, many observers concluded, the uncompromising hard-right tone of the document was simply unacceptable to the vast majority of Ontario voters.

When the election was finally called, for 8 June 1995, the common assumption of an easy Liberal victory found ready support: a typical poll in the first week of the campaign put the Liberals at 52 percent, the Tories at 26 percent, and the NDP at 17 percent.[21] And yet, all was not what it seemed on the surface. The Tories (who disavowed the term "Conservative" lest they be tarred with lingering public distaste for their federal brethren) were in the final stages of a remarkable return from the political scrap heap.[22]

The party, which had been effectively taken over by a small band of young, committed ideologues, had paid off most of its debt, rebuilt its organization, and established a strong policy agenda. Strategists had crafted a clear, straightforward image for the party and the leader and had worked out in intricate detail a plan for setting the agenda during the campaign and positioning itself to reap the rewards. Party polling and focus groups confirmed not only that *The Common Sense Revolution* had struck a positive chord with many Ontarians but also that significant electoral gains were to be made by pushing such political "hot buttons" as anti-welfare sentiment and opposition to employment equity. Once the election was under way, the Tories' carefully laid plans were executed with almost flawless precision.

If the Conservatives' brilliantly conceived and expertly conducted campaign did just about everything right, the Liberals' campaign was misdirected and prone to error. Liberal strategists underestimated the Conservatives until well into the campaign, and they incorrectly believed that they could repeat the impressive success of the 1993 federal Liberal campaign built around unveiling a "red book" of detailed policy statements. The Liberals entered the election without making it clear why people should vote for them rather than against the other parties. Their leader was little known yet saddled with a "flip-flop" image based on a well-publicized reversal of her stand on gay rights. The Liberals' red book policies came across either as confusingly complex or as watered-down versions of the Tories' Common Sense Revolution proposals.

The New Democrats were never really in the running and mounted a curious "no promises" campaign, whose main objective was ensuring the party's continued existence as a viable political force.

By midway through the campaign, the Tories were surging in the polls while the Liberals' support had crumbled. For a few days, a minority government – perhaps Tory, perhaps Grit – seemed possible, but the Conservatives continued to widen their lead over the Liberals. Election night saw 82 Conservatives returned on 45 percent of the vote; the Liberals garnered 31 percent of the vote, good for 30 seats; the NDP managed 17 seats on 21 percent of the vote; 1 seat went to an independent.

Mike Harris would be premier and his Common Sense Revolution would transfix Ontario. The Tories had come from nowhere to capture the government of Canada's wealthiest, most populous province, but surely a party so far distant from power so recently would be unprepared to govern. In the event, they proved extraordinarily ready to take power. As in the electoral realm, the Conservatives demonstrated remarkable foresight and self-confidence in their transition planning, as will be seen in subsequent chapters.

But before examining the Tory transition, let us set the stage by sketching out Ontario's experience with two previous transitions, in 1985 and 1990.

2
The 1985 and 1990 Transitions

Until 1985, Ontario politicians and bureaucrats saw government transitions as exotic rituals that happened elsewhere. The most recent Ontario transition had taken place in 1943; since then, the Progressive Conservatives had ruled Ontario with scarcely a serious challenge to their hegemony. Then in barely five years, the unthinkable happened twice: well-entrenched parties lost power in astonishing political reversals.

This chapter examines the transitions that occurred in 1985 when David Peterson's Liberals took over from the Conservatives under Frank Miller and in 1990 when the Peterson government was itself vanquished by Bob Rae's New Democrats. The Liberal transition was by any standard remarkably smooth and successful, though good luck played almost as prominent a role in its success as good management. By contrast, one key participant aptly dubbed the NDP transition "the transition from hell." In large measure, the difficulties that the New Democrats encountered stemmed from their ambitious goals, their anti-establishment ideology, and their inexperience. In addition, the public service's response to the NDP, and the often-strained relations that developed between the NDP and the bureaucracy, contributed to the roughness of the transition. The role played by the public service in the 1990 transition stands in sharp contrast to the roles it played in 1985 and 1995.

An account of the two preceding transitions thus provides necessary background and context for the 1995 transition, and also offers useful insights into the transition process generally. The chapter begins with a discussion of some key similarities and differences between the two transitions and then examines how they unfolded, with special attention to the parties' relations with the bureaucracy and their moves towards government restructuring.[1]

Similarities and Differences

Conservative Frank Miller and Liberal David Peterson both called elections while holding seemingly insurmountable leads in the polls. Both fell victim to a popular mood for change and to inept campaign management the dimensions of which were evident only in retrospect.[2] Thus both in 1985 and in 1990, the eventual winners were totally unprepared to govern. In both instances internal party polls indicated that victory was possible only about a week before election day. Accordingly, neither the Liberals nor the NDP had devoted a scintilla of thought to the question of transition until immediately before the vote. At that, precious little attention was devoted to transition until after the ballots were counted. Not only were both new governments unprepared, they were completely inexperienced and staggeringly ignorant about the operation of the Ontario Government.

So, too, the bureaucracy was almost entirely unprepared for changes of government either in 1985 or in 1990. Like everyone else, the bureaucrats expected the Miller and Peterson governments to be easily returned and were caught as short as the parties when major transition exercises had to be mounted; in 1990 some deputy ministers were away on vacation during the election.

These similarities tend to obscure fundamental differences between the two transitions, many of which derived from differences in party ideology and in party culture. In terms of the role of the state in the economy, the proper mix of social welfare measures, and the like, the ideological differences between the Ontario Liberal Party and the Ontario NDP are substantial. New Democrats prefer a more interventionist state and envision society in quite different ways than Liberals. Once in office the NDP wanted to make substantially more far-reaching policy changes than had the Liberals.

Also significant are differences between the Liberals and the NDP in orientation to the governing process. In opposition, the Liberals had criticized the Conservatives for patronage, for a secretive style of governing, and for excluding those outside the Anglo-Celtic mainstream of Ontario society. In these realms, the Liberals did make significant efforts to operate differently. Still, their philosophy of governance did not differ greatly from that of the Conservatives; they were generally comfortable with the structures and processes they inherited. As a party of social activists, suspicious of established centres of power, the NDP was much less accepting of the traditional operations of government. New Democrats believe that they bring a "different approach" to governing that is neither understood nor accepted by the senior bureaucracy. The hostility they exhibit towards the public service is rooted in philosophy and is thus more difficult to dispel than the Liberals' suspicion of partisan tendencies in the bureaucracy. (Right-wing parties often exhibit a similar hostility to the public service, though its roots are quite different, reflecting a general distaste for big, interventionist government.)

Another key difference between the two transitions lay in the circumstances of the new governments coming into office. The NDP victory in 1990 was clear and unequivocal; with 74 of 130 seats the NDP knew immediately that it would be forming a majority government. On election night 1985, by contrast, it initially seemed that the ruling Conservatives would hang on to power; they took fifty-two seats to the Liberals' forty-eight and the NDP's twenty-five. (In 1975, the Tories had managed to retain office with marginally fewer seats.) Protracted inter-party negotiations produced an unusual Liberal-NDP "Accord" that spelled out the terms of NDP support for a Liberal government by setting out a long list of policy commitments. The Accord's importance for the Liberal transition can hardly be underestimated: it established, with unmistakable force and clarity, the government's policy agenda and priorities. This effectively removed the need for the incoming government to spend time and energy sorting out its policy priorities, and it gave clear direction to the bureaucracy; as one senior bureaucrat put it, "The deputy ministers just had to do what was in the Accord." The direction provided by the Accord greatly simplified the Liberal transition. By contrast, the NDP's 1990 "Agenda for People" had been hurriedly assembled during the election campaign with no thought that it might have to be implemented. It was a rendering of NDP policy views for electoral purposes, not a blueprint for governing. And to the extent that the Accord and "Agenda for People" reflected the ideological direction of the Liberal and NDP governments, respectively, the Accord was clearly a more mainstream document, calling for less sweeping change.

The Liberals also had the luxury of a relatively long period for their transition. In 1990 the NDP government was sworn in on 1 October, twenty-five days after the election. In 1985, election day was 2 May, but because of the political manoeuvring around the Accord and the Tories' attempt to retain power even after their defeat was assured, the Liberal government did not take office until 26 June, some fifty-five days later. (By some standards, of course, even twenty-five days constitutes a very long transition; the British prime minister, for example, is expected to vacate 10 Downing Street the day after losing an election.)

The task of dealing with inexperienced MPPs – introducing them to the arcane ways of legislature, setting up their offices, and evaluating their talent was far more difficult for the New Democrats than for the Liberals. Of forty-eight Liberals elected in 1985, twenty-five were new to the legislature, whereas fifty seven of the seventy-four New Democratic MPPs were first-term members.

Finally, the Liberals enjoyed the great good fortune to be coming into office just as the provincial economy, and thus the provincial coffers, was beginning a remarkable expansion. By contrast, the hapless NDP began its term just as Ontario was descending into the worst economic downturn since the Great Depression.

The Liberal Transition

The Liberal transition had two distinct organizational bases. A small group of highly experienced political insiders, most of whom had been with Peterson in opposition, made the key decisions. A larger, more formally organized Transition Advisory Group dealt with specific projects and handled many of the details of the transition. This arrangement proved highly effective.

It was not until it had become clear – nearly three weeks after the election – that a deal would be struck with the NDP to vault the Liberals into office that the transition team began to take shape. The idea for the team came directly from David Peterson. He recognized from his business experience that he needed what one associate called "an outside board" to assist with the transition. Peterson asked an old friend, Martin Connell, head of Conwest Explorations, to chair the team. Beyond personal friendship, Connell had no political ties to Peterson and was not a member of the Liberal Party. He knew little about how Queen's Park operated. He did, however, enjoy Peterson's complete trust and was, in the words of one member of the team, "a terrific manager."

The Transition Advisory Group's contribution lay not solely in its operational functions; it also carried great public symbolic value. Its ten members were carefully chosen to be representative not only of the province's regions but also of "the new face of Ontario," which the Liberals were targeting politically. Included were several women, a black, an Aboriginal, and a South Asian: a striking symbol of the Liberals' commitment to open the Ontario political process to previously excluded groups and interests.

Six working groups were established: on structure of government; staffing of ministers' offices and the Premier's Office; conflict of interest; briefing material for ministers; moving-day logistics; and organization of an orientation seminar for ministers. A number of the team members served on more than one working group. Liaison with Peterson took place chiefly through Gordon Ashworth, one of his principal advisors. Staff support for the team was limited; the Liberal Opposition Office provided some assistance, and a group of volunteers developed a computerized database of job applicants. Although the entire team met weekly, most of the work was carried out on an individual basis; members concentrated on their specific assignments and often had little contact with each other. Connell's office and the Liberals' Queen's Park offices were the principal work sites; several of the transition team members effectively worked full time in the month leading up to the swearing-in.

With the Accord in place, the Liberals' policy priorities were clearly settled. The transition team, accordingly, was concerned with policy only insofar as one of the working groups was assembling briefing material for new ministers (a compilation of government-produced summaries of existing policy and Liberal campaign promises and public statements). Rather than develop policy or set overall priorities, the objective of the transition team, in the words of one member, "was to ease the process of transition ... It was a technical nuts and bolts operation." Another member stated that "there was a group of insiders who had already made many of the basic political decisions and told us what they wanted ... We were outriders ... They were the Executive Committee." The transition team looked after the details so that the insiders could be free to concentrate on more fundamental concerns. Team members recognized that, as one put it, "the real action was elsewhere," and took it in stride when one of the insiders told them that something they had been discussing had already been decided.

Some on the transition team argued that the transition would benefit significantly from a delay of several weeks once the Conservatives were defeated in the House. Peterson rejected this view, emphasizing that it was crucial for the new government to establish a sense of dynamism by starting to do things right away. Thus, the lieutenant governor called upon Peterson to form a government on 19 June (the day after the Miller government fell on a confidence vote), and on 26 June the Liberals were sworn into office. Six days later the legislature resumed with a major policy statement by the new premier.

The 1985 Ontario election took place less than a year after the triumph of the Mulroney Conservatives. Consequently many Ottawa Liberals were at loose ends and eager to return to positions of power. Yet the image of the Peterson government as a breath of fresh air stood to be compromised by association with their discredited Ottawa colleagues. Thus while the Ontario Liberals did want the benefit of their experience, they wished to avoid appearing to be influenced by figures from the Trudeau years.

While a number of federal Liberals surfaced during and after the transition, three key insiders in particular who were close to Peterson came from the Ottawa milieu: Hershell Ezrin, Gordon Ashworth, and Michael Kirby (though Ezrin had been with Peterson for several years). Members of the transition team differ in their assessments of the Ottawa influence on the transition and on the approach of the Peterson government. Some saw the Ottawa connection as fostering a secretive, manipulative, elitist approach. Others discounted its influence, particularly as the Ontario Liberals gained experience and confidence. In terms of policy substance, ministers were sceptical of advice from the Ottawa Liberals, who were not particularly knowledgeable about Ontario issues and conditions. All the same, as one participant put it, the Ontario Liberals "had no other resource to draw upon other than Ottawa." "It was our only frame of reference," said another. Thus, to the extent that the Liberal transition was influenced by previous experience, the source of that influence was Ottawa.

With few exceptions, the elected members of the legislature – even those assured of cabinet positions – were not involved in the transition. Sean Conway had early on been designated the education minister to deal with the critical issue of separate school funding, but this was the only instance of an MPP specifically being assigned to a portfolio in advance of the swearing-in.

One member of the team interviewed all members of caucus to ascertain whether their personal finances or family business ties might give rise to possible conflicts of interest. The results were reported only to Peterson, shortly before he chose his cabinet. The evaluation of the little-known, newly elected MPPs was, as one insider admitted, "very imperfect." Judgments were based on how they had performed as candidates in the election, on checks into their pasts for possible problems, and on their record of achievement in previous careers.

The cabinet was intentionally kept small at twenty-two ministers plus the premier. In part this reflected a limited talent pool, but it was also based on the principle that the fewer included, the less the offence to those left out and the more compelling the incentives to remain team players for those who sought cabinet rank. Some veteran MPPs were included in cabinet "because David Peterson owed people" – long-time loyalty was important and was rewarded. Still, ten of the twenty-three ministers were newcomers, leaving ten returning MPPs out of cabinet. More significantly, perhaps, according to one Peterson advisor, it was "a true MacGregor Dawson cabinet": long on representativeness, with such factors as region, ethnicity, sex, and ideological persuasion all given voice within cabinet.[3]

Contacts between the outgoing Conservatives and the Liberals, though infrequent, were civil. The Tories did not go out of their way to assist the new government but neither did they engage in "scorched earth" tactics. On the mechanics of the transfer of power, they were cooperative and professional, thereby greatly simplifying the task of the transition team.

The Liberals adroitly used the swearing-in ceremony to symbolize their new approach to government. Traditionally, ministers were sworn in in the lieutenant governor's suite in the Legislative Building with only family and senior party figures in attendance. The Liberals moved the ceremony to the legislature's spacious front lawn and invited the public to attend. Several thousand spectators witnessed Peterson pledge government "without walls or barriers" and accepted his invitation into the

Legislative Building for strawberry tarts and a glimpse of the premier's office and the cabinet room.

A key event was a day-long gathering of all ministers and deputies at a downtown hotel one day after the swearing-in. Officials gave presentations on the process of cabinet decision making and on central agencies. In addition, each minister met his or her deputy privately for several hours. A social gathering in the evening helped dispel a good deal of the tension between ministers and bureaucrats. Peterson began the after-dinner activities by telling humorous stories at the expense of a popular and colourful deputy minister with whom he had roomed in university; the deputy minister replied with reminiscences in a similar vein about the premier. This good-natured exchange set the tone for the evening, by the end of which relations between deputies and ministers had warmed markedly.

A "school for ministers" followed on the next day. The focus of the sessions, many of which were led by Ottawa figures, was on the practicalities of being a minister: handling Question Period, dealing with staff, preserving a semblance of personal life, and the like.

When the House resumed on 2 July the ministers had been settled into their offices efficiently and the formal transition was effectively over. The transition team, its task completed, disbanded. For about a year, members of the transition team met regularly for dinner with Peterson and his top ministers and advisors, but the talk was of politics, policy, and strategy. The group made no attempt to monitor the effectiveness of the government's structures and processes or to evaluate how the longer-term transition issues, such as relations with the bureaucracy, were unfolding. To the extent that this happened, it was confined to a few top officials in the Premier's Office.

The Liberals and the Bureaucracy

In opposition, the Liberals had been occasionally given to dark mutterings about "hit lists" of bureaucrats to be dispatched should they ever come to power. Very early in the transition process, however, a firm decision was made to avoid even the appearance of a witch-hunt. This decision reflected not only an appreciation of the professionalism of the Ontario public service but also a stark recognition that the Liberals would need to depend very heavily on the bureaucracy.

Within two days of the election – that is, while the Conservatives still clung to power – Peterson had quietly begun to contact senior public servants to reassure the bureaucrats that the Liberals were anxious to establish a professional, cooperative relationship with the bureaucracy.

Throughout the process, top Peterson advisors and members of the transition team met with deputy ministers. With the Conservatives attempting to stay in office, discussions necessarily remained at a general, bridge-building level. Information on finances and programs was not provided to the transition team by the bureaucracy until the lieutenant governor called on Peterson to form a government, and even then a good deal of important briefing material was not turned over to the Liberals until the new government was sworn in.

The Liberals, and Peterson in particular, paid special attention to cultivating good relations with the bureaucracy. Retiring cabinet secretary Ed Stewart was asked to stay on to assist with the transition. This was highly significant because the Liberals had repeatedly attacked Stewart publicly for his close connection to Premier Davis. Stewart served not only as cabinet secretary but also as deputy minister in the Premier's Office, and accordingly wielded formidable power; for Liberal MPPs, he epitomized the unseemly "blue tinge" to the Ontario public service. By indicating his confidence in Stewart, and by publicly praising his professionalism and his contribution to the transition process, Peterson sent a powerful message to the public service. This message was reinforced by the choice of Robert Carman as the new cabinet secretary. Carman was a respected career public servant, but among bureaucratic insiders it was widely believed that he had blotted his copy book irredeemably by his close and public involvement in Frank Miller's transition earlier in the year.

Still, the public service found itself with mixed reactions to the new government. For all of Peterson's protestations of goodwill and his symbolic gestures of trust, the notion of having a new set of political masters, most of whom were largely unknown quantities, was unsettling. After all, no change of government had occurred in Ontario within any public servant's working life. Conversely, however, the Liberals brought with them a full, activist agenda, which came as a welcome change from what many bureaucrats regarded as the stagnation of the final Davis years and the right-wing threat of the Miller government. The advent of a new government reopened all sorts of apparently closed policy possibilities and promised exciting times. Certainly, insecurity and confusion were widespread within the bureaucracy, but at the same time the Liberals' ingenuous overtures of faith quickly won over a good many public servants. In the words of one senior Liberal, "We quickly established the transition in the minds of the public service ... The question in their minds was no longer 'Is my job safe?' but 'How am I going to get them to adopt my pet project?'"

The politicians and their staff also had adjustments to make, but for the most part their experiences were positive; as one Liberal put it, "You were constantly surprised when you met them [bureaucrats] in the flesh and found that they weren't ogres." Another commented, "It was like going to university and having your profs write your papers," referring to how

Peterson or his senior staff would muse vaguely on some issue and within a day or two receive, unsolicited, a crisp, thoughtful policy paper on it. None of the small but highly visible group of senior bureaucrats with strong links to the Conservative Party was dismissed, though it was made clear to them that they were under scrutiny (and several left before long). The Liberals did, however, fire two civil servants "who jerked us around." This was important, one insider said, "because it showed enough of the fist to show that we were in charge" and indicated that though partisanship was not a criterion, high standards would be expected of the bureaucracy.

In dealing with the senior mandarinate, the Liberals were not hesitant to make changes, but they made them selectively so as not to upset the career bureaucracy. At the end of the summer, after two and a half months in office, the Liberals announced their first shuffle of deputy ministers. Eight deputies found themselves in new ministries, three assistant deputy ministers were promoted to deputy minister, and two outsiders were brought in at the deputy level (one had been a federal bureaucrat and the other had been a senior university administrator).[4] After a year in office nineteen of twenty-nine deputies from the Miller administration remained in deputy minister positions; most of the balance had been appointed to major government agencies or to other senior positions.[5]

Though the Liberals worked diligently at developing good relations with the public service, they did harbour suspicions about the loyalty of some bureaucrats, and were concerned about the possibility of being "captured" by the public service. One Liberal insider noted that in the early dealings with the bureaucracy, "we played on our own naïveté," but it was also made very clear to deputy ministers that the government's commitment to the policies set out in the Accord was firm and that the government expected them to get on with it.

As in so many other aspects of the transition, the Liberals benefited from a combination of good luck and good management as potentially debilitating effects of the lack of civil service preparation did not materialize. The public service had not been prepared for a change in government, but the long delay from election day to swearing-in, together with the clear policy directions of the Accord, enabled them to make up for lost time.

Restructuring under the Liberals
Looking back on the transition process after several years, one Liberal indicated that, in retrospect, more thought should have been given to the structures of government, commenting, "We left a lot to chance." Another subsequently came to realize that, as a group, the Liberals – ministers and top staff – had only limited understanding of the dynamics of large organizations, how and why they work and the nature and significance of corporate culture.

For all that, however, the Liberal transition did pay a good deal of attention to the *organization* of government. Perhaps because of its inherently more complex and nebulous nature, the *process* of government decision making was not considered nearly as extensively.

One of the working groups of the transition team dealt with the machinery of government issues. For them and for those close to Peterson, the foremost structural question was how to organize the Premier's Office. The basic principle was universally agreed upon: that the effective fusion of the Premier's Office and Cabinet Office under one extremely powerful figure should be ended – "the separation of church and state," in one Liberal's words. This decision reflected both altruism and self-interest. The Liberals genuinely believed it inappropriate to meld the bureaucratic and political as the Tories had done. At the same time, they recognized that no Liberal knew the process and the personnel of the Ontario Government well enough to serve as cabinet secretary. Nor were the Liberals about to trust their political fate to a bureaucrat. After much discussion, it was decided to establish a three-pillared organization. Cabinet Office, under the cabinet secretary, would be shorn away from the Premier's Office. The Premier's Office was divided in two, with responsibility for policy, planning, and communications assigned to Principal Secretary Hershell Ezrin and responsibility for operations and party liaison assigned to Executive Director Gordon Ashworth. Both reported directly to the premier.

Beyond revamping the Cabinet Office-Premier's Office nexus, the Liberals made few structural changes. They did immediately abolish the three small policy secretariats established early in the Davis era and the ministerial posts associated with them. However, they retained the three sectoral cabinet committees that derived from the secretariats. Indeed, the cabinet committee system adopted by the Liberals was unchanged in structural essentials from that of the Davis years. Once the Liberals were in power, substantial thought went into possible restructuring of the cabinet committee system, but it was not until 1989 that a major overhaul took place.

One small but important structural change introduced by the Liberals was the establishment of a small policy unit in the Premier's Office. The analysts in this unit reviewed emerging policy from a partisan viewpoint. In this way not only was a clear Liberal stamp put on policy development but the separation of the political from the bureaucratic was enhanced. The policy unit worked closely with Cabinet Office staff; by and large the relationship was an agreeable, complementary one.

Another set of structures had its genesis in this period, although it was not formally implemented until some months later. Recognizing the difficulty of combining long-term strategic policy development with the activist agenda of the Accord, which kept ministers and senior officials alike fully occupied, the Liberals established so-called Premier's Councils on health and on economic and technological development. These amounted to think tanks combining elected and appointed public officials, private sector representatives, and policy experts.

Although some thought was devoted to revamping the jurisdictional boundaries between ministries, in the end only very limited restructuring occurred. Overall, the Liberals accepted the existing structures in part because, as one senior Liberal put it, the transition was "quite traumatic for the bureaucracy." This led to an approach designed "not to create more anxiety [for the bureaucracy] than already exists."

The NDP Transition

Members of the NDP transition team made no attempt to learn how the Liberal transition had been effected in 1985. In part this reflected a view that differing circumstances – the long lead time in 1985 and the crucial role of the Accord – rendered the Liberal experience of limited value. The NDP also believed that they were very different from the Liberals, and would make far more fundamental changes. "There was not a lot to learn from their approach, which was to leave the entire apparatus untouched and intact" was the assessment of one transition team member. This choice exemplified the inward-looking, at times cliquish approach that the NDP adopted towards taking power. The day after the election, when the core of the NDP transition team met to determine what should be done, they began by asking themselves, in the words of one insider, "Who do we know from our tribe who's done this before?" This sense of tribalism was one of several aspects of the NDP transition that differed substantially from the Liberal transition.

The NDP did not, for example, adopt the Liberal approach of a public transition team composed only partly of partisans. It was simply inconceivable that anyone other than an active long-time New Democrat, well known to the Queen's Park insiders and trusted by them, could serve on the transition team. Inevitably the central election campaign team in effect became the transition team, headed by former Ontario NDP Leader Stephen Lewis. Lewis's high public profile beyond the party proved significant, for he served as a contact point for people who wanted to offer assistance but who were not linked to the regular party networks.

David Agnew, Rae's closest advisor, who subsequently became principal secretary to the premier, became de facto co-head of the transition team. A rough division of labour was worked out among the members of the transition team, though responsibilities "very rapidly got all fuzzed over." A good many people took on supporting roles, but only about a dozen were centrally involved in the transition. Given the enormity of the task at hand and the very limited time available, members of the transition team found themselves too busy to delegate: "You were so overwhelmed with myriad tasks that had to be done immediately that you tried to do it all yourself." Physical exhaustion was a problem, for the campaign team had been working flat out during the six weeks of the election and was now putting in long hours under intense pressure. More than one member of the transition team spoke of falling asleep in meetings.

All of the NDP transition team members were highly experienced politicos with fierce dedication to the party. However, not only were they generally ignorant of the workings of the Ontario Government, but only Lewis had any significant experience with large bureaucratic organizations. In retrospect, several members of the transition team recognized this as a significant failing; one commented that it would have been useful to have either professional bureaucrats or people with extensive administrative experience "giving us a more brutal assessment of the realities of government." The transition team did seek direction from what were termed "friendly bureaucrats," most of whom had worked in Manitoba and had been recruited into the Ontario public service by the Liberals.

Valuable advice was also forthcoming from New Democrats with governmental experience in western Canada. Former premiers Allan Blakeney and Howard Pawley met with the transition team, as did Wilson Parasiuk and Michael Decter, former cabinet secretaries in Manitoba NDP governments. (Parasiuk was also involved in transition planning for the British Columbia NDP.) Still, the transition team had difficulty knowing how to use the experience of other NDP governments; comments to the effect that "Manitoba is very interesting, but it's like Guelph" became common in meetings. This was only in part Upper Canadian conceit; it was also recognition that, as one team member remarked, "scale changes the nature of things."

Members of the team tended to work in isolation, in part because of seriously inadequate logistics; there were not enough phones or computers, and members of the transition team were scattered throughout the Legislative Building. However, given that in the clearly successful Liberal and Conservative transitions similar patterns of team members operating for the most part independently prevailed, the logistical difficulties experienced by the NDP rate more as annoyance than as debilitating problem. The entire transition team did meet each evening. In retrospective consensus, far too much collective meeting time was devoted to trivial details – the design of the premier's stationery, the guest list for the swearing-in, and the like – so that the "big picture" was not always in focus.

Indeed, the purpose of the transition team was not to develop strategic plans but to smooth the way for the new government. One member of the team commented that their purpose was "to deal with mundane realities – prepare briefing books, hire staff, organize the swearing-in ... Nobody wanted to think great thoughts, just serve as custodians until the government came in." The larger strategic questions were largely left to Rae and his close advisors. When creative ideas about governance did emerge they weren't so much rejected as lost in the shuffle because, as one person put it, the government was "just overwhelmed with the task ... mired in survival."

Atop the priorities list was the task of getting the ministers' offices and the Premier's Office up and running by 1 October. This entailed a massive screening and recruitment process; estimates of the number of résumés received in the first week varied between 2,000 and 5,000. The concentration was on ministers' executive assistants (who would assume chief of staff responsibilities) and communications assistants. Executive assistants were seen as critical since they had to be tough and strong lest the ministers be victimized by the public service: "We were quite suspicious of a bureaucracy that had never worked with an NDP government."

Another key decision was to strive for gender balance and affirmative action on ministers' staff. It turned out that the party's links with the various ethnic communities weren't extensive enough to produce many good candidates for "EA" or "CA" positions; nor were there many Native, disabled, or francophone possibilities. Talented women, however, were in plentiful supply and in the end more than half of the initial batch of executive assistants were women. It went without saying that anyone considered for a position in a minister's office had to be a party stalwart who had paid the requisite dues over the years. Save a handful of executive assistant recruits who had worked for NDP ministers in Manitoba, precious few of the top candidates had significant government experience or equivalent experience in large organizations. The qualities sought in executive assistants were good organizational skills, good political judgment, good human relations skills, and (least in importance) capacity to deal with policy. The closest analogue within the NDP sphere of reference was a good campaign manager, and indeed a high proportion of executive assistants came from that background. The typical NDP campaign manager had little experience dealing with the professional bureaucracy of the Ontario Government, but then few in the party did.

Ministerial staffing decisions followed the election organization model in another way. By and large, the transition team assigned executive assistants to ministers, though ministers were usually offered one or two alternatives and were given the opportunity to interview those selected to work for them. Specific requests were accommodated from some of the veteran MPPs named to cabinet who had made known their staff preferences. It was, however, very clear that the executive assistants had been recruited by, and were responsible to, the Premier's Office. Thomas Walkom explains the central assignment of ministerial staff as follows: "The idea here was to emulate the NDP's election-campaign structure, one in which candidates did not choose their campaign managers but were assigned them by party headquarters. In elections, this allowed the NDP's central organization to ensure that its candidates didn't do anything too nutty. The hope was that a cadre of experienced aides working with inexperienced ministers could perform the same service for the government."[6]

The executive assistants did most of the subsequent hiring of ministerial staff, although some variations did occur across ministers' offices, particularly with respect to the degree of involvement by the ministers. For this hiring, the EAs made extensive use of the data bank of applicants assembled by the transition team. In a few instances, the transition team had to "dehire" staff who had been taken on by overenthusiastic MPPs but who were later thought not up to standards.

Given the complexities of the process and the numbers involved, the upshot was that some ministers spent their first few weeks in office without executive assistants, and with skeletal personal staffs. Among other things, this meant that in the first round of briefings, some ministers met with the public service without any personal or political staff in attendance. Some deputy ministers seconded able but non-threatening public servants for a few weeks to help the ministers get their offices running smoothly. This seems to have occurred on a hit-and-miss basis, however; more than one bureaucrat in ministries where this did not occur commented that in retrospect the practice should have been more widely followed.

All told, the transition team spent an enormous amount of time and energy reviewing proposed appointments of EAs and CAs, senior Premier's Office staff, and consultants; it was, lamented one insider, "a résumé mill."

Rae took little direct part in the work of the transition team. His advisors wanted him to conserve his time and energy for more critical tasks. Rae would not have been inclined to become involved in any event, for he is by nature uninterested in organization and process. Nor did any of the NDP MPPs – even the veterans assured of cabinet posts – play more than a peripheral role in the transition. They were strongly advised simply to go home and to recover from the election.

Constructing a cabinet was rather more difficult for Rae than it had been for Peterson because so many of the new MPPs were unknown. Rae personally interviewed most of the caucus, his advisors did a good deal of "plain old-fashioned résumé reading," and party figures offered advice, and yet some cabinet choices remained essentially unknown. In part this reflected Rae's decision to have a cabinet with a very strong contingent of women (in the end, eleven of twenty-seven ministers were women). Taken in concert with the traditional imperative of regional representation, this significantly reduced the talent pool; as one advisor put it, "You go to [Region A], assume affirmative action, and you end up with [X] ... and no one knew who [X] was." All but three of the seventeen experienced MPPs became ministers; they were joined by thirteen neophyte MPPs.

Although it might have made administrative sense to push the swearing-in back by two or three weeks, politically this was just not on: "We had to show that we were in control and knew what we were doing even though we didn't." Some on the transition team pushed to have the ministers named a week before the actual swearing-in so that they could be taken away on retreat to learn how to be ministers and also to get a head start on ministry briefings. This did not happen because of what one team member termed "an absurd obeisance to convention" among members of the team, reinforced by the traditionalist views being put forward by Cabinet Office.

The swearing-in matched the Liberals' ceremony in symbolism, with a distinctive NDP tinge. Well over 2,000 party faithful packed the University of Toronto's Convocation Hall for an occasion that was part pomp, part revival meeting, part family reunion, and part love-in. Leaders of all of Toronto's major religions – Islam, Buddhism, Hinduism, Judaism, as well as the principal Christian denominations – shared the stage with the new cabinet. The choir captured the spirit and the hopes of the new government with its first selection, "Side by Side," the meaning of which was not lost on the crowd or the news media: "Oh we ain't got a barrel of money / Maybe we're ragged and funny / But we're traveling along, singing a song / Side by side."

One set of problems faced by the NDP transition team that the Liberals had not encountered arose from pending decisions on pressing issues. On election day, Rae and his top advisors had decided that they would support Toronto's bid to host the 1996 Olympics (an immediate decision was needed because the International Olympic Committee was slated to meet in Tokyo in ten days to make its decision). Within days, the transition team was inundated with requests from the bureaucracy for decisions on a host of issues requiring immediate attention. This served as yet another signal to the transition team how little they knew about governing. Even those who for years had been living Ontario politics daily in the Opposition Office were unfamiliar with many of the issues in question. The transition team rapidly reached the conclusion that very few of the issues the public service was putting forward as requiring urgent attention were all that pressing. This contributed to the transition team's feeling of being manipulated by the bureaucrats and significantly worsened the already uneasy relationship between the New Democrats and the bureaucrats.

Shortly after the swearing-in, a two-day seminar was held for the new ministers. It included briefings from central agency bureaucrats on governmental process and a panel discussion of former Manitoba NDP ministers on the realities of ministerial life. A more extended "Legislative

Academy" was mounted for newly elected MPPs. In trying to help the ministers find their way, it became evident that "some things are not learnable until ministers reach a certain stage": only after ministers have a certain amount of experience can they recognize the meaning and the value of the advice they've been offered. Ministers first elected only a few weeks earlier sometimes lacked the political experience and savvy of the veteran MPPs, whereas some who did have experience took time to make the psychological transition from opposition to government. In some cases what emerged was "an opposition mentality with ministerial letterhead" – a failure to recognize that ministers of the crown cannot operate with the free rein of opposition critics.

Given that the transition team members who remained in government all went to the Premier's Office, and that they neither wanted nor trusted Cabinet Office to coordinate government during the first difficult weeks in office, it was scarcely surprising that the Premier's Office should play a crucial role. "We were," one senior New Democrat explained, "centralist by default – it was not heavy-handed, it was basic survival." From the outset, the transition team was determined "to put in place in the Premier's Office a political core that would function as a collective that could provide support and leadership to ministerial staff, so that the political stamp of the government would be strong ... [consequently] for a period we had fairly severe central control." Another remarked that the problem with the Premier's Office in the early days was not being overly centralist but rather being too overburdened to control anything.

Like the Liberals, the NDP did not have to contend with a "scorched earth" policy left by their predecessors. "The Liberals weren't horrible; they just disappeared," commented one New Democrat. Of course, the Liberals, like the Conservatives before them, were not about to do their successors any favours. On taking office, ministers typically found little more than bare walls and (sometimes) furniture. At the same time, individual Liberals were of significant help. Several Liberal ministers met privately with their NDP successors to offer advice and assistance. Other Liberals who had held senior positions in the Premier's Office offered similar help to the New Democrats who replaced them, some out of personal friendship, some out of professional courtesy. And one member of the NDP transition team held "quiet chats with my red Tory friends" about how the Conservatives had run the government.

The task of monitoring the transition after 1 October – for it was widely recognized that the transition would continue for many weeks – fell to the Premier's Office. Insiders' opinions diverge substantially as to how effectively this was done. One group in the Premier's Office felt confident that the office was quite reflective about the process and was "acutely aware of where the system [was] not working," whereas another group felt that they had been so badly swamped by day-to-day crisis management that this function was not performed at all well.

The transition team, as noted above, had put off policy decisions until the cabinet could deal with them. Hence, "Once we were in place [after 1 October] there was a mad scramble to get our priorities sorted out." Although the process for putting together a Throne Speech proved successful in determining government priorities, most of those involved thought in retrospect that a serious mistake had been made in calling the House back too early (on 20 November, seven weeks after the swearing-in).

Perhaps the most significant shortcoming of the NDP transition, which several of the transition team members subsequently recognized, was that insufficient attention was paid to learning about the levers of power. NDP chronicler Desmond Morton commented that "a problem the Ontario NDP faces and is experiencing is that they're paying the price of many years of almost superstitious refusal to inform themselves about the issues of public administration: managing the Ontario government."[7] A saltier rendering of the same point was made by a senior official in the Premier's Office: "We had the passion and theory. But we didn't have a fucking idea how to make things work."[8] One bureaucrat perceptively observed that "for the NDP, management is a dirty word; policy is what matters." Among members of the transition team, as among New Democrats generally, it was widely presumed that once the content of policy was settled, the process of implementing and administering it would be straightforward and would require little attention from the political decision makers. A related concern was that if the political side took an active interest in the administrative process it would be sucked into the bureaucrats' game and bog down in management detail to the detriment of policy development.

The NDP and the Bureaucracy

Publicly, the New Democrats gave encouraging signs to the bureaucracy. Shortly after the election, Bob Rae told the press, "I've been called the son of many things, but I'm the son of a professional civil servant. And I understand well their sense of professionalism and their sense of public service."[9] Six deputy ministers up for renewal in September were reappointed.

Behind the scenes, however, the relationship was less amicable. Although Rae insisted privately, as he had in public, that he had confidence in the professionalism of the public service, many New Democrats came to power with a profound mistrust of the bureaucracy. Whereas the Liberals' doubts about partisan taint in the public service were assuaged with relative ease, the NDP's distrust was rooted in ideology and was therefore more difficult to dislodge. By and large, the NDP accepted that the public service was professional and non-partisan but believed that its conservatism was a major impediment to reform and that, given half a chance, the bureaucrats would pursue their own agenda over that of the government.

Although some of the NDP antipathy towards the bureaucracy was rooted in a deep-seated distrust of their motives ("We all have copies of *A Very British Coup*"), more fundamental was the culture clash between the NDP and the public service.[10] The sentiment expressed by one member of the transition team, "We do things differently ... We have a whole different way of operating," was echoed by virtually every New Democrat interviewed. When pressed as to the nature of this difference, though, most were vague.

Cabinet Office had been caught as off guard as anyone else by the astounding electoral results. Although staff had been assigned to keep track of the three main parties' platforms during the election, little had been done in anticipation of a change in government. Senior Cabinet Office officials had been concentrating their attention on the "Tomorrow Project," a wide-ranging reorganization and reorientation of management practices that struck the New Democrats as a pointless bureaucratic exercise. In consequence, "the transition team was asking for something much different" from what Cabinet Office wanted to talk about.

Surprisingly, the transition experience just five years earlier had little influence on how the bureaucracy handled the 1990 transition. To some extent the line ministries were able to build on their experiences in 1985, though even here one senior official commented that many in the Ontario public service were "completely flummoxed as to what to do ... There were no lessons learned from 1985, no institutional memory."

At Cabinet Office the situation was even worse, since virtually no one there had been at the centre in 1985. The problems arising from this lack of continuity were exacerbated by the suspicious approach of the NDP transition team, which provided little direction as to how Cabinet Office could best help it beyond assembling vast amounts of policy-related information from the ministries.

With some exceptions, the transition team did not feel victimized by systematic bureaucratic manipulation, but they were firmly of the view that the public service simply did not understand their needs, priorities, and methods. A telling case in point involved briefing material. Within a few days of the election the public service delivered an extensive set of briefing books that set out the background and substance of current policy. Initially delighted at this display of cooperation, the New Democrats soon concluded that the material lacked sufficient detail and analytic rigour and would therefore have to be redone. For some on the transition team, this was simply a function of the bureaucracy taking time to adjust to the NDP approach; one insider remarked, "From the outset the bureaucracy's attitude was 'Tell us what you want and we'll do it,'" adding that there was a good deal of uncertainty as to what the New Democrats were about. Others were far less complimentary: "They gave us briefing books that had to be returned, sometimes twice. They were unbelievable. Insubstantial, pre-digested pablum that did not serve our purposes at all."[11] One senior public servant acknowledged that some ministries' patent lack of sympathy for the NDP and its agenda was evident in their uncooperative attitude. Another, who was involved in the preparation of briefing material, argues that a good deal of the problem stemmed from the lack of communication from the transition team; ministries provided reams of information that disappeared into a black hole without response or feedback.

Early in the transition, each ministry was asked to provide a short list of reform initiatives that could be quickly implemented so that the new government could gain momentum. Ministries were also asked to review "The Agenda for People" and produce ideas for turning it into concrete policy. The transition team found the results to be profoundly disappointing, not only in terms of the paucity of feasible policy ideas but also because they revealed that, as one insider remarked, "most ministries are brain-dead in terms of strategic planning." Except with regards to one or two ministries, the transition team did not interpret this episode as a wilful attempt at subversion, but as a lack of capacity on the part of the public service. Nonetheless, it did serve to lower the New Democrats' estimation of the public service.

While "no one wanted a purge," the pros and cons of early extensive changes of deputy ministers were debated at length in the transition team. The decision – viewed in retrospect as an error by some on the team – was to shift few deputies immediately. As one insider explained, "We'd been enough of a shock to the political system ... We didn't want to make it worse" by firing deputy ministers, thereby creating uncertainty and fear. At the same time, the transition team wanted to avoid repeating what they saw as the wholesale "capture" of the Liberal ministers by the senior bureaucracy, termed by one as "the invasion of the body snatchers." Similarly, many on the team strongly believed that, given the NDP's ideological bent, it was essential that key bureaucratic positions be filled by persons who shared the commitment to social democratic values or, at a minimum, had experience working for an NDP government.

In retrospect, senior NDP officials came to recognize that they had sent mixed messages to the bureaucracy. Although both Cabinet Secretary Peter Barnes and Deputy Secretary Bernard Shapiro were closely associated with the approach of the Liberal government, Barnes was retained while Shapiro was replaced. One NDP insider commented that the attempts by the public service to understand the pattern and the purpose of similar, apparently contradictory changes to the bureaucracy were largely in vain since there was no coherent plan or approach.

Over the course of their first year in office, the New Democrats moved in a measured way to put their stamp on the senior bureaucracy. Several long-serving deputies retired and several others whose performance or approach did not meet with NDP approval were removed. Of the thirty-one deputy ministers in place a year after the NDP came to power, seventeen had been deputies under the Liberals (though few remained in the same post).[12] Of the fourteen new appointments, half came from within the Ontario public service (almost all were women) and half were outsiders. This record could not in the remotest way be construed as a purge. Yet it occasioned far more resentment within the public service than the Liberals' similar record since those with experience serving NDP governments seemed unduly favoured. (Five deputies, plus the head of Ontario Hydro, had once been public servants in Manitoba. Often lost sight of, though, were two key facts: all but one were career bureaucrats and most had been recruited under the Liberals.)[13]

The hostility and suspicion of the bureaucracy that characterized the transition team also became evident among the ministers and their staffs. As one Cabinet Office official observed, "There was immense distrust of the public service, especially from those [ministers] without experience ... We were the establishment as much as Bay Street was." A related problem, which plagued the NDP long after the transition, was the enormous hostility to the bureaucracy among senior ministerial staff, much of it born of unfamiliarity. Bureaucrats suggested that the New Democrats' inexperienced staff failed to understand their role as liaison between their ministers and the bureaucrats; many public servants contributed to the problem by failing to recognize the insecurity of the ministers and their staffs. The extent of the NDP's dissatisfaction with the public service is illustrated in the comments of one transition member about the relatively junior staff in the Premier's Correspondence Unit in Cabinet Office: "They were not our people and they didn't write letters we liked."

At the same time, as one long-time official commented, "senior bureaucrats gave them every reason to be distrustful ... There were and are many bureaucrats who act as if nothing has changed ... [Others exhibited] an unprofessional attitude that 'They're not going to listen anyway.'"

Relations between the new government and the public service deteriorated during the NDP's first months in office. Within a few weeks senior bureaucrats had taken to referring to the New Democrats as "the Clampetts" after the simple-minded rubes in the *Beverly Hillbillies* television series. As for the New Democrats, they interpreted many of the delays in implementing their policies and the problems they encountered (for example, the public relations disaster of their first budget) as bureaucratic obstruction: "The resistance from the mandarinate was more formidable than we expected."

The New Democrats' attempts to reduce the bureaucrats' influence included abolishing the "mirror committees" of deputy ministers, which under the Liberals had paralleled the cabinet committees, and instituting a "ministers only" session at the beginning of cabinet committee meetings. These discussions without bureaucrats (though often with political staff) might last anywhere from ten or fifteen minutes to over an hour. This made it difficult for the bureaucrats to implement decisions, especially in politically sensitive areas, since the public servants were not aware of the considerations underlying decisions. When the bureaucrats raised concerns about implementation, these were often dismissed "as just cheap arguments about policy and borderline insubordination."

Over time, as the New Democrats and the senior public service came to understand one another, relations began to improve, though tensions remained noticeably higher than during the Liberal era. A year into the mandate, one top New Democrat observed, only partly in jest, "We've taken office, but we haven't taken power yet."

Restructuring under the NDP

The New Democrats made virtually no significant changes to ministry jurisdictions. Their prime structural concerns focused on the role of Cabinet Office and on the cabinet decision-making process.

The key question of how best to organize the planning function for a social democratic government was handled primarily by Stephen Lewis and Gerry Caplan, a close Lewis associate and former national NDP secretary. They met with Ontario bureaucrats and with bureaucrats, ministers, and premiers from western Canadian NDP governments. Their operative premise was that a strong central planning apparatus was essential to keep the government from being overwhelmed by the minutiae of governing and to maintain a clear focus on policy development. After considerable reflection they recommended locating the planning function in Cabinet Office rather than in the Premier's Office to emphasize professional planning. They proposed a radically expanded Cabinet Office along the lines of the large central planning agencies of NDP governments in Manitoba and Saskatchewan.

The "Saskatchewan model" was not universally favoured by senior New Democrats. Some specifically wanted to avoid an "all-powerful politburo," which was seen as having caused enormous problems in Manitoba and which would not likely mesh with existing structures. Doubts were also expressed about whether stripping ministries of their already inadequate strategic planning capacities in order to beef up Cabinet Office would be a wise course. As well, the premier was said to be uncomfortable with the politicization of the public service that creation of such a powerful, politically engaged agency would entail.[14] Accordingly, Rae and Agnew decided to proceed with a hybrid, compromise model for Cabinet Office. Deputy Cabinet Secretary Michael Mendelson was given a mandate to build up the government's policy planning capacity, chiefly through Cabinet Office. Overall, however (press reports and the perceptions of line ministry officials to the contrary), the staff complement at Cabinet Office expanded only marginally; virtually all new appointments came from within the public service.

Early on it was decided that certain particularly important policy projects would in effect be moved into Cabinet Office. Auto insurance (a central plank in the NDP program) was handled in this fashion with several dozen people working on policy development under the direction of Cabinet Office.

The new government also moved to restructure the cabinet decision-making process. The principle underpinning this exercise was that the process should be suited to the New Democrats' priorities and approaches. Rae and his senior ministers made a strong commitment to emphasize collegiality in the cabinet. In part this reflected their distaste for what they viewed to be the unhealthy concentration of power in a handful of ministers during the Peterson government. More fundamentally, though, their preference for collegiality arose from the NDP culture, which stresses participation and collective decision making. Thus, in a remarkable departure from past Ontario experience, in which the Premier's Office and Cabinet Office put together the Throne Speech, every item incorporated into the New Democrats' first Throne Speech in November was thrashed out either in full cabinet or in the Policy and Priorities Committee. This made for very long cabinet meetings but, as had been hoped, it also forced cabinet to coalesce into an effective, collegial, decision-making body. (So, too, a number of key issues, such as the decision not to fund Toronto's Ballet-Opera House, were subject to extensive debate in full cabinet.)

The new government wished to avoid the "decision-making paralysis" that, in their view, resulted from the proliferation of cabinet committees under the Liberals. The basic division of policy into a small number of sectoral cabinet committees was retained, with some modifications to their mandates. Other cabinet committees, however, were not revived. In particular, the New Democrats rejected what they saw as the "marginalization" of concerns such as women's issues and race relations into specific cabinet committees. These sorts of problems, they believed, had to be addressed on a government-wide basis, as part of the overall decision-making process, not just in individual (and minor) cabinet committees.

An Ottawa-inspired Operations Committee was established, but its mandate was never clear and it was abolished within a year. Rather more significantly, the wheels were set in motion for a far-reaching restructuring of the expenditure process. Cabinet Office had been contemplating possible changes to financial decision making, and the New Democrats' desperately straitened financial position inclined them towards more effective means of expenditure control. Some time into the new year the Management Board was replaced by a Treasury Board. This change was far more than cosmetic. The new Treasury Board had a much clearer, more focused mandate (expenditure control) than the old, multi-faceted Management Board, which was widely believed to have outlived its usefulness. Treasury Board was also given substantially more clout, though its relations to the Ministry of Treasury and Economics and to Cabinet Office, and indeed its place in the overall cabinet decision-making process, were not immediately clear.

Conclusion

Chapter 1 framed the study of transitions in terms of the interplay of party program, government structures, and the personnel of government, emphasizing the importance of the relationship between politicians and senior bureaucrats. Much about the 1985 and 1990 transitions can be understood in terms of the nature and the degree of friction between these components. From this perspective, several themes germane to our inquiry into the 1995 transition emerge from a review of the 1985 and 1990 transitions. First, preparation – or more accurately, lack of preparation – on the part of both the political parties and the public service was a central concern. It was not simply that appropriate documents and processes had not been developed; neither the politicians nor the bureaucrats were psychologically prepared for a change of government. For a variety of reasons, the Liberals were notably more successful in overcoming the general unpreparedness for taking power than were the New Democrats. As we will see, lessons about the importance of being prepared were not lost on the key players as the 1995 election approached.

A second persistent theme involves the relationship between the incoming government – ministers and their political staff – and the permanent bureaucracy, especially those at senior levels. This is at once a crucial and highly problematic relationship, which relies heavily on trust at a time when trust may be in short supply. Questions of loyalty, partisanship, competence, and political orientation loom large as the new government assesses the public service and sets it to work. So, too, the public service has its own questions about the policies, approaches, and management style of the government. A smooth transition leading to effective governance requires careful management of relations with the bureaucrats.

Third, much depends on what the new government wants to do. The clarity of its policy objectives, its commitment to moving ahead quickly, and its willingness to consider alternatives or modifications all bear on what it requires, expects, and experiences during the transition.

Before examining these and other issues in detail for the 1995 transition, it is important to be clear about the political-constitutional context of transitions, particularly with respect to relations between the politicians and the bureaucrats and to the "mandate" of the incoming government. We now turn to these matters.

3
Transition Building Blocks: Bureaucrats, Politicians, and Mandates

Doubtless some universal truths apply to all transitions in democratic polities, regardless of regime type. Our focus, though, is on transitions within parliamentary systems conforming to the Westminster "responsible government" model. As with other aspects of the parliamentary system, transitions are surrounded, supported, and defined by various and sundry principles, conventions, expectations, settled practices, and traditions.

A study such as ours, conceived with both explanation and practical reform in mind, needs to make the more important of these principles and practices explicit. This will assist us in understanding the behaviour of the critical actors in the transition game. As well, such an exercise will help clarify the constitutional and political constraints within which transitions take place. This entails distinguishing between what is and is not constitutionally permissible, on the one hand, and what is and is not politically wise or expedient on the other. Without worrying overly about finer gradations in constitutional conventions and customs, it is important to recognize that some powerful, long-established practices, such as collective cabinet responsibility, form the central pillars of our constitutional regime, while other powerful, long-established practices, such as party discipline, simply reflect the political interests of key political players, such as the political parties. Finally, this examination will also make it possible to assess relevant principles and practices to determine which are essential to good and effective transitions and which inhibit them. In turn, this analysis may point to areas in need of reform.

In this chapter, therefore, we discuss a number of practices and principles underpinning the Canadian version of parliamentary government that seem particularly important to the tale we are telling. The chapter is largely about the political-bureaucratic interface: linkages, expectations, and frictions – both formal and informal – in the relationship between the politicians (both ministers and members of the opposition) and public servants, particularly senior bureaucrats. We also briefly consider a critical element of the context within which political-bureaucratic relations unfold: the program the incoming party wishes to implement – its mandate.

Central to any transition is the intersection of the incoming government's political agenda and approach and the permanent bureaucracy's capacity and outlook. In an important sense, transitions are special – very special, we suggest – cases of the critical relationship between politicians and bureaucrats. Accordingly, to appreciate how this relationship develops during a transition we must step back and examine the fundamental principles defining the nature of the public service in our parliamentary system.

We begin with the recognition that one of the principal constitutional doctrines of responsible government speaks directly to the role and operation of the public service. Simply put, "The notion of an apolitical or non-partisan civil service has been an important foundation of modern responsible government."[1] We further recognize that constitutional precepts (and their realization in practical politics) in this realm have undergone significant evolution over the past century, and that the evolution continues.

At the core of responsible government is the principle of ministerial responsibility – individual and collective – to the elected assembly, which entails that elected ministers, rather than appointed bureaucrats, are accountable to parliament. The corollary, which is that ministers accept both the plaudits and the blame for actions taken in their name, requires that public servants refrain from political involvement. A politically neutral civil service is an important pillar of our system of governance for other reasons as well; Sharon Sutherland offers the following persuasive interpretation: "The political importance of a permanent civil service [under responsible government] is that it enlarges the realm of actions over which the political system can rule by protecting a core of memory and administrative professionalism at the heart of the state. Thus it can be said that all of the conventions that guide the behaviour of administrators to keep them out of the heat of political action, restrict their freedom of speech, and which entitle them to the protection of ministers, are secondary conventions that are deduced from the rules allocating political capacity and responsibility."[2]

Particularly with the expansion of the Canadian state in the early decades of the twentieth century, the benefits of a public service premised on merit rather than patronage and political favouritism became increasingly evident.

Depoliticizing the Public Service: The Triumph of Merit
One important thread in the political history of Canada that is highly germane to our story is the transformation of the relationship between

politics and the public service as a result of the country's growth and modernization. Political patronage dominated the connections between government and bureaucracy in the decades following Confederation, both at the federal and provincial level, and the spoils system for the allocation of government jobs and benefits was a notable reality of public life.[3] To a substantially greater degree than is the case today, patronage defined the relationship between those holding political power and those in the public service, and loyalty to the ruling party was an indispensable requirement for nomination to many administrative positions. A newspaper item from 1906 illustrates this point well: "There was a meeting of the Liberal Association on Thursday, with a full attendance of delegates. The object of the meeting was to nominate a successor to the position of Customs officer in (Havelock) made vacant by the death of the late A. Fiddes."[4]

By the early years of the twentieth century, in Canada and many other Western countries it was increasingly evident that a public administration rooted in the spoils system was inadequate to support the growing size and complexity of modern government. Giving government jobs to loyal party workers may have been acceptable when they were working on roads with picks and shovels, or delivering the mail. Party loyalty, however, was hardly sufficient qualification to conduct a country's foreign policy, prosecute a war, oversee increasingly sophisticated industrial processes, or manage the nation's finances. Technical and educational qualifications were coming to be seen as highly desirable if civil servants were to provide good government in increasingly complex times.

The long struggle for civil service reform in this country was in fact largely a battle to eliminate or contain the scourge of patronage. Between 1867 and 1918, no less than six major inquiries into the federal bureaucracy dealt at length with the "patronage evil."[5] Over time, the spoils system was pushed back, replaced by the merit system, which came to prevail throughout government operations. Ottawa led the way in reform. The Civil Service Commission of Canada was established in 1908, requiring that civil servants in Ottawa be hired on the basis of merit; in 1918, with the passage of the Civil Service Act, this requirement was extended to federal government positions outside of Ottawa. Political patronage ceased to be the operating principle for nomination to the bulk of departmental posts, and a system was created designed to foster appointment by open, competitive examination and interview and to establish job tenure protected from removal on partisan grounds. Vacancies were advertised, necessary qualifications were specified, and a public service commission that ensured the integrity and fairness of the process oversaw the filling of positions. Thus was the professional, non-partisan character of the public service to be guaranteed. The provinces followed a similar path, though they were usually several steps behind the pace set by Ottawa; the key developments in Ontario unfolded in uneven steps in the three or four decades following the 1918 amendments to the Civil Service Act.[6]

These initiatives were important steps in establishing the government bureaucracies that have been features of our public life throughout most of this century, namely, organizations based largely on the merit principle, with open competition for advertised positions, some security of tenure, and a general prohibition on partisan political activity. It was organizations such as these, in both the public and parapublic sectors, that played such a critical role in the post-war construction of the Canadian welfare state. As the role of patronage was reduced, the modes of operation of the civil service shifted and the principles governing the relationship between politician and bureaucrat altered as well.

The merit principle is now universally accepted as the proper basis on which to organize a modern government bureaucracy. Although in practice sometimes honoured in the breach, it has been enormously important in guiding the conduct of both bureaucrats and politicians. Its contemporary meaning and significance is typically brought into bold relief when new governments take power. The decisions that new governments make about staffing the key senior civil service positions are watched with morbid fascination by journalists, by opposition party members, and especially, of course, by public servants themselves. Observers are quick to judge whether the new government is undermining the merit principle, handing out jobs to its political friends, or politicizing the bureaucracy.

Politicizing the Bureaucracy?
With merit ascendant, should it not be easy to detect when violations, in the form of politicizing the public service, occur? In fact, making fair and reasonable judgments about these matters is more difficult than it might seem at first blush. This is true for several reasons, and the difficulties are both conceptual – delineating just what politicization means at the highest reaches of the public service – and empirical – ascertaining whether a particular appointment or action constitutes politicization.

First and foremost, the most senior positions in the public service are Order-in-Council appointments (that is to say direct cabinet decisions) and in that respect indistinguishable from other patronage appointments a prime minister or premier is entitled to make. Both federally and provincially, deputy ministers, the most senior bureaucrats, are selected and appointed not through a competitive process overseen by an independent public service commission, but by personal choice of the head of government. In addition, deputy ministers hold office at the pleasure of their political "masters," and can be dismissed at any time, with or without cause. There is good reason for this arrangement. A deputy minister operates at the nexus between politics and administration. A minister and deputy minister exist in a state of mutually dependent professional intimacy; neither can do his or her job properly without the other's assistance and support. While it is formally the responsibility of the minister to give political direction to the deputy and the department, it is the task of the deputy to offer advice to the minister. It would be a grave error to believe that this advice has only to do with the implementation of political decisions or with the administration of the department over which the two preside. One of the most common responses of deputy ministers, when asked to identify their most crucial responsibility, is "to keep my minister out of trouble." A deputy not equipped with highly sensitive political antennae will not last long.

What, then, does the merit principle mean for a deputy minister? Most will have come up through the ranks, where the merit principle holds sway. But it would be naïve to think that it is the merit principle, as understood in the public service commission, that is consistently the crucial factor in getting named deputy minister. Indeed, why should it be? One can reasonably expect that the upper reaches of the public service are populated by highly competent, talented officials who have the technical requirements, professional qualifications, and experience necessary for the top position. But all of this, though desirable, is not enough.

An incoming prime minister or premier will have been elected to move the government in certain directions, to achieve certain public goals. He or she is entitled to construct the team of key people best able to move in that direction and achieve those goals. That is why a first minister's most significant and most blatant act of patronage is not even recognized as such: the selection of his or her cabinet ministers. It is, equally, why the top public service jobs remain directly in the gift of the premier or prime minister. Deputy ministers are a crucial part of the first minister's team, and are critical to the government's success or failure; it is only appropriate, therefore, that the premier be able to choose whom he or she wants. A capacity to work well with a given minister, the need to have a new face, the "comfort level" that exists between a new government and an official, an ability to work effectively on the government's agenda – these are all legitimate considerations that, in addition to professional competence, a premier or prime minister may have in mind when selecting deputy ministers or altering their assignments.[7]

The propriety – indeed, sometimes the need – for new governments intent on pursuing a strong policy agenda to make deputy-level appointments of people in whom they have confidence is argued not only by NDP premiers[8] but also by figures such as Hugh Segal, an unabashed Tory partisan who once held a senior bureaucratic post in the Ontario government: "To suggest rather blithely that while governments may come and go, there is at the apex of both power and influence an elite public service that should always stay, is, in my view, to sanction a fundamental subversion of both the democratic and parliamentary processes ... Newly elected administrations in Canada [are] sometimes reluctant to make the kind of large-scale and fundamental change necessary to ensure that those who voted for them get not only politicians chosen at the ballot box, but also policy-making and policy-development at the bureaucratic level which responds to the decision made by the electorate."[9]

A second reason why allegations about politicizing the bureaucracy are easy to make, but difficult to substantiate, has to do with the nature of the public service itself. To argue that the public service is not politically partisan is not to establish that the public service has no interests.[10] For starters, many members of the public service have an interest in preserving a non-partisan public service; they can be expected to resist efforts to alter the foundation on which they judge their conception of the public service to rest. Beyond that, however, members of the public service may be expected to have an interest in that service being treated with respect; other things being equal, most civil servants would quite naturally prefer to work with a government that not only respected the merit principle but also regarded them and the work they do as valuable. When Brian Mulroney, in the 1984 election campaign, declared that as prime minister he intended to give civil servants "pink slips and running shoes," it may have been a good line and good politics, but it sent a powerful message to the federal bureaucracy about how they were regarded.[11] Bureaucrats have an interest in working with a government that wants to work with them.

It is also clear that civil servants can over time develop an interest in the preservation of the governmental status quo. A political party that lasts an extended time in office, such as the Conservatives in Ontario after the Second World War or the Liberals in Ottawa under Pierre Trudeau, will become known by the public service, and vice versa. Close professional and personal relationships between politicians and bureaucrats will be built up over time; commonly understood ways of doing business, even shared views about the broad purposes of government, link the fortunes and predispositions of politicians and public servants. A change from this pattern will be disruptive. Thus it is perfectly possible for a generation of civil servants to develop a view of the public sector, of public policy, of the appropriate focus and sphere of government action, that derives largely from the concrete experience of working with a single political party as government over an extended period of time. In some sense, bureaucrats in this situation will have an interest in preserving those patterns and ways of doing things, and will be disgruntled or resistant if confronted with the necessity to change. For similar reasons, bureaucrats will often have become leery of opposition parties and politicians whom they will most likely know only as confrontational critics who are none too particular about distinguishing civil servants from politicians in their public attacks on the government. Whether the opposition goes after public servants out of partisan motives or because they don't know any better matters little.

This brings us to the third reason why it is sometimes difficult to sort out what politicization really means. The vocabulary most readily available to a civil servant wishing to speak of the relationship between the public service and the politicians is that of the merit principle and the professionalism of the public service. These are words and concepts that can be used to construct some barriers to inhibit political interventions that the public servant finds inappropriate or distasteful. Sometimes this discourse will be directed to issues that almost everyone would agree raise genuine questions of principle; at other times, that may be less clear, but the discourse will continue to be employed nevertheless. Charges of politicization may be made, not because of a direct assault on the merit principle, but because the directions in which the duly elected government wants to go seem alien or ill advised to bureaucrats. A left-wing government, for example, may hold views about labour-management relations that are very different from those of its centrist predecessor, and may begin to refashion the position of organized labour, even within the public service itself, in ways that seem more appropriate to it and more consistent with its values. A right-wing government may terminate social programs dear to the hearts of liberally minded officials. These are ideological and party issues, and need not have anything directly to do with the principles of a non-partisan public service, but they can be easily assimilated into that discourse.

Such thoughts indicate that the notion of politicizing a public service is a good deal more complex than might first appear. By way of illustration, the simple-minded notion that partisanship is the key indicator of politicization is misleading on two counts. On the one hand, previous partisan activity is by no means incompatible with effective, politically neutral bureaucratic service. In Ontario, Conservative, Liberal, and NDP governments have all appointed former partisans to senior public service positions, and most proved themselves effective, professional bureaucrats. (Though it entailed a unique situation, it is worth recalling that one of Conservative Premier John Robarts's speechwriter-advisors was a former Communist MPP.) On the other hand, one need not be a card-carrying party member to adopt a highly political stance either promoting the political, as opposed to governmental, interests of the governing party or obstructing the policies of the government for political reasons. Certainly it was concern with the latter prospect that led the Rae government (as it had led other governments of both left and right in western Canada) to install in senior bureaucratic posts officials who could be counted on to understand and to support its policy agenda (most were career bureaucrats with experience working for NDP governments).

Politicization entailing wholesale replacement of career public servants with partisan camp followers throughout the bureaucracy, motivated by a desire for patronage and party advantage, is readily detected and patently unacceptable in our system. No Ontario government has engaged in such behaviour for decades. What, however, are we to make of a small number of strategic placements of overt partisans or ideological soulmates into senior bureaucratic posts in order to promote the government's policy agenda? Purists might argue that all such appointments are inappropriate; realists, such as Segal, would counter that governments are justified in ensuring that staff of like mind hold posts central to the attainment of their policy agendas.

Even if we can sort out such issues, we must be careful about attributing politicization to situations that may appear rooted in partisan considerations but on closer inspection turn out to be less clear-cut. Two illustrations from the experience of the Rae government are instructive. First, Rae's appointment as deputy minister of intergovernmental affairs of close friend Jeff Rose, the former president of the Canadian Union of Public Employees and an undoubted NDP partisan, was widely cited as evidence of untoward politicization. According to *Toronto Star* columnist Thomas Walkom, however, the Rose appointment was more personal than partisan; referring to Rose, Walkom wrote, "The bureaucrats who had influence under Rae did so not because they were New Democrats but because they instinctively understood the notoriously uncommunicative Premier without his having to explain himself."[12] A second episode, which generated even more disapprobation than the Rose appointment, was the elevation of David Agnew, Rae's principal secretary and closest political advisor, to the position of cabinet secretary – in effect the government's top bureaucrat. In his book, *Rae Days,* Walkom disputes the notion that this controversial move represented the "ultimate attempt to politicize the civil service," remarking, "In fact it was the opposite. It was the bureaucratization of politics. By placing his most trusted aide in charge of the civil service, Rae had given deputy ministers – the top bureaucrats – direct access to his ear ... the lines of power no longer went through the ministers to Agnew and the premier's office and finally to Rae. Instead they went from the bureaucracy to the deputies ... effectively bypassing the politicians."[13] Much of what was seen in the higher reaches of the Ontario public service as politicization during the Rae era, one NDP insider argues, was in fact bureaucratic centralization.[14]

Finally, one must recognize that in organizations as large as the public services of Ottawa and the larger provinces, interests and constituencies exist within the bureaucracy itself – groups of deputies linked with a network of other officials throughout the system who may have ties of affinity, origin, point of entry into the service, long-time association, and the like binding them together. A new government might inadvertently or purposely remove a group of officials such as this from proximity to the key levers of bureaucratic power. It would not be surprising if these officials regarded such action as illegitimate interference in the non-partisan functioning of the public service, and viewed their subsequent return to the centre under a new government as the re-establishment of order and propriety.

It would be unwise, therefore, to take charges of politicization at their face value without examining the reality of the situation that lies beneath. The interlocking principles that give shape to a non-partisan administrative function in government are complex; they become embedded in concrete situations that render them more complex still.

Change in the Public Service and Its Role

A series of changes in recent years is once again altering the nature of the public service and its relationship to the political executive. Particularly following the advent of the Charter of Rights and Freedoms most Canadian jurisdictions have loosened the restrictions on public servants' political activity within specified limits. The Rae government's 1993 amendments to the Public Service Act significantly widened the scope for Ontario's civil servants to engage in political activity. Another change of note in the legal framework of public service has been the passage of "whistle-blowing" legislation, which protects bureaucrats who bring to public attention government wrongdoing or impropriety. (Significantly, however, this protection remains unrealized since neither the Rae nor the Harris government has seen fit to proclaim it into law.) A change of much deeper significance has been the willingness of governments to violate one of the central constitutional precepts of responsible governments by publicly blaming public servants for politically embarrassing gaffes. The "Al-Mashat Affair," in which a senior federal public servant was offered as a scapegoat to protect the ministers responsible, stands perhaps as the most noteworthy illustration of this trend.[15]

Recent large-scale efforts to "re-engineer" government and to substantially reduce the role of the state in society have resulted in sweeping changes to the functions of government, the size of the bureaucracy, and the status and activities of civil servants. In turn this has altered the assumed conditions, the implicit "social contract," of employment with respect to job tenure, wage scales, work assignments, and the essential character of government employment that many public servants took as given.

Parliamentary government, then, has shown itself capable of substantial, and sometimes radical, adaptation over time. So has the public service. A significant alteration in the one is matched, almost inevitably, by a parallel alteration in the other. The organizational and administrative requirements of modern government invited the emergence of the modern public service; the perceived overextension of government towards the end of the millennium is now leading to its trimming and redefinition. The relationship between government and bureaucracy is symbiotic – almost biological; as one part of the organism of the modern state adapts to a change in its environment, so too does its sister element.[16]

Let us conclude this section with three observations. First, change in behaviour within a parliamentary system is not always reform and it does not always move in a consistent direction. Second, different regimes converge and diverge for reasons that sometimes have little to do with the alleged logic of the political system they largely share. Third, government behaviour is often dressed up as a matter of principle when in fact it is little more than a contemporary practice or, sometimes, a passing preference. It is worth bearing these observations in mind when one hears a stout defence of the enduring principles that should underlie any proper government transition in a parliamentary system.

What Is Policy and What Is Administration?
A certain set of distinctions is perceived by many to be of vital importance to the proper functioning of modern constitutional government. These distinctions have to do with establishing and patrolling the frontier that is understood to exist between politics and public administration. One is the distinction between the political and administrative functions, and another is the distinction between politicians and bureaucrats. Others include the distinctions between policy making and policy implementation, between taking a decision and implementing it, between the minister and the deputy minister, and between the political staff and the professional civil servants.

These distinctions are useful, and probably essential, in the effort to designate and disentangle some of the roles that must be performed in modern government. Without them, it would not be possible to talk of a professional public service. Without them, it would be difficult if not impossible to make cabinet government work in a modern industrialized state. Without them, it is hard to imagine fashioning a robust system for establishing civilian control over the armed forces.

Yet a careful scrutiny of the situation leads to the realization that these distinctions point to part of the truth, but by no means the whole truth. We have seen above in the section discussing the issue of bureaucratic politicization that the understanding of these distinctions has evolved, and that there are positions, such as that of deputy minister, where the status of the incumbents is intentionally blurred. This is in recognition of the other part of the truth, namely, that the fabric connecting politics and administration is much more seamless than we sometimes acknowledge.

One of the reasons for this can be glimpsed by examining the policy process in a bit more detail. What are the main elements in the policy and program cycle to which one must pay heed? With respect to policy making, we would identify the following: problem or issue identification; policy development; policy approval; and policy implementation. With respect to the program area, the following seem to be the distinguishable elements: program design; program approval, including authorization of staff and financial resources; program implementation; program administration; program review; and the decision to continue, alter, or terminate the program.

To break the policy and program cycle out in this way is to begin to see the artificiality of a clean distinction between policy and administration. Ed Stewart, long-time deputy minister and cabinet secretary during the Davis regime, has written: "The notion that you can keep administrative responsibilities and political considerations in distinct compartments at the highest levels of decision-making, including many of the responsibilities which involve the deputy ... is naïve and non-productive ... A deputy who claims that political considerations never influence his or her thinking, or the advice that he or she is giving to the government, is either trying to deceive the public or is of limited value to the Premier and Minister whom he or she serves."[17] Civil servants might be involved in every stage of the policy process, and they frequently are. Politicians may take an interest in every step of the program implementation process, and they often do. Their motives, perspectives, and interests may differ, but it is naïve to think that a clean break between policy and administration can hold true in the real world: "My job as a politician is to make policy. Your job as a civil servant is to implement it." It is not as simple as that. Indeed, "the distinction between policy and administration, between deciding and implementing, resembles the fabled Cheshire cat – upon examination, its substance fades, leaving only a mocking smile."[18] Yet, as one leading authority on the links between politicians and bureaucrats confirms, unrealistic outlooks live on: "Although there are now precious few students of public administration who still adhere to the politics-administration dichotomy to explain how the real world of government actually works, the principle still haunts many public services and individual government services."[19]

The less experience of government that a political party possesses at the time it assumes office, the more likely will its members be to overestimate the gulf between politics and public service – or perhaps more precisely, to fail to appreciate the complex linkages between politics and administration. Opposition parties, particularly those far from office, are given to sweeping policy pronouncements with little concern for the practicalities of implementation or for qualifications, nuances, and caveats, all of which are central to bureaucratic approaches. The more explicit and detailed are the policy commitments a new government brings with it into office, the more inclined both politicians and civil servants will be to exaggerate the distinction between the political and administrative function. Because this misconstrues the reality and distorts the genuine roles of each set of participants, an overestimation or an exaggeration of this sort can lead to complications. We will see some evidence of this in the transition we are about to examine.

To reject as a false dichotomy the policy-administration distinction is by no means to slip into some governmental equivalent of moral relativism, seeing politicians and bureaucrats as performing roles distinguishable only in terms of constantly changing context. Legally, functionally, and culturally, bureaucrats are very different from politicians, even at the apex of power. Aberbach, Putnam, and Rockman's landmark comparative study of the higher reaches of government, *Bureaucrats and Politicians in Western Democracies,* captures some of the key differences between officials and their political masters: "Politicians are passionate, partisan, idealistic, even ideological; bureaucrats are, by contrast, prudent, centrist, practical, pragmatic. Politicians seek publicity, raise innovative issues, and are energizing to the policy system whereas bureaucrats prefer the back room, manage incremental adjustments and provide policy equilibrium ... The skills and experience of the bureaucrats lead them to seek technically appropriate solutions to more precisely defined problems ... The politicians define problems chiefly in terms of political principle and political advantage."[20] Notice that these differences have nothing to do with legal status; rather they are cultural, reflecting far-reaching differences in experience and world view. Little wonder that "bureaucrats and politicians gravitate naturally toward different definitions of the same problem."[21]

This is not the only possible way of looking at the two groups and their interrelationships. Indeed, the passage quoted above is only one of four "images" Aberbach, Putnam, and Rockman put forward of the perceptions, role definitions, and relationships of bureaucrats and politicians. Over time, they contend, writing and thinking about politicians and bureaucrats has progressed through four images. Image 1 is simply the old policy-administration dichotomy: "Politicians make decisions; bureaucrats merely implement them."[22] Image 2 "assumes that *both* politicians and civil servants participate in making policy, but that they make distinctive contributions. Civil servants bring facts and knowledge; politicians, interests and values."[23] Ed Stewart's observation that deputy ministers don't have to be partisan to be political[24] fits well with Image 3, which accepts that politicians and senior bureaucrats engage in both policy making and politics, but in ways reflective of their respective strengths and mindsets: "The politicians energize the political system, the bureaucrats provide ballast and equilibrium."[25] It is to Image 3 that the passages quoted in the previous paragraph relate. Image 4 is more speculative, postulating that progressive politicization of the bureaucracy and bureaucratization of politics is leading towards a "pure hybrid" in which role differentiation between politicians and bureaucrats all but disappears.[26] This interpretation is most convincing as it pertains to non-Westminster systems.

The survey data on top policy makers in Western political systems presented in Aberbach, Putnam, and Rockman's book are most consistent with Image 3, though some elements of Image 2 also find support. Colin Campbell has argued the validity of Image 4, even in Canada, Britain, and Australia, in which "the breadth of some officials' interests and/or the depths of their personal commitments to desired outcomes become indistinguishable from those of their political masters."[27]

Though we will not directly apply this framework to particular aspects of the transition, the insights it offers are useful in coming to grips with the complex interaction between bureaucrats and politicians, particularly with regards to misunderstandings and misperceptions stemming from discordance in the images that the two groups hold of one another and of their relations.

Never the Twain Shall Meet: Contact between the Public Service and Opposition Parties

Our political system is premised on an explicitly adversarial, zero-sum relationship between the government and the opposition, each on opposite sides of every question with virtually no common ground between. The parliamentary system institutionalizes team combat as the best way of doing politics and as the device most likely to produce effective government. Government and opposition are arrayed directly across from one another in the legislature, two swords' lengths apart. Question Period is a systematic assault by the opposition on the party in government. Few forums exist in which there are genuine opportunities and genuine incentives for the opposing forces to work together, and those that do exist – such as the meetings of party House leaders to organize the business of the House, as well as certain parliamentary committees – operate out of the public eye, frequently on relatively minor matters.

The government controls and is supported by the public service, which offers sophisticated backup to cabinet ministers in the conduct of their duties and in defending their positions in the legislature and in public;

over time relationships of trust and mutual confidence, and frequently friendship, build up between politicians and bureaucrats, and the sense of working together on the same team sometimes becomes solidly established. A party long out of power receives none of these benefits. Indeed, the bureaucracy over time becomes terra incognita to such a party, and government processes of policy making and program implementation begin to appear increasingly arcane. In these circumstances, it is easy for the opposition to begin to demonize the public servants together with the politicians for whom those public servants work, and to vow retribution and radical correction once office is secured.

Many civil servants, for their part, avoid opposition party members like the plague, rightly regarding contact with them as being fraught with danger. Although bureaucrats understand that they work for the government rather than the governing party, the political reality, which is also well understood by bureaucrats, is that the interests of the two are inextricably bound together and that their political masters are less inclined to make that distinction than they are. Bureaucrats possess highly sensitive information about the plans of the government; they are aware of the internal difficulties that ministers are wrestling with as well as divisions within cabinet, either of which, if made public, could prove intensely embarrassing for the government. Contacts with members of the opposition are high-risk moments and even appearances before legislative committees are approached with extreme caution. Bureaucrats have much to lose from such encounters and very little to gain, fearing that they may be accused of fraternizing with the enemy. Just as the opposition has trouble understanding that bureaucrats do not work to further the government's partisan political interests, so too ministers and government backbenchers often fail to grasp that public servants' interchanges with members of the opposition are not tantamount to attempts to undermine the government politically. It is common for cabinet ministers and leaders of governments to regard such contacts with suspicion, in part because the definition of loyalty that is central to partisan politics is very different from the notion of loyalty and honour that informs the continuing, professional public service. How can these people serve us loyally, then turn around the day after the election and work with equal loyalty for our political opponents? That is a question that lies at the back of the minds of many cabinet ministers as they carry on their work with professional public servants. The civil servants, for their part, conceive loyalty to be bound up with professional and conscientious service to the government of the day – loyalty to the office as much as to the transitory officeholder. Loyalty is to the state and to the political actors in the system only insofar as they are the authorized representatives of the state.

This condition of isolation and mutual ignorance is not a circumstance in which it is easy to envisage a smooth takeover of power by an opposition party, flushed with success after winning a general election. Even if one discounts the bad feelings that may have built up during the previous period, the opposition party's sheer ignorance of government operations, its incomprehension of the bureaucracy, and the public service's reciprocal lack of knowledge of the party assuming the responsibilities of government make an effective transition unlikely.

While it would be naïve to think that these tensions could be entirely dissipated, it is, in our opinion, not at all unrealistic to think that the situation could be very different and much improved. It is possible to diminish the gulf that exists between the public service and the opposition parties without undermining the principles and operation of parliamentary government and without compromising the government of the day. This requires a degree of political maturity that, as a political society, we have not yet achieved and a commitment, beyond partisan advantage, to the interests of good government that is too little in evidence. We shall have some proposals to make relating to this matter in Chapter 7.

The Appearance of Defeatism

Given the current state of development of transition thinking, a government party that licenses the bureaucracy to prepare itself effectively for a possible transition exposes itself to the charge that it is anticipating electoral defeat. This can be a sensitive matter within the ranks of the governing party as it assumes electoral battle stations. What is more, helping the opposition to replace them in office, should it win election, is unlikely to make a powerful appeal to governing party members and is certain to be low on their list of priorities.

The jurisdiction that has routinized the transition process to the greatest extent in this country is the Government of Canada. For some years, it has been the practice of federal officials to go through a fairly elaborate transition planning exercise prior to a federal campaign, and in some cases the federal bureaucracy has boldly offered its ideas on substantive policy directions to an incoming government. Just prior to the 1984 election campaign, the Trudeau government agreed to meetings of transition teams with senior government officials for briefings on departmental policies and operations. These briefings were conducted on the same basis as those that for some time had been held with opposition critics and were subject to three conditions: "The prime minister approved the meeting in advance; the subject matter was known and approved in advance; and the briefing was factual and did not provide advice."[28] It was probably not coincidental that this foray into openness only occurred after the practice of extensive transition planning had been institutionalized within the public service.

At the same time, even in Ottawa, such contacts are limited. Nor have they been able to overcome more than a portion of the profound ignorance of government and its workings (rooted not in lack of intellectual horsepower, but in inexperience) that characterizes most opposition parties. Writing of federal transitions, two public servants emphasize "the isolation of the political transition planners from their counterparts in the public service – perhaps an inevitable result of the distinctively Canadian tradition of one-party dominance, which has meant that whole generations of major-party politicians have known government only from the opposition benches ... This isolation can exact a high price when parties must make a rapid transition from politics to governing."[29]

Despite partisan constraints, a serious transition planning process that includes contact between civil servants and opposition parties is possible. In Canada, when this has occurred, we suspect it has owed more to a set of particular circumstances than to settled practices and expectations. Our belief is that the partisan sting could be drawn from this process to the extent that it becomes routinized, normal, and conventional. If governments, whatever their circumstances or partisan stripe, did this as a matter of course, charges of defeatism and much of the political sensitivity of the practice would wither away.

Electoral Platforms and Government Policy

Our prime focus in studying transitions is to understand how incoming governments get into position to implement their policies. The substance of those policies is not a central concern, but the form, clarity, and comprehensiveness of the new government's policy agenda is directly relevant to the transition process.

As in so many other aspects of the transition process, elemental questions emerge about the linkage between the political and the bureaucratic. However, though the relationship of would-be ministers and their staff in the opposition to senior public servants is even more problematic than the more standard relations between ministers and their staff to the bureaucrats. Developing a platform and campaigning on it by definition occur without public service assistance. Yet it is essential for the bureaucracy to understand what a party means in its campaign pronouncements, how serious the party's specific policy commitments are, and the party's willingness to accept modifications to its plans once the realities of implementation arise. Indeed, the party itself, or more accurately its top leadership, must also know the answers to these questions. Such is not always the case.

The relationship between what political parties stand for during elections and what they do in office has been the subject of intense public debate and extensive scrutiny on the part of political scientists.[30] More precisely, the question of whether a political party receives a mandate during an election campaign to implement specific policies once it takes office has attracted the attention of academics, practitioners, press, and citizens.

There is an impressive array of reasons, both conceptual and practical, why the mandate theory of representative democracy is deeply problematic. This having been said, the belief that a successful political party should be understood as having won not just the right to rule, but the right to do X as well as the obligation not to do Y, remains a durable feature of our political culture. Yet in Canadian parliamentary practice, both at the federal and at the provincial levels, the notion that a political party should present a coherent electoral platform on which it is prepared to be elected and held accountable has not struck very deep roots, certainly not among the political parties themselves.

To be sure, Canadian political parties have not been shy about making promises on the hustings, and indeed have a long history of issuing formal electoral manifestos. Such documents, however, have often been vague and more rhetorical than substantive. More significantly, formal platforms have frequently not been taken very seriously. The parties well know that most elections are decided far more by voter reaction to leadership and party image than by issues. And voters have become increasingly cynical about politicians' commitments to fulfilling their election-time promises. Bad enough that governments may prove unwilling or unable to avoid breaking electoral promises, but voters' outlooks are also coloured by 180-degree policy reversals following election victories, such as Pierre Trudeau's imposition of wage and price controls shortly after he had ridiculed them in the 1974 election and Brian Mulroney's shift to support of free trade from the opposition he had voiced against it shortly before the 1984 election.

In recent years, in part to counter public cynicism, opposition parties have been laying greater stress on their electoral platforms. The federal Liberals under Jean Chrétien prepared their "Red Book" – a detailed manifesto of policy commitments – prior to the 1993 federal election. At the time it was regarded as a modest innovation, and some observers wondered whether it might prove to be more of a hostage to fortune than a help to Liberal re-election strategy. It turned out to be a useful and strategically very helpful element in their successful campaign, but most observers would acknowledge that it derived its benefit from the context in which it was placed. What was important about the Red Book was not its substance, but its existence – a signal that the party had a plan and that it was serious about keeping its commitments. Had the electorate not been weary and cynical about the capacity of politicians to say what they would do and then do it, the necessity and the political impact of the Red Book would have been much reduced. While the Liberals did produce a Red

Book, Mark 2, for the 1997 general election, it was not a central element in their campaign.

The Ontario NDP experience in 1990 is also instructive. Upon its surprise electoral victory, the NDP found itself burdened with an elaborate and unrealistic set of policy commitments assembled purely for campaign purposes in the belief that the party stood no chance of victory. While some NDP militants took the view that certain policy commitments, such as the introduction of public auto insurance, were sacrosanct and therefore required conscientious follow-through, the public at large appeared to approach the matter very differently, recognizing that the NDP had won mostly by default and contenting itself generally with hoping for the best. The tension between the two views caused the New Democrats a great deal of political trouble.

The 8 June 1995 Ontario election, which brought the Mike Harris Tories to power, was a very different matter. In this case, the party running third was led by a conviction politician with clear, hard-edged policy commitments that had been laid out far in advance of the election. Vote for the Mike Harris Tories and you will get the policies contained in *The Common Sense Revolution*. Every one of them. The strong Conservative win, attracting an impressive 45 percent of the vote share in a three-party race, gave Mike Harris and his colleagues an unusually clear mandate to govern, and to implement the policies they had campaigned on. The voting public had formed a very clear notion of what the Tories were proposing, and, in voting for them, had no reason not to expect that this was what they would get.

This certainly was the Conservatives' preferred interpretation, but less clear-cut readings are also possible. In terms of a mandate, it could be argued that, aside from a few central "hot-button" issues such as welfare reform, the Harris victory was less an explicit acceptance of the whole *Common Sense Revolution* – which few voters likely read and digested in its entirety – than a more inchoate search for change among many dissatisfied with the status quo. As in 1990, when the clear choice for those seeking change was the NDP, Harris's strong campaign established him as the voice of change. Moreover, *The Common Sense Revolution* is a less detailed road map to change than is sometimes imagined. For every precise commitment (a 30 percent cut in provincial income tax rate), is a vaguely worded commitment – "rationalize the regional and municipal levels to avoid the overlap and duplication that now exists"[31] – or a broad policy swath not addressed. (The document is entirely silent on environmental issues.)

Whatever the nature of the mandate to implement the Common Sense Revolution, a second aspect of the Tories' situation vis-à-vis their electoral platform was unquestionably unusual. A cynic might suggest that what distinguished the Conservatives was the fact that they really believed in what they proposed to do, but a more accurate rendering would be that they not only believed in what they said but had thought through how they could realize their promises. As we will see later, the Ontario Conservatives had, to an unusual degree, engaged in a serious policy formulation process, undertaken on the working assumption that they would implement these policies if elected. They had done their policy work with what one might call "a governing mindset." They had formed their analysis of the set of problems that the province was confronting, developed the policies, costed them, and road-tested them around the province. As a party, they were earnestly committed to their implementation. They wanted not just to win the election, but to govern so as to be able to put these policies into effect. This unusually intense, policy-driven approach structured the Tories' campaign, and it structured their governing style. As we will see, it profoundly shaped the way that they took power as well.

Let us turn now to the transition itself.

4
Bureaucratic Preparations

Bureaucratic preparations for a change of power occur in two places: in the line ministries, which may expect to find themselves with a new minister representing a new governing party after an election; and at the centre, where the incoming prime minister or premier and his or her colleagues encounter the public servants responsible for the corporate well-being and central direction of the government. Often, when a new party takes power, early political decisions result in a second, bureaucratic transition, echoing and flowing out of the first, as key senior officials are released, shuffled, and recruited to meet the needs of the incoming government. Important as this may be, there is little the bureaucrats can do to prepare for it; we therefore examine the bureaucratic transition in Chapter 6. Let us turn first to the preparations that were made at the centre.

The Central Process
On the bureaucratic side, the success of the 1995 transition could be traced directly to the problems encountered in the 1990 transition. Both Premier Rae and Cabinet Secretary David Agnew, a key NDP figure in 1990 (and thus on the receiving end of the transition), had unhappy first-hand experience with the lack of transition planning in 1990 and were determined to mount a more effective, professional transition. Noting what he terms an "adversarial immaturity" in our political system, Rae says in his memoirs, *From Protest to Power:* "[David Peterson] and his staff slipped away without sharing very many tips of office organization, management or pending political issues. When we moved into our offices on October 1, 1990, the room was completely bare. Inside the empty desk were the words, 'Good luck, David Peterson' ... Months before our election in 1995, I asked David Agnew to approach both the other parties about a possible transition. I told him to give them briefing books, and to prepare the way for whatever might happen. This was done."[1]

In order to be clear that the preparations for transition had his sanction and to allay fears that they constituted some sort of bureaucratic sabotage, Rae raised the matter in cabinet. Ministers we spoke to were too preoccupied with getting on with their work and gearing up for the election to pay much attention to the transition exercise.

With this backing from the premier, Agnew set to work organizing the first comprehensive bureaucratic transition planning exercise in Ontario history. He met with officials who had worked on recent federal transitions and with previous clerks of the Privy Council to get a feel for the issues involved and to draw on their experiences. Late in 1994, he drew together a small team in the Cabinet Office to organize the project. Since the Ontario Cabinet Office lacked any analogue of the federal Privy Council Office's Machinery of Government unit, this team was put together in an informal, ad hoc manner. The core group was never larger than three or four people, though others were brought into the process as needed for specific tasks. Preliminary work commenced late in 1994; serious work began early in 1995. (This might seem to have been rather far into the government's mandate, but Agnew was in a particularly good position to judge the proximity of an election given his close personal ties to the premier.)

Initial work centred on thinking through how the public service could best meet the needs of a new government, and what preparations would be necessary so that the bureaucracy would be ready for the task. Persons involved with the 1990 transition and with transitions in other jurisdictions were canvassed, documents from 1990 were reviewed (though they proved of little assistance), and the opposition parties were consulted on an off-the-record basis. Savoie's *Taking Power: Managing Government Transitions*, the only book on transitions in Canada, was used extensively. One official, who referred to it as "the bible," indicated that the volume's importance was not so much as a source of new ideas but as a means of legitimizing plans that were looked at askance in some bureaucratic circles.

The focus of the exercise was to provide the incoming government with the information and support it would need to be able to exercise power quickly and effectively. The emphasis was thus on practical, nuts and bolts information rather than on what one person described as "big Ottawa-style think pieces." A subsidiary purpose was to prepare the Ontario public service (OPS) both psychologically and logistically for the organizational and policy changes that would follow the establishment of any new government.

Agnew met with the deputy ministers in March 1995 to explain the transition planning process; a follow-up memo underlined the importance of the exercise, as did a reference to the effectiveness of transition planning in the deputies' performance contract letters. Each deputy was asked to nominate a staff member for a coordinating committee. Most were executive assistants to deputies, communications directors, or others holding central or coordinating positions in ministries; they tended not to be the regular set of policy advisors who served as Cabinet Office's usual ministry contacts.

Cabinet Office used this group not only to disseminate and coordinate requests and directives to the ministries but as advisors and as catalysts for transition. Inevitably, the quality of the group and its members' enthusiasm for its task were uneven; ministry contacts varied a good deal in experience and capacity. Four meetings were held, under Cabinet Office direction, to explain the transition process, to develop procedures and information protocols, to advise the centre on line ministry problems and perspectives, and to ensure consistency and coordination. Three meetings took place during the run-up to the election and the last was held a week after the election was called. The Cabinet Office officials in charge of the project were also in regular contact with the group via fax and e-mail.

Undercurrents of unease, suspicion, and hostility marked the first meetings of the contact group. To some extent this reflected the novelty of the process. As one deputy noted, "There is no culture in the Ontario Government to plan about such things ... It is at times perceived as sacrilegious." In order to soothe concerns about political overtones, the word "transition" was not used; rather, the operative term was "election planning procedures." Framing the exercise in terms of the entire election period (for example, by including issues such as the status of ministerial decisions made during the election) helped dispel some of the unease. The deeply ingrained culture of decentralization in the Ontario Government, amplified by the traditional weakness of the central agencies, was also a factor in ministry reservations about the central transition planning. Distrust of central agencies is doubtless a universal phenomenon in modern government, but Ontario ministries were generally unused to extensive demands for detailed information from Cabinet Office. "Why do they want to know this?" was commonly asked about Cabinet Office requests. Moreover, ministries typically saw their tasks and operations as unique and thus resisted the centre's insistence that material or information be presented according to a standardized format.

Some in the line ministries suggested that the level of detail required by Cabinet Office went far beyond what an incoming government or minister needed to know in the early going. How essential was it, they asked, to know who the bargaining agents were in collective agreements affecting ministries? Looking back at the process, one central agency official recognized that ministries experienced some legitimate concerns about whether certain information sought for the briefing books was subject to cabinet confidentiality provisions.

In some quarters, "Why do they want to know this?" was a coded expression of distrust of Cabinet Office's political orientation. A significant segment of the higher reaches of the OPS remained deeply suspicious of David Agnew, who had been appointed cabinet secretary after having been Rae's closest political advisor. One deputy commented that it seemed "bizarre" that the public service was assembling material to be forwarded to the NDP's 1990 campaign manager, though the ministry was complying fully with Cabinet Office's information requests. It was reported that some ministries were holding back information because of their concerns about partisan taint.

OPS concern about possible partisan use of the material is difficult to fathom, since, as the legitimate government, the NDP was entitled to the information held by ministries and was, after all, preparing the OPS for a possible *change* in government. Furthermore, it is hard to believe that the type of transition material that was being prepared could be of any partisan use to the NDP in electioneering. Moreover, any ministries or officials who did actively withhold material on these grounds were behaving – to put it as charitably as possible – inconsistently: if the neutrality of the public service had been compromised through NDP appointments and activities, surely subversion of the transition planning process was not the appropriate bureaucratic response.

Some of those we interviewed spoke of outright subversion on the part of some old-line OPS figures, motivated in part by personal vindictiveness against David Agnew, who had made clear his personal commitment to the transition exercise. One career public servant observed: "Not cooperating [with the transition] was a way for non-NDP sympathizers to make life difficult for the outgoing secretary of cabinet, and possibly undermine his attempts to leave with grace and a good reputation. Of course, this behaviour could be self-justified as virtuous: it is no sin to skirt someone who is not really a public servant ... A sense that Agnew's days were numbered reduced the risk of this subversive behaviour."

Opinion in the OPS was divided on Agnew and his motivations: some interpreted his actions as self-serving and politically inspired; others expressed sentiments along the lines of those voiced by one bureaucrat close to the transition who said that Agnew turned in "one of the most consummately professional civil service performances I've ever seen." Interestingly, no such ambivalence was evident among the politicos of the Tory transition team. To a one, the Conservative operatives we interviewed were unstinting in their praise of Agnew's professionalism and cooperation.

Not all of the OPS's political qualms about the transition exercise were responses to the actions or motives of key government bureaucrats. Cabinet Office had originally specified that the ministry briefing books contain photographs of senior staff. The idea was premised on what seemed to be a straightforward exercise in human relations – to literally "put a face" to the bureaucracy. Since new ministers are inundated with unfamiliar information and people, it seemed sensible to help them connect names to faces in this way. Some ministries balked at the prospect of including staff photos in the briefing books, on the grounds that they might be used by a new government's political "hit men." In the end, photos were made optional.

On a less paranoid level, partially because no precedent existed for such systematic transition planning, OPS staff needed a good deal of reassurance that this endeavour was neither disloyal to the existing government nor political. The centre portrayed the preparations as an apolitical exercise in good government. Most of the material assembled by the ministries, it was pointed out, would be useful not only to a new government but also to the existing government should it be returned.

Still, as one official pointed out, the Cabinet Office's briefing requirements could be problematic for bureaucrats trying to distance themselves from the old regime: "Prudence would dictate forwarding the least information possible, especially if one wished not to be drawn into explaining the motivation behind programs and policies of the outgoing government, and by so doing, taint oneself by association. In this sense, a briefing book exercise run from Cabinet Office made it even more difficult for some bureaucrats to figure out how best to 'turn the page' on the NDP regime, and present a 'neutral' face to the incoming government."

Although Cabinet Office's formal transition plans made no allowance for it, most senior and experienced officials, including those at the centre, recognized that in addition to a political transition, a bureaucratic transition was in the offing. As a close political associate of Bob Rae's, David Agnew would almost certainly be replaced as cabinet secretary, which would have significant repercussions not only for Cabinet Office but also for the entire OPS. As well, the likelihood was high that a new government would replace Jay Kaufman, the deputy treasurer and Treasury Board secretary; Michael Mendelson (on leave from his position as deputy cabinet secretary); and Intergovernmental Affairs Deputy Jeff Rose. Changes at the top of these central agencies also portended a major upheaval. (It was less predictable that Management Board Secretary Jim Thomas would also be fired, so that the Conservative government began with new deputies at all central agencies.) A further portent of bureaucratic transition was the "staffing down" of Cabinet Office's policy capacity on the premise that a new government might want to adopt a different advisory structure and likely different staff as well. This entailed returning seconded staff to their home ministries and moving other staff to other positions in the OPS; in this process the entire "Jobs Secretariat" in Cabinet Office was dismantled.

Over the course of its meetings, the ministry contact group experienced some success in overcoming line ministry resistance and concern about the need for and the form of transition planning, though, as the flap over the staff photos illustrated, anxieties ran high. The group also served to convey useful ideas and intelligence to the centre from the ministries (not least as to the depth of unease about the whole enterprise). One of the group members who had been seconded into a minister's office in the 1990 transition was able to offer valuable insights into the transition process from a non-bureaucratic perspective.

The members of the group and the Cabinet Office staff we interviewed thought that, overall, the contact group had proven effective at coordination and information exchange and at improving acceptance for the idea of transition planning. The representation of some ministries by junior staff without adequate experience or access to their deputy ministers was seen as problematic, as was the essentially reactive nature of the enterprise. As well, aside from during the actual meetings, communication almost entirely consisted of bilateral exchanges between the centre and individual ministries or between the centre and all ministries; contact between ministries on transition issues was minimal.

Although the Cabinet Office-driven project had as an important goal the energizing and mobilization of the OPS for transition, its primary tangible objective was assembling a series of what were termed "products." These were briefing books mostly designed for use by the political transition team.

Each ministry was to prepare a briefing binder for the ministers and their political staff. Detailed guidelines were developed by Cabinet Office for these binders, which were to follow a prescribed format (for which templates and computer disks were distributed). One reason for the hypersensitivity to seemingly minor details – even the type size and font were prescribed – was to avoid the impression of inconsistency and lack of coherence across ministries conveyed by the tremendous variation in form and style of the 1990 briefing books ("a dog's breakfast" in the words of one person who reviewed them). In this, and in other more substantive aspects of the transition, a concerted effort was made to show the new government that "they're taking over a government, not twenty-three fiefdoms [ministries]," as one official put it.

The binders were to be completed and forwarded to Cabinet Office a week before the election; by and large they were. They set out, among other things, the ministry's basic objectives and mandate and the policy environment within which it operated, its principal clients and stakeholders, its organizational structure (including agencies, boards, and commissions), staff complement, operating and financial expenditures, and summaries of ministry policies and programs. As well, they detailed support services available to the minister and to the minister's office (briefing routines, administrative support, ministerial correspondence procedures, and the like). Most ministries supplemented these binders with additional briefing material.

Ministries were also required to submit material, again following a prescribed format, for two binders to be given to the premier and the political transition team. Short (seven- to eight-page) profiles of ministry structures, activities, and finances were incorporated into a binder offering an overview of government organization and operation.

This "Organization of Government and Ministries" binder was one of a set of eight binders put together for the incoming premier and the political transition team.[2] The Ministry of Finance put together a detailed look at the province's economy and the state of government finance. The Public Appointments Secretariat (an odd organizational hybrid staffed by public servants in Management Board but run by a political appointee from the Premier's Office) was responsible for a binder containing an overview of the appointments process and identifying positions coming up for renewal or appointment. This included a selected list of "key appointments" to be made over the next six months and complete lists of all "premier's prerogative" and "ministers' prerogative" appointments in the same period.

Cabinet Office itself prepared several binders: an update of the "Minister's Handbook"; a detailed explanation of its own operation and the existing cabinet decision-making system; material of a personal nature for the new premier (salary and benefits, security matters, support services, and the like); and a binder entitled "Post Election Decisions and Procedures." This was an extensive nuts-and-bolts treatment of the matters that an incoming government would face, from organization of the cabinet, to scheduling the first cabinet meeting and recalling the House, to arrangements for the swearing-in ceremony and the Speech from the Throne, to setting up ministers' offices. Various options and timelines were sketched out, and the binder included a calendar of key events (such as the annual premiers conference and provincial-territorial ministers and deputy ministers meetings) and comprehensive checklists of decisions to be made and items to be considered.

A separate binder, prepared by the ministries and Cabinet Office, was devoted to "critical issues" – matters requiring a very early, if not immediate, decision from the new government. This was an especially sensitive, problematic area. Attention to such issues is essential, since government faces some significant, inflexible deadlines; in 1990, by way of illustration, the NDP had to decide before assuming office whether to proceed with Toronto's Olympic bid. Yet the opportunity to present pending policy decisions as "critical" is a temptation for bureaucrats to take advantage of a new government's inexperience. We were told of issues put forward to the NDP in 1990 as critical – requiring immediate decision – which remained unresolved years later, without apparent ill effect. Changes in government are ideal times for bureaucrats to resuscitate long-dormant projects rejected or deferred by previous governments. Such game-playing not only leads to hasty, ill-considered decisions, it can also sour the politicians' relationship with the public service by raising the politicians' hackles and suspicions, as clearly occurred in 1990. Accordingly, special care was taken to screen items put forward by ministries to ensure that they truly were critical. A preliminary list was solicited early in the election campaign and its content was vetted by Cabinet Office analysts and by the cabinet secretary. A final set of briefing notes, which required sign-off by the responsible deputy ministers, was prepared just before election day and passed to the transition team. In addition to material from the Ministry of Finance relating to the provision of spending authority once the existing "special warrants" (under which the government may spend money without legislative approval if the Assembly is prorogued) were exhausted, only seven "potentially critical issues" were deemed of sufficient importance to warrant special immediate attention from the incoming government. These included such matters as the province's position on federal social policy reforms, a private sector firm's time-sensitive proposal for a strategic partnership with government in a high-tech field, and pending court cases relating to adoption by same-sex couples.

The central process deliberately rejected any notion of analyzing or costing out the policies and changes promised in the Liberals' Red Book of campaign commitments or the Conservatives' *Common Sense Revolution*. This reflected the project's consistent emphasis on administration rather than on policy. As well, Cabinet Office had concerns over the political consequences should an extensive analysis/costing leak out. Finance officials did some work on the Liberal and Conservative fiscal plans so as to be able to do an overlay of a new government's approach on the baseline data. As well, individual ministries reviewed and analyzed the opposition parties' promises in various ways and to quite different degrees, though David Agnew explicitly directed deputies to restrain such activities, lest their purpose be misconstrued. In keeping with the neutral tenor of the briefing documents, the finance binder was premised on a "no policy change" fiscal plan, which sought to bleach out any party policy directions (including the NDP's), for example, in assumptions about how and whether reductions in federal transfers would be reflected in spending cuts.

One of the clearest and most easily acted on lessons from the 1990 transition was the need for good logistical support for the political transition team. A sizable space was prepared in the Whitney Block, just across the street from the Legislative Building and literally down the hall from key Cabinet Office contacts. Additional phone lines were installed, as were computers, fax machines, photocopiers, and other necessary amenities and facilities.

In the weeks prior to the election, Cabinet Office officials spoke to ministers' political staff to encourage them to distinguish between their personal, political, and governmental papers on the premise that if this was not done before the electoral battle was joined, it would not be done.

In addition to these preparations in anticipation of a change in government, a series of routine bureaucratic processes were triggered with the issuance of the election writ. These included a Cabinet Office memo to all ministries setting out the caretaker nature of governance during the election period, an OPS-wide fax outlining public servants' political rights, and a Treasury Board memo on financial matters in light of the need to run the government on special warrants in the absence of a budget.

With minority government always a possibility in Ontario's three-party system, work was done in Cabinet Office to prepare for such an eventuality. Background and briefing papers were prepared for the new government and for the lieutenant governor and discreet contact was made with procedural and constitutional experts in Ottawa and elsewhere in case their expertise should be required.

At the Ministry Level

We found no line ministry that had not engaged in substantial planning in anticipation of a change of government and the arrival of a new minister. Some started earlier, planned more thoroughly, and performed more creatively than others, but even those that were by no means leading the pack had done a fair amount of work by election day. The vigorous Cabinet Office initiative at the centre clearly prompted a number of line departments to engage in transition planning earlier and more seriously than would otherwise have been the case. Indeed, this was one of the benefits of the central operation, which also offered something of a template against which to measure individual plans.

Individual ministries varied tremendously in their overall approaches to the transition and in the specific measures they developed in anticipation of a change in government. This should not be surprising, given the diversity of ministry mandates and activities, the differences in style and approach among deputy ministers, and the deeply ingrained variations in ministry cultures that characterize the Ontario public service. Moreover, the lack of cross-ministry communication on transition planning evident in the ministry contact group was also found at more senior levels. Aside from some general discussion at the Deputy Ministers Council and isolated instances of informal comparing of notes, deputies appear to have engaged in little exchange of ideas or experiences on the subject of transition. Partly this was a function of divisions, hostilities, and uncertainties within the deputy minister community, reflecting differing perspectives, career paths, and views on the contentious question of NDP politicization of senior OPS appointments. It was widely assumed that a change in government would entail significant firings of deputies, though just who might be in and who might be out was highly speculative. The result, as one deputy put it at the time, was that deputies were not being very open with one another and that "myriad, myriad games [were] being played."

Most ministries put together small internal transition teams, though their mandates and ultimately their effectiveness varied a good deal. The better teams, which were typically composed of staff with corporate rather than line responsibilities, not only oversaw compilation of briefing materials (beyond those required by the centre) but worked through logistical preparations. This entailed identifying ministry staff for secondment to the minister's office until political staff were in place, ensuring quick action on small but symbolic details such as parking permits and security passes for the minister's staff, and anticipating the administrative needs of the new minister and his or her staff. In some ministries, political staff were asked directly for suggestions about smoothing the transition process, based on their experiences in 1990, but in others the bureaucrats planning for transition pointedly avoided raising the matter with their ministers and their political advisors.

Politically astute bureaucrats were aware that they had to walk a fine line between, on the one hand, demonstrating their competence and preparedness and, on the other hand, coming across as pushy and presumptuous. The idea, as one ministry transition-team official put it, was for the minister "to find a system that [was] up and running and ready for direction, without imposing anything on them." This entailed not so much developing responses for every possible contingency or assembling tremendous masses of detailed information as having people in place ready to respond quickly to what the minister wanted. The more astute ministry transition teams recognized that the new ministers' knowledge of their ministries' policy fields would vary enormously, as would their personal preferences on how they wished to be briefed. As one deputy commented, with any new minister, "you don't know if you'll get a reader, a listener, or a talker."

Accordingly, although ministries prepared extensive plans for formal briefings, most recognized that they had to be ready to alter their plans or to scrap them altogether, though some were nonplussed and put off balance when ministers rejected their proposed format or the priorities they had set for briefing topics. Capacity to respond quickly to ministerial requests required a clear and efficient contact point with the ministry bureaucracy. This primarily meant the deputy minister, though several ministries ensured that ministers and their political staff had home phone numbers for key officials; one ministry put two central managers on twenty-four-hour call, so that "they'll only have to push two buttons to get what they need."

In terms of process, the approach to transition at the ministry level tended not to be qualitatively different from that employed for a change in ministers. Indeed, some ministries explicitly premised their briefing materials and preparations on the models they had used when ministers were shuffled. Substantively, however, the issues were far trickier. It is difficult enough to guide neophyte ministers through the intricacies of ministry policy and organization in a neutral yet effective manner. It is more problematic still to ensure that initial contacts with the new government were positive and established a good, trusting relationship. As one experienced deputy put it, "If you get off on the wrong foot, you never recover, though when people [i.e., a new government] come in with predispositions, building trust may be impossible." As part of the attempt to build that critical trust, this deputy had taken special pains to ensure that the new minister's executive assistant/chief of staff was treated well and given clear demonstrations of the public service's commitment to supporting the minister and his or her staff in every way possible. Another official put the issue of meeting the needs of newly appointed ministers in a larger context, noting that the OPS was generally not very adroit at orientation, with newly hired bureaucrats often receiving little useful orientation before being assigned to their tasks. And given the extensive turnover in the higher echelons of the OPS in the 1990s and late 1980s, the lack of corporate memory among senior bureaucrats (either of the OPS generally or of their specific positions) proved problematic for effective transition planning in some ministries. Not all ministries were lacking in continuity; in one, for example, two of the six persons on the internal transition team had been involved in the 1990 transition and one had also worked on the 1985 transition.

For the most part, efforts focused on winning trust by demonstrating competence, dedication, and responsiveness during the minister's first days and weeks. Briefings were critical to this process. Some ministries insisted on inundating the new ministers with endless programmatic and administrative detail, but most preferred to present "big picture" accounts of their policy environments, the nature and approach of their client groups, and the range of their activities. One deputy, who thought the Cabinet Office briefing material was "short, dull, and boring," concentrated on developing a strategic "game plan" that would allow the new minister to assess the major issues facing the ministry and possible policy choices.

Although the Cabinet Office templates made for a certain uniformity of information and approach at the centre, the watchword at the ministry level was variability. For example, while most ministries seem to have constructed their own list of "critical issues" that the new ministers would face, some commissioned policy option papers on them whereas others explicitly rejected such a course. ("We'll wait for our marching orders," said one official.)

Some ministry transition teams made determined efforts to retain a human perspective in planning their briefings. "Just imagine," said one official, "what it would be like [as an outsider] receiving all this briefing material," adding that if the material proves too detailed or is not presented in a comprehensible way, sooner or later most people "will blank out, freak out, or tune out." To avoid this, several ministries developed what came to be known in one as the "Berlitz Guide" – initial briefing material, very short and summary in character, providing information on where you have landed, what language the natives speak, local customs, and so forth. A deputy who had been involved in ministerial briefings during the 1990 transition recognized, with the benefit of hindsight, and sought to correct a significant weakness in the process: the inadvertent creation of situations in which the new minister is hesitant about revealing ignorance of the ministry's policy field. Among this same deputy's efforts at providing the new minister with a firm political and policy footing were the development of lists of people and organizations that the new minister should contact in his or her first forty-eight hours and first two weeks in office as well as proposals for an early reception for key stakeholders and industry leaders, for a press conference for the industry media, and for get-acquainted trips to regional offices. Other ministries worked out similar practical ideas to ease the transition process, such as dry runs of ministerial briefings.

Not all ministries were so thorough or so imaginative. Some quite simply did not take the transition process very seriously until after the election was under way or failed to think through the needs of a new minister and new ministerial staff. One middle-level official involved in the transition remarked on being "surprised at the lack of comprehension [by ministry staff] of the value of the transition exercise; people were not taking time to organize thoughtful briefing processes." By way of illustration, this official's ministry prepared reams of substantive policy detail but left unexplained important processes that bureaucrats take for granted but that are unfamiliar and confusing to politicians, especially inexperienced politicians. Some ministries had only incomplete tracking of policy statements and speeches by opposition leaders and critics, and thus found themselves with limited awareness of opposition priorities and positions (not to mention the personal preferences of their critics, who stood to become their ministers). This variation across ministries was consistent with longer-term differences in personal links to opposition critics. Ministries where bureaucrats had been in regular personal contact with the critics were unusual. To some extent, the uneven attention to the positions and statements of opposition critics reflected a general lack of political savvy among middle-range bureaucrats. One official recalled being asked by a co-worker why anyone planning for transition would be interested in assembling speeches made by opposition critics. Another mentioned having difficulty explaining to those in the Management Board Secretariat compiling a new edition of the government telephone directory why its publication should be delayed until the composition of the new government was settled.

All of the ministries we reviewed were anticipating a severe round of cost-cutting and administrative contraction, no matter which party – including the NDP – won office. One deputy declared that any of his colleagues who was *not* preparing significant measures to reduce public sector expenditures in his or her domain was not doing a proper job. Some ministries' plans were more elaborate than were others; several had prepared scenarios for cost reductions in the ranges of 20, 30, and 40 percent. The ministries we examined did not offer unsolicited analyses or implementation plans for opposition campaign promises, but were in a position to respond if asked. They had generally done some work on issues of particular importance to the opposition parties. In one ministry, for example, the policy unit prepared short papers (including cost estimates) on key opposition commitments and the deputy had "frank discussions with my [assistant deputy ministers] in case they have to do this [implement them]." The Ministry of Environment and Energy went through a full-scale review, designed to acclimatize ministry personnel to the prospect of substantial change; to identify core functions across the ministry, regardless of the administrative unit within which they happened to be located; and to make it possible to offer a new government the opportunity to make strategic, rather than across-the-board cuts, which would protect core functions while reducing costs. In this case, the deputy used the prospect of a change of government to push through a ministerial exercise of fundamental redefinition.

More modestly, several ministries found that the transition planning exercise offered them the chance to tidy up some administrative confusions and inefficiencies that had emerged in the course of the previous mandate. For example, several ministries recaptured bureaucratic responsibility for the correspondence unit, which had migrated to the minister's office during the tenure of the outgoing minister. One ministry reformed its grants administration procedures, with a view to both simplifying them and making them more sensitive to the political rhythms experienced by the minister. In a good many cases, then, ministries experienced the transition planning exercise as an opportune moment for reassessment and stock-taking, from which they emerged more self aware and more capable of providing effective service, both to their political masters and to the citizens they were serving.

Some of our interviews were conducted midway through the election campaign, when it was obvious that Liberal support was waning but it was not yet clear how well the Conservatives were faring. Thus a minority government seemed, for a time at least, a distinct possibility. Yet this was one contingency for which the line ministries had not planned. One deputy, when asked about this prospect, responded, "I'll slit my wrists!"; another confessed to having no idea about how a minority might impinge on the transition process. Overall, the consensus among bureaucrats was that the only sensible response would be to proceed with established plans and modify them as necessary as the transition unfolded.

As the election neared, and the probability of a Conservative victory grew, activities intensified substantially at some ministries that felt substantively and psychologically unprepared for the dramatic changes that a Conservative government would entail.

Common Threads

A number of recurrent patterns emerged out of our discussions with deputies and senior officials in a variety of line ministries. It seemed that a fair amount of informal sharing of information and testing of approaches was going on among ministries, and it was clear that a few deputies whose experience and political sensitivity were widely respected were regularly consulted by their colleagues.

We spoke with Arthur Kroeger, a retired federal deputy minister with vast experience in a range of Ottawa departments, about his understanding of what was most important for civil servants in mounting an effective transition. Without Kroeger realizing it, his observations touched on many of the common themes we encountered in our interviews with Queen's Park officials.

First, Kroeger spoke of the need to keep things simple. Bureaucrats cumulatively possess a huge amount of information and knowledge, but cannot expect it to be transmitted to an incoming minister and his or her political staff in real time. You cannot dump piles of thick binders on people's desks and expect them to absorb their contents. How can they?

Second, everything depends on the quality of the relationship between the minister and political staff, on the one hand, and the deputy and senior officials, on the other. Thus building trust and establishing frank and open communications are the most important elements in the first days. Politicians are likely to assume competence; officials have been around for a long time, they are specialized staff, they know a lot. But politicians can't assume that they can trust officials. After all, a few days ago these same officials were loyally serving the politicians' political opponents. A transition is the equivalent of arms control negotiations; you are always trying to build trust.

Third, it is vital that senior departmental officials be flexible and open-minded. The insecurity of a minister and political staff walking into a new ministry is almost inconceivable. It's a huge job. Often they know nothing about it. The people in the department know everything. Will they play games, hoard information, or decline to provide crucial advice? It is important that a department not feed the politicians' insecurity; the best way to proceed is to be very open and flexible. Invite the minister to indicate how he or she wishes to proceed, and be responsive to expressed preferences and priorities. Kroeger recounted the story of a newly appointed federal minister who, feeling more secure in his legislative office on Parliament Hill, decided to stay there and tried, with one secretary and three telephone lines, to handle the hundreds of calls that were coming in. They were completely swamped. Meanwhile, his department had staff, telephone lines, and administrative resources available by the bushel. But the minister at first was very hesitant to go over and put himself in the thrall of the department. (It is worth noting, parenthetically, that, in the case of the Tory takeover of Queen's Park, there was nervousness, occasionally mounting to high anxiety, on the bureaucratic side as well.)

Each of these three points – the need for simplicity, for building trust, and for flexibility and responsiveness – was made in one form or another by most of the deputies and senior officials to whom we spoke. In a number of cases, the lessons were hard won from earlier experiences in which a different manner and approach had been employed, very often involving an attempt to load the new minister down with masses of detailed information without stopping to ask the unsuspecting victim what he or she would like to know and the way in which he or she would like to learn about it. Officials in one department consulted the chief of staff in the NDP minister's office about the 1990 briefing. "Too much paper, too much detail, too much talking," was his reply.

The information compiled by Cabinet Office and by the individual ministries certainly could have been used as raw material for major government reorganization, but it was neither organized nor presented in a fashion to promote reorganization. Options were not developed as to possible ministry consolidations or eliminations. In part this was a function of wishing to refrain from putting forward the bureaucracy's policy preferences to the new government (for if on the surface such changes might appear simply as administrative issues, in fact they bespeak substantial underlying political choices and powerful political signals). As well, this approach embodied the premise that David Agnew and several other deputies sought to impress on whatever government took power: it is possible for a new administration to carry out sweeping policy change or to engage in major government reorganization, but not to do both at the same time. And since the evidence was clear that both the Liberals and the Conservatives planned a host of far-reaching policy changes, they should be encouraged to concentrate their attention on policy and make only limited structural changes. Furthermore, the extensive staff cutbacks and the reduction in the scope of state activity promised by the opposition parties would entail significant bureaucratic readjustment – reason enough not to dissipate energy on designing and implementing a major restructuring.

5
The Parties Prepare for Power

We have seen how and why the Ontario Public Service (OPS) prepared itself for what it believed would certainly be a change of government. The thoroughness with which the OPS was able to accomplish the transition exercise was fostered by the willingness of the premier and his cabinet colleagues to see this done. The tacit or explicit operating assumption of the public servants engaged in transition planning, until the closing days of the election, was the same as that of most citizens and observers of the Ontario political scene, namely, that the Liberal Party would win the election, and probably win it decisively.

As support for the Conservatives surged in the latter part of the campaign, however, the OPS shifted its focus. Many senior public servants began to closely scrutinize *The Common Sense Revolution* and to review the transition material they had prepared and the plans they had made, in the light of the probable victory of the Tories. Much of the "boiler plate" material and plans still held good, but the policy-sensitive issues needed in some cases to be rethought.

What of the transition preparations of the political parties? With respect to the New Democratic Party, the answer is clear and simple: there were none. No one in the party seriously believed that they would be returned to government; if they were, they would presumably carry on with what they were doing. The main contribution of the NDP government was to license and support the transition work of the Ontario bureaucracy, and to facilitate the handover of power to the new government. For the serious contenders, however, the situation was very different.

Preparations of the Conservative Party
By any reckoning it was a remarkable political achievement. When Premier Bob Rae called the election on 28 April 1995, it seemed clear to everyone that the Ontario NDP government was destined to go down in defeat. The NDP was running consistently below 20 percent in public opinion

polls, reflecting a widespread sense that Ontarians were simply waiting quietly for the opportunity to kick out the incumbents.

The expectation that the beneficiary of this deep voter discontent would be the Liberal Party, led by Lyn McLeod, was close to universal. For months polls had been showing that the Liberals were sailing along near 50 percent in popular support. It seemed as if they had to do little more than wait, avoid error, and take over responsibility for the governing of Canada's largest province. Their platform and political strategy reflected this perception.

Alas, for the Liberals, it was not to be. The Tories, under leader Mike Harris, stole a march on the Liberals in the election and seized victory from under the noses of the astonished Liberal Party. That a party with a hard-edged, radical right-wing agenda – trailing the first-place, middle-of-the-road Liberals by about 25 points at the start of the campaign – could upset the Liberal apple cart and win 45 percent of the popular vote and 82 out of 130 seats astonished most observers. Because of the impact of Ontario's active three-party system, it was the best showing the Conservatives had made in popular vote since 1963. In the nine elections held since then, only the Liberals in 1987 had achieved a higher share of the vote.

What was equally surprising, though less remarked on, was that the Conservatives, coming from so far behind, were so well prepared to take control of the levers of government after the election. It had something of the flavour of a hostile takeover in the private sector. The new guys gained control of the company; they came in and made it instantly clear who was in charge; they knew what they wanted to do; and they got right down to business, restructuring the organization, stanching the flow of red ink, discarding unprofitable product lines, consolidating productive operations, and setting the company on a new course. Classic private sector turnaround management.

The foundation of the Conservatives' transition achievement had been laid several years before, and in fact was part and parcel of the party's response to its galling defeat in the September 1990 election, which brought Bob Rae's NDP to power. It was in the aftermath of that experience that the Conservative Party of Ontario began to prepare itself for the long march back to power. Transition planning was one of the integral elements of the policy and strategy exercise.

The Tory Leadership Convention and the 1990 Election
Mike Harris became leader of the Progressive Conservative Party of Ontario on 12 May 1990. He was elected Tory leader by a process that the Tories had never used before, and that was, indeed, novel in Canadian politics at that time – a modified one-member/one-vote election in which 24,000 Progressive Conservatives from across Ontario cast their ballots.[1]

This process, which replaced the conventional delegate method of selecting a new leader, transformed the leader's relationship to his party. The new system meant that lines of accountability ran right back to the party rank and file, instead of to the party elites; the leader was connected to the mass membership of the party, having been directly elected by its members, and was not dependent on the traditional political elites who had historically been so important.[2] Tory activists argue that this populist model meant that the principle of staying close to the people – both Tory militants and Ontario voters – became a central element in the reconstruction of the party: the main planks of the platform were designed to respond to the key concerns expressed by the people the Tories encountered at innumerable meetings across the province.

The shift in the method of electing the leader appears to have had two other implications as well. First, it tended to downgrade the significance of the party's traditional governing elites, both at the centre and in the constituencies. The virtual abolition of the central office and its paid staff as a cost-cutting measure amplified this effect. The second implication was that the reforms created more space and increased the influence of volunteers, in particular, the small band of dedicated Harris loyalists who worked intensively on the creation of a new-model Tory Party.

The simultaneous presence of populism and highly centralized control is a phenomenon well known in other grassroots, populist movements. In the case of the Harris Tories, it is illuminated by the following surprising fact: *The Common Sense Revolution*, the most comprehensive and authoritative statement of Conservative Party policy and the centrepiece of the Tory campaign, was never approved by a party policy convention or by any other party body. It was prepared by a small group of Harris advisors, approved by the leader, and released directly to the public in May 1994.

That there was no apparent party resistance to this procedure, and no complaint after the fact, could be explained in different ways. One possible explanation is that in a party with a mass base, but with no powerful headquarters staff and no significant intermediary institutions, the capacity for resistance to the will of the leader is very limited. Another explanation is that the widespread party policy discussion that preceded the preparation of *The Common Sense Revolution* meant that in a sense the leader and his advisors were simply "writing up" a broad, already existing party consensus.

Premier Harris's advisors would clearly place the emphasis on the second explanation.[3] On the other hand, Etobicoke-Lakeshore MPP Morley Kells, a long-standing Ontario Conservative and Davis-era minister, begged to differ in a surprisingly candid article in the *Toronto Star* that ran shortly after the 1995 election. An aggrieved Kells declared that, with the Harris victory, he "had been hoping for a new era of grass-roots participation in the political process, not a return to the backroom politics of the past." He added that he had not expected "the new revolution to reinvigorate the old imperialism, let alone, in a more rigidly controlled format."[4]

At any rate, less than three months after Mike Harris had won the Tory leadership in the party's first experience with direct democracy, David Peterson launched the 1990 provincial election campaign. Conventional wisdom, buttressed by the Liberals' commanding lead in opinion polls, had it that David Peterson and the Liberal Party were unbeatable. In the event, both the premier and the party were eminently beatable, as a cranky, restive electorate gave the NDP the victory on election night in a three-way voting split. The Conservatives, under their new leader, Mike Harris, had been utterly unprepared to contest the election, more than half of the ridings, for example, were without nominated candidates at the start of the campaign, and the party began the campaign underfinanced and without a platform or an election strategy. Nevertheless, Harris's presentation of himself during the election as the "tax fighter," though not effectively developed as a policy or campaign strategy, prefigured a central element in what was to become the Common Sense Revolution. Given their disarray, the Tories heaved a sigh of relief on election night, when they won twenty seats in the legislature. But Mike Harris, himself easily re-elected in Nipissing, swore he would never again allow himself or his party to be so unprepared.

Mission '97

When we asked a senior Conservative Party staffer to account for the effectiveness of the transition in 1995, he quoted the comedian who said that it took him twenty years to become an overnight sensation.

After the 1990 election, Mike Harris put the Conservatives through a full-scale corporate-style planning exercise. The party rank and file, constituency organizations, business supporters, and party advisors were asked to help determine what the Conservative Party stood for and where its main strengths, weaknesses, and areas of opportunity lay. Party strategists concluded that the party was suffering from four deficits, all of which needed to be corrected if the Tories were to win back the confidence of Ontarians.[5]

The first and most obvious was the fiscal deficit. The party came out of the 1990 campaign $5.4 million in debt, a staggering sum that stood in the way of everything the Tories wanted to do. Second was the organizational deficit. Many Conservatives had drifted away from the party over the last several years, weakening the organizational base of the party and limiting its capacity to function effectively. The third deficit was intellectual. The party seemed bereft of new ideas and out of touch with the thinking of "ordinary" Ontarians. The final deficit was strategic. Once the goals were established, the finances were back in order, and the membership was motivated and growing, the party still had to figure out the best way to achieve its ambitions.

These deficiencies were gradually addressed through a series of conferences (in Barrie, 1991; Windsor, 1992; and Richmond Hill, 1994), through a set of party task forces, and through a good deal of hard work and tough choices, such as the decision to effectively shut down the party's provincial office and lay off its permanent paid staff as a cost-cutting measure.

Overall, the process of rebuilding the Ontario Conservative Party from the foundation up proved remarkably successful.[6] Paradoxically, it helped that the party's fortunes seemed so dismal, since this made it relatively easy for a small band of young, dedicated ideologues to effectively take it over and to shape it along their preferred lines. This group was ideologically and strategically in tune with Harris and together they launched a massive rethinking, rebuilding exercise that was explicitly premised on a private sector corporate reorganization model.

Harris toured the province extensively, holding endless meetings with small groups of business people, party faithful, and anyone else who was prepared to come and talk. Some fourteen Policy Advisory Councils and four Regional Advisory Councils, each with about two dozen members, were struck, "comprising MPPs, legislative staff, party executive members and volunteers (who were not necessarily party members)."[7] These bodies explored various policy issues, including reform of the structure of government, and fed into a major policy conference in early 1994. The party also published a series of policy papers, entitled *New Directions*. These processes linked policy development and organizational reconstruction. A concerted fundraising effort substantially reduced the party's debt. Finally, extensive polling and focus group meetings provided the raw material for innovative "war gaming" exercises in which the Conservatives worked out a bold and unconventional election strategy based on conclusions about the approaches the other parties would adopt.

As part of these policy and strategy development processes, about twenty Tory activists met for a weekend at the Guild Inn in east-end Toronto in the early autumn of 1992 to prepare a statement of purpose in anticipation of the Windsor meeting. They drew on the results of two rounds of discussion held in the late spring and summer of that year that involved caucus members, riding presidents, the party executive, and Progressive Conservative women's, youth, and campus associations. The result was a twelve-page booklet entitled *Mission '97*. (See Appendix B for excerpts.) The title was chosen consciously to underline the fact that the party's ambition was not simply to win the next election, but to govern Ontario (the next election was expected in 1994 or 1995, so that by 1997 the victorious party would be well into its mandate). The document declares that the party's actions "should focus not only on getting elected but on how we will govern after that election."

The document is a classic mission statement. The Conservatives' overarching commitment – to build a safe and prosperous Ontario – is translated into three strategic elements, each of which is further subdivided into a list of actions to be taken, with measurable results and timelines.[8]

The first element is "adhering to shared values based on individual rights and responsibilities, fairness and equality of opportunity." The second, "implementing innovative, consistent and responsible policies," refers in the action category to the development of a comprehensive policy framework, a policy development process, and a policy implementation plan, each to be accomplished in a series of steps prior to the next provincial election. Meeting these requirements led to the release of *The Common Sense Revolution* in May 1994. The third element is "governing with responsive, competent and principled leadership." The implementation steps required by this element include the early recruitment of a first-rate team of volunteers, staff, and candidates; an election campaign strategy; methods for involving the public directly in governing themselves; and – from our point of view, the most significant – a commitment to fashion a transition strategy.

Almost three years before the election, then, the party had set for itself the requirement to plan for the takeover of the provincial government after winning the election – specifically, to "complete the development of a detailed, integrated transition strategy 6 months prior to the next election." The drafters of the mission statement saw this as a natural consequence of adopting a governance focus, and it was in fact put into effect pretty much as scheduled.

Mission '97 was designed to foster internal party discussion about how the mission statement could be most effectively implemented at the riding and the provincial level. It contained suggestions about how party members could get involved and the best way to use the document. A series of discussion questions was included at the end, together with a blank page for party members to jot down their suggestions and ideas. *Mission '97* was presented at the party's general meeting in Windsor, 16-18 October 1992, and became the road map for the Conservatives.

The Common Sense Revolution
The work of the policy advisory committees and the results of Harris's numerous meetings with local notables, party activists, and ordinary voters confirmed the party's decided tilt to the right, in line with Harris's own views and those of his close advisors. Their polling and their electoral strategizing exercise told the Conservatives that the policies they espoused –

tax reduction, welfare reform, reduction of state intrusiveness, and the like – resonated with many Ontario voters but that few Ontarians identified the Tories with these policies. This disjuncture led to a bold move: publication of their uncompromising, hard-right platform months in advance of the election call. Thus was born the document known as *The Common Sense Revolution*.

Over several months in the winter of 1993-4 a small group of key Tory advisors drafted, redrafted, and refined the document. Most of the members of this Bradgate Group (named for the uptown restaurant they frequented) were the new core of young Harris insiders, such as David Lindsay, Leslie Noble, Tom Long, and Alistair Campbell, but also included were figures such as Consumers Distributing CEO Bill Young and Tom Campbell, a former Ontario deputy treasurer and Ontario Hydro CEO with extensive ties to the senior levels of the OPS. Drawing together the policies developed over the previous two years and Harris's personal outlooks and preferences, *The Common Sense Revolution* was a twenty-one-page combination of clear, unequivocal promises – a 30 percent cut in provincial income tax rates over three years, creation of 725,000 jobs and a balanced budget within four years, a reduction of 13,000 OPS positions, and so on – and vague indications of general policy direction on issues such as municipal governance and health care. Public finance and the need to reform government structure and operations received extensive treatment, but some important policy fields such as the environment and transportation were mentioned not at all.

For our purposes, the importance of the CSR (as it came to be called, first by Tory insiders, later by bureaucrats and observers of Ontario politics) lies less in its specific nostrums and ideological coloration as in its drafters' concern with ensuring its feasibility. One of its authors notes that it was written with the following question very much in mind: "What if you had to implement what you're saying you're going to do?" As journalist John Ibbitson put it, "The CSR was both an election strategy and a statement of neo-conservative political philosophy ... Producing a detailed policy document that would double as an election platform, and producing it well in advance of the next election, the Bradgate Group believed, would both win them the election and anchor the government."[9] The commitments in it were extensively examined in terms of their practicality; they may have been radical, but in their creators' eyes they were "doable." The CSR, in short, was created very much with a governing mindset.

Serious Planning for Transition Begins

Context
In the years prior to the election the Conservatives were engaged in three

overlapping streams of preparatory work: election strategy and candidate recruitment; policy development; and transition planning. The first two were closely interrelated and were managed by the same core group of activists. For example, all but one of the Tory candidates were nominated after the publication of *The Common Sense Revolution*, so they knew what set of policies they were signing on for; indeed, they were tested on their knowledge of the CSR at the candidates training school so that they would know Mike Harris took the program seriously and also so that they would be equipped to defend it effectively during the campaign.

Transition planning, the third stream of activity, was kept to one side as a separate process. While the inner circle of party officials was aware of or involved in all three streams, the party at large was not drawn in to the transition work. When the election campaign began, the Tories, rather like the Liberals, had two separate teams, one responsible for running the campaign and the other responsible for preparing to take over the government, should the election be won. Three factors underlay this division of responsibility.

First, with the party running in the mid-20s in the polls, open talk of transition planning would be risible, both inside and outside of the party. Second, taking the reins of governmental power is, in some respects, a technical matter about which the views of party militants are of slight significance; it calls for a knowledge of government, not politics or electioneering, and the people with useful views and experience are not likely to be found in large numbers in the party rank and file. Third, the division allowed for the effective use of scarce human resources.

The Transition Co-Chairs Begin Their Work
The core of the transition team was established in January 1994, simultaneous with the nomination of Harris loyalists Tom Long and Leslie Noble as campaign chair and campaign manager, respectively. William Farlinger, retired chairman of Ernst and Young, a large accounting and management consulting firm, and David Lindsay, a senior Harris advisor, were named transition co-chairs. This was not announced publicly for the reasons indicated above, though those who read the party's public pronouncements carefully would have been aware that a transition exercise was under way.[10] Both Farlinger and Lindsay were and remain close confidants of Mike Harris. With the Conservatives in office, David Lindsay became the premier's principal secretary and subsequently head of the Ontario Jobs and Investment Board (a key element in the Tories' re-election strategy); William Farlinger became chair of Ontario Hydro. Tom Long had some involvement in transition planning at the beginning, but was soon drawn off on election issues.

By mid-1994, two key players – Tom Campbell and George Boddington –

had joined the transition team. Boddington was a public policy consultant and lobbyist who had served in important staff positions to Dennis Timbrell, one of Bill Davis's top ministers. Campbell and Boddington were not only the first recruits to the transition team but were also the longest serving, staying on longest after the election. Other former bureaucrats were added a bit later.

While the general policy, strategic, and recruitment work of the party was under way during 1994, Lindsay and Farlinger began to address transition matters. They did not put a lot of concentrated work into it at the beginning, but they started to think about some of the problems that the Conservatives would confront should they win the election. They talked to people with transition experience, such as Stanley Hartt, former chief of staff to Brian Mulroney, and Martin Connell, who had headed David Peterson's transition team in 1985, and they examined what had happened during the 1985 Davis-to-Miller transition in Ontario and the federal Conservative Party's 1984 takeover of power in Ottawa under Brian Mulroney. They bought a half-dozen copies of the Institute of Public Administration of Canada book, *Taking Power,* for distribution to people with some responsibility for the transition within the party. The book proved helpful, not so much in providing a checklist of do's and don'ts, but in offering a context and some general ideas. The transition co-chairs also began to review the senior personnel situation in the Ontario public service. During this period, David Lindsay, and often William Farlinger as well, would meet on Fridays at the King Edward Hotel with Leslie Noble and Tom Long to plan the campaign, thus ensuring that there was close liaison between the transition work and other elements of the Tory strategy. Once the election was under way, a one-day retreat was held with members of both the campaign and the transition teams; the two subsequently went ahead with their tasks quite separately.

In the early days, the transition planning group, apart from Lindsay and Farlinger, tended to be loosely defined, with various people moving in and out of the process. The core group of about half a dozen people met roughly every two weeks in Harris's Queen's Park office during the winter of 1994-5. As the election approached, the group became somewhat larger, more formal, and more structured. Although the transition team included politicians and political activists from the Davis era, and people with some links to the Mulroney government, it depended heavily on several former Ontario deputy ministers. Everyone on the transition team worked on a volunteer basis.

In line with the principle that the party needed not just a strong platform but also the capacity to deliver on its promises was a process set in motion in the summer of 1994 (which is to say after the release of *The Common Sense Revolution*). Harris, Lindsay, Long, and Noble spent two days in Boston learning about change management from key people at Monitor, the well-known consulting firm of management guru Michael Porter. The meetings were arranged by one of the Tories' private sector advisors, who was involved with the firm. In developing a framework for change and for transition planning following this trip, a series of policy committees was struck to look at such areas as privatization and contracting out, welfare, and education. These committees brought together interested party members and sympathetic outsiders, all on a voluntary basis. The watchword was implementation; the central idea was to identify potential roadblocks and barriers to achieving the policy objectives the Tories had in mind. In this way, Lindsay and others on the transition team were forced to think seriously about policy implementation. Across the various committees both the process and the product were uneven; the welfare group delivered a detailed 130-page report, whereas other committees produced much less impressive results.

In March and April of 1995, Harris was presented with the results. This exercise significantly enhanced Harris's ability to respond to questions of feasibility and implementation of the party's general policy objectives. One Conservative involved in the process explained its value in terms of "increasing our comfort level that what we wanted to do could be done" and also establishing groups of knowledgeable, friendly advisors "who gave us the right questions to ask and could tell us later on how we were doing." Some thought had been given to formally incorporating these policy committees into the government structure once the Tories took power, but this idea had to be abandoned out of concern that it would unduly intrude into the public service's domain.

Members of the transition team wrote memos on topics such as the cabinet decision-making system and ministry restructuring; short, point-form documents were also developed on specific issues. Overall, however, the transition team produced relatively little paper, partially on the assumption that the civil service would provide extensive, high-quality briefing books and partially as a consequence of Farlinger and Harris's preference for action over lengthy documents. Harris met occasionally with the transition team to discuss overall direction and progress, but for the most part his communication with the team came through regular briefings by Farlinger. Typically, when the team needed decisions or directions from Harris, they would be sought and received through these briefings.

Planning to Take Control of the Public Service
The transition team viewed an incoming government's relationship with the public service as the most important element in taking power effectively, and it sought and received a good deal of advice from former public servants who knew the system and the senior players well. It quickly

became clear that there was a widely held view among many present and former senior bureaucrats that the NDP had politicized the public service during their tenure of office; members of the transition team heard strong talk about "the U-Hauls from Manitoba" and about "the NDP polluting the public service with their own people." As we have noted, the appointment in 1992 of Premier Bob Rae's principal secretary and chief political advisor, David Agnew, as cabinet secretary was never accepted by many senior officials in the OPS. Despite his professional conduct and his apparent acceptance of the norms of public service, they regarded him as an NDP operative with little claim to their loyalty or acceptance.

After the Agnew appointment, a group of former deputy ministers who still enjoyed close ties to the bureaucracy got together to discuss the situation and consider whether anything might be done about their concerns. A representative of the Public Policy Forum, a non-profit organization interested in promoting better governance and closely tied to senior levels of the business community and the federal and provincial public services, was asked to attend as well. The group, expanded to include some other former deputies, did not continue after the second or third meeting because of differences about whether there was a real problem and, if so, what its dimensions were. Nevertheless, the initiative did have consequences for the transition process.

Several members of the group began to provide external advice about the public service to the opposition parties, in some cases, to both parties at the same time. One of the Tory politicos on the transition team indicated that they knew the Liberals were consulting some of their advisors but were untroubled since they were aboard for their bureaucratic expertise, not their politics. In the end the Tory transition team included several former Ontario deputies.

The transition team made a presentation to Harris in January 1995. Its recommendations regarding senior personnel were based on two criteria: competence and "the degree of comfort" with the policy directions of *The Common Sense Revolution*. Senior civil servants could be strongly committed to what the Conservatives were trying to achieve, but be incapable of delivering – which would be unsatisfactory – or they could be highly competent, but deeply out of sympathy with Tory policy goals – unsatisfactory as well.

They concluded that there was a need for some adjustment, but that it would be unwise to engage in wholesale personnel changes if the government intended to engage in wholesale policy reform. Some people would have to be moved, some released, some perhaps brought in, but the decision was made to confirm the party's belief in a professional public service, and not to introduce a lot of people from outside or from party ranks into the senior bureaucracy. As one member of the Conservative transition team said cynically, "We knew we had a bureaucracy that would love us. So we decided that we would make love to them."

Advice on Cabinet Formation and Cabinet Structure
The transition team prepared alternative cabinet scenarios for the leader. In developing their ideas, they took into account the fact that most of the Conservative candidates were not experienced politicians and certainly had no prior government experience. Various plans for cabinets of anywhere from thirteen to twenty-two posts were worked out, including the organizational and ministerial implications of each, and Mike Harris accepted these principles just before the election campaign began.

Some thought was given in advance to what would be the most appropriate central government decision-making process, given the program the Tories would be bringing into government if they won the election. Several of the former deputies drafted a memo on the choices and decisions that would have to be made in designing a cabinet system, set within the context of the structural implications of the CSR's policy priorities. The memo examined various models of cabinet decision making in Ontario back to the days of the Committee on Government Productivity of the early 1970s, but did not review the experience of other jurisdictions, such as New Zealand or Alberta, which had revamped their cabinet systems to accommodate sweeping, CSR-like programs.

A central conclusion was that a Harris government would focus on a narrow, tough fiscal agenda, and that to succeed, such an agenda would have to be driven from the top. In turn, the system should see senior ministry staff primarily responding to direction from the top rather than sending ideas and proposals up the line for approval (traditionally the bulk of cabinet activity). This analysis pointed to the need for a lean cabinet and cabinet committee system, designed for action rather than for interminable discussion. The exact nature of the arrangements awaited determination in the course of the campaign and the days immediately following the election.

The Involvement of the Public Policy Forum
Some of the former deputies concerned about the direction of the OPS enlisted the Public Policy Forum's assistance in spurring the opposition parties to develop their ideas about governance issues. The response to the Public Policy Forum's attempt to do the same for the federal Liberals during the 1993 election had been disappointing, and the Forum was interested in developing a presence at Queen's Park.

The Forum prepared a document entitled "Public Service Reform in Ontario: Key Messages for Party Leaders," which tackled the need to bridge the gap between the business and public service cultures. This document was partially based on research the Forum had commissioned, which took the form of a series of interviews with present and former deputies. Meetings were requested with the opposition leaders; Mike Harris obliged and met with Forum representatives; Lyn McLeod delegated the meeting to her transition team. The Liberal transition team asked the Forum to put together some thoughts on what messages McLeod might send at a first meeting with deputy ministers. The Forum complied, giving this material to the Tories as well. (See Appendix A for the Public Policy Forum material.) As we will see in Chapter 6, this advice on appropriate messages for the deputies was used substantially by Harris in his first speech to deputy ministers after the election.

Finally, with the NDP government's agreement, the Forum sponsored two meetings between several key deputy ministers and members of the Liberal and Conservative transition teams. Chaired by former Ontario Deputy Treasurer Mary Mogford, these meetings, which took place on successive days about a month before the election, were stilted and awkward affairs, particularly for the civil servants involved, but all sides agree that they were of benefit, at least in providing some modest reality checks for the transition teams and in putting faces to names. The meetings, which were conducted on an off-the-record basis with an understanding from the parties that they would not be used for political gain, focused on process rather than on substantive issues.

Preparations of the Liberal Party

Transition planning for the front-running Liberals bore strong similarities to the work the Conservatives did in preparation for taking power, in broad outline if not always in detail. One member of the Liberal transition team recalls watching the Tory transition and thinking on many specifics, "That's exactly what we would have done." Like the Tories, the Liberals began their transition planning far in advance of the election and devoted their principal attention to issues of organizational design, staffing of key political and bureaucratic posts, and the practicalities of implementing their election platform. The two parties' transition preparations did differ in certain respects, however. The Liberals drew on more recent experience in government and, for most of the time that they spent working on transition, they felt a stronger sense of certainty that they would be forming the next government. Their approach was more formally organized and it generated more detailed transition planning documents. Finally, although the Tories' *Common Sense Revolution* portended far more radical changes to the role of the state in Ontario society, the Liberals developed a more sweeping reorganization of Ontario Government structures.

Whereas the previous Liberal experience with transition in 1985 had been a scramble to learn about government and about exercising power, in this case a more sophisticated quest underpinned the Liberals' efforts. One key figure put the party's objective this way: "how to use the transition as a way to frame the activities of government to be able to make the changes you want early." As a senior minister in the Peterson government, Liberal Leader Lyn McLeod had developed a keen appreciation that devising policy ideas counted for little without the administrative capacity to implement change. In her words, "How government works – the implementation process – is critical and has to be integrated into policy development ... We thought about how to implement our policy continuously; we had rigorously thought out the changes in the civil service that would have been necessary to bring about our policies; we were extremely practical, perhaps to a fault."[11]

Since becoming leader in 1992, McLeod had been promoting a wide range of policy reviews. Some of this work was made public in a series of policy papers, but the culmination of the process was the campaign publication of *The Liberal Plan for Ontario* (popularly called the "Red Book"), a detailed inventory of the Liberals' program, complete with explicit commitments as to timing (various promises were to be realized within thirty days, ninety days, or one year of a Liberal government taking office). Those working on policy, in the party's platform committee and elsewhere, had almost no formal contact with those preparing for transition, but this did not, as might be surmised, make for a problematic hiatus between substantive policy decisions and issues of transition, organization, and implementation. Rather, the policies and the timing benchmarks established in the Red Book served as parameters for transition planning. Those preparing for transition worked from the premise that their job was to create the conditions necessary to implement Liberal policies.

Thus the policy program drove the transition process. To an extent, this represented recognition of a key lesson from the 1985 transition, in which the Liberal-NDP "Accord" had played such a central role. As one insider suggested, "When you have an agenda it's much easier," meaning that with clear policy objectives, the system is forced to accept and to adapt to the political agenda and schedule so that transition issues become more straightforward: "When push comes to shove [with the bureaucracy putting forth arguments about insufficient time and the like] you have the stick – this is what the premier was elected on."

In a sense McLeod had been thinking about transition issues since before becoming leader; as she put it, "The central theme of the leadership campaign and of the Red Book was rethinking government – we wanted to make it less top down and hierarchical and more responsive to regional and local sensibilities and to give a stronger role to those on the front line delivering the services." Accordingly, she took a leading role in creating a serious transition planning exercise; this was "the only responsible thing to do as a party with a good chance of forming the next government ... We had serious concerns about the need for effective management and about the civil service; also we had to show that we could take control quickly – we were aware that we would only have a very small window to establish the tone of our government."

Organizing for a Liberal Transition
The Liberals' transition planning began in the summer of 1994 and organizational work began that fall. This timing was premised on a strongly held view that the NDP would not call an election until very near the end of their mandate, which would be late spring or summer of 1995. Initially, the formulation of a basic approach and the assembling of a transition team were done by Bob Richardson, McLeod's principal secretary. Although Richardson remained a key liaison between McLeod and the transition team and occasionally attended meetings, he played a limited role in the actual work of the transition team.

McLeod asked retired cabinet colleague and close confidant John Sweeney, co-chair of her leadership campaign in 1992, to head the transition team. In turn, Sweeney recommended that former Treasurer Robert Nixon share responsibility for directing the transition. In consultation with McLeod, Sweeney selected the others to serve in the transition exercise. Karen Pitre, a former member of Nixon's ministerial staff, was asked to take on the critical role of coordinating the exercise. Pitre was the only person who worked close to full-time on the transition during the run-up to the election and, in the words of one transition team member, "ended up driving the whole project." She was the only person paid to work on the transition.

All told only about a dozen people were involved in a significant way in the Liberal transition planning, though others took on limited responsibilities. The team included former Ontario bureaucrats, private sector Liberals with extensive governmental experience, and former ministerial staff. "A very deliberate choice was made," said one senior figure, "not to have Queen's Park staff or MPPs involved in transition planning ... We had an election to win ... [and besides] there is way too much self-interest." Of the Liberal caucus, only veteran MPP Sean Conway, who was likely to become deputy premier, had more than passing involvement with the transition. Like the Conservatives, the Liberals consciously kept transition planning quite separate from election planning, with only Richardson – like David Lindsay in the Tory camp – linking the two processes at the top.

At one point, Pitre did take part in discussions leading to the finalization of the Red Book, the Liberal policy compendium. She argued vociferously but unsuccessfully against the inclusion of commitments to introduce certain hallmark bills within thirty days of the government's taking office since this would require calling the House into session, thus seriously constraining the government's options in its early days. (She was at least successful in scuppering thoughts of promising to *pass* these bills within a short time; such a commitment could have proven highly problematic.)

By and large, those involved in the 1985 transition had little to do with Liberal transition planning a decade later. Only Senator Michael Kirby and Tom Zizys, a top Peterson aide throughout the opposition and government years, brought experience from 1985 to the transition team. At that, they were brought on board because of their skills and contacts rather than because of what they knew of the 1985 exercise (also important in Kirby's case was his central role in the 1993 federal Liberal transition).

Indeed, the experience of the Peterson transition was of limited relevance to planning for a 1995 return to office. In 1985, the Liberals had no inkling that they might form a government until election night, and thus found themselves thrown into transition with no prior thought or planning. By contrast, the McLeod Liberals were odds-on favourites to depose the Rae government and were engaged in serious, systematic planning months before the expected election call. More significantly, perhaps, whereas in 1985 experience was all but non-existent, in 1995 it was in plentiful supply. The Liberal front bench was replete with former ministers who were knowledgeable about government and about specific portfolios; as well, many senior Liberal staff from the Peterson era, who had worked for Liberal ministers in a range of portfolios, either remained at Queen's Park or were readily available. Whereas in 1985 everyone was new to government and thus knew neither the structures nor the players, in 1995 the Liberal transition planners were highly knowledgeable about government, as evidenced by one team member's comment that "we felt comfortable moving the boxes [organizational units] around and we knew many of the individuals in the boxes."

At the outset McLeod met with the transition team to outline its mandate and to explore the approaches she wanted it to take. A few subsequent meetings occurred between McLeod and the transition team, and she met with Sweeney, Pitre, and Kirby on an as needed basis. Generally, though, McLeod adopted a hands-off stance on transition planning. She had thought through a number of transition issues but was for the most part content with having set out her ideas during the initial meetings or conveying them to the team via Richardson. She took an active interest in major issues such as cabinet organization and ministry structure but left matters of detail to the transition team.

Beyond a small office and computer equipment to handle résumés and job applications, the Queen's Park caucus provided little in the way of logistical support for the transition team. In fact, no formal headquarters existed; team members tended to work individually on their specific assignments. This minimalist organizational approach was not imposed for want of resources; more formal arrangements were not thought necessary.

The transition team called on a number of people to advise on specific issues or to undertake specific tasks. Many, though not all, had ties to the party; some, whose partisan leanings were unknown, were personal friends of team members or of McLeod. Though the value of the contributions received in this manner varied a good deal, overall the approach was judged to be a success (not least because those whom the transition team approached broke no confidences). Some outsiders responded out of a sense of public service, others doubtless calculated that enjoying the favour of the new government would be personally and professionally beneficial.

In several instances, the Liberals found themselves seeking ideas and information from people who were also advising the Conservatives. The knowledge that the transition team was dealing with "people who had feet in both camps" caused some disquiet among Liberals on the periphery of the process, but was not a concern for the central transition team members, who viewed their work as primarily administrative, some distance removed from the partisan fray.

Early on, four main areas emerged as warranting close attention: conflict of interest review, logistics, human resources, and structures of government/policy implementation. Conflict of interest – primarily procedures for vetting potential ministers – was handed over to a Toronto lawyer. It was a relatively straightforward exercise that was wrapped up well before the election. In the other three areas, working groups of three or four transition team members were established.

Though no hard and fast division of labour existed, Sweeney was primarily involved with the group dealing with governmental structures and policy implementation and Nixon's main attention was devoted to the appointment of ministerial staff and to senior public service positions. The logistics group, which was to see to settling ministers and staff into office and to schedule and organize events and activities, such as the swearing-in ceremony, came under Pitre (who, by virtue of her role as the central staff person for the transition, was also heavily involved in the other groups).

For the first few months, the full transition team met roughly every month, as did each of the working groups. In the new year, according to one team member, it had become evident that the team had not jelled as a unit and effectively ceased to meet in plenary session. The subgroups continued to meet every two weeks and, as the election approached, weekly.

Considerable internal discussion took place over whether to follow the approach of the Chrétien Liberals in 1993 in which the transition team simply got on with the job, with no public face. In the end McLeod decided on a public transition team, largely separate from the "real" transition team, on the premise that a public transition team would be useful "to provide cover to get work done and to send people [who wanted to contact the new government] to." This had been the course followed in 1985.

One of the reasons for keeping the transition team small was to avoid drawing attention to it. One central figure in the transition noted the concern with avoiding publicity about the party's transition planning: "We were sensitive about being perceived as just waltzing into government." Another added that a party planning for a transition is seen to be arrogant, so that "the nature of the [transition] process is that you don't go public." Even two years after the election, McLeod was at once proud of the quality of the Liberals' transition preparations and reticent about discussing it lest it feed the image of overconfident presumptuousness and complacency.[12] Transition planning may well be politically dangerous, yet it is a telling indictment of our political culture that a party with very good prospects of forming a government believes that its political interests are better served by hiding rather than advertising the fact that it is taking seriously its responsibility to be prepared for governing.

The transition team and the party leadership did encounter a problem of Liberals with little or no connection to the transition exercise portraying themselves as transition insiders. The difficulty arose from their unauthorized and sometimes outlandish claims about which public servants were on "hit lists" and about other facets of the Liberals' plans. This situation was one of the factors leading to the party's low-key approach and to the winding down of gatherings of the full transition team.

Members of the transition team did not engage in extensive research into governance ideas from other jurisdictions. A few travelled to Ottawa to meet with those who had managed the 1993 federal transition. Some read the Institute of Public Administration of Canada book, *Taking Power*, and found it useful for providing context and for stimulating thought about issues that otherwise might not have found their way onto the agenda. Discussions were held with a small number of consultants and former officials from other jurisdictions about possible ways of restructuring the Ontario Government. On balance, however, the transition team members recognized that they were working within the constraints of the existing system. As one put it in reference to the alignment of ministries and to the overall decision-making process, "We're restructuring not reinventing ... We can shuffle the deck but we have to work with the deck we're given."

Liberal transition planning was more inclined than its Conservative counterpart to proceed by way of discussion papers and other documents. It was not, however, essentially a paper-driven exercise, in part since, as one participant commented, the potential for embarrassing leaks meant "We were gun-shy politically about having too much paper floating around." Still, a key product of the transition planning was a detailed binder prepared for delivery to McLeod on election night. The idea was to set out as many of the key decisions that McLeod would have to make in the briefing book. Pitre was to be in Thunder Bay, McLeod's home riding, for an all-day briefing on the day after the election focusing on issues requiring quick decisions. (A meeting of the full transition team in Toronto was planned for the Saturday following the Thursday election.)

Material in the binder covered four main areas: government structure and process, appointments (political and bureaucratic), communications to key governmental actors, and critical event schedules.[13] Government structures and processes were examined in considerable detail, with extensive specific recommendations to the leader on such matters as ministry structure, design of the cabinet decision-making system, and relations of the government caucus to the cabinet. A "Minister's Office Staffing Manual" was developed prescribing staffing levels, job descriptions, hiring processes, and the like for ministerial offices. Also included was a detailed draft agenda for the government's first thirty days, premised on the need to take quick, decisive action on the economic front and on a host of specific campaign promises laid out in the Red Book. This document set out not only a list of items, organized by ministry, requiring action (legislative or otherwise) in the first thirty or ninety days, but even proposed agendas specifying when cabinet and cabinet committees would deal with these issues.

The recommendations flowed from a discussion paper entitled "The Liberal Approach to Organization, Management, and Decision-Making in the Government of Ontario," which derived practical reform proposals from general principles such as the need for more open consultative government, clearer focus on individual citizens, and more flexible and accountable government. Prepared by three transition team members, this paper was reviewed and approved by McLeod after extensive discussions and revisions. The paper was framed to indicate the Liberal philosophy of governance to senior OPS officials; among other things, it was to be appended to the mandate letters from the premier to the deputy ministers. Consideration had also been given to publishing the paper during the campaign as a demonstration of the Liberals' commitment to change and of the thoroughness of their plan. This was not done in part because organizational issues were not thought to be politically sexy and in part because as the election unfolded the campaign team worried that publishing such a paper might come across as desperation or as lack of realism.

The paper, which is reproduced as Appendix C, put into concrete form many of McLeod's ideas for revamping the premises of government that she had been formulating since her leadership campaign. It called for thoroughgoing change in the scope and nature of state activities – for example, through reductions in program and service delivery – and in methods of governance – through an emphasis on flexible, consultative, responsive structures and processes. At the same time, it consciously avoided the market language and assumptions so prevalent in the "reinventing government" mindset and attempted to ensure that government-as-business thinking was tempered with recognition of the uniqueness and importance of the public sector: "Liberals believe that government needs to be reformed, not destroyed ... with an emphasis on fairness and social justice."[14]

An unstated but critical assumption underlay the paper and indeed the entire thrust of Liberal transition planning. The transition team was strongly of the view that extensive structural and personnel changes were needed in government and that change had to be effected early in the mandate.

Relations with the OPS

Like their Tory counterparts, the Liberal transition planners were very much of the view that the NDP had politicized the upper levels of the OPS. This view was reinforced by a small group of former deputy ministers who approached a senior caucus member with their concerns about bureaucratic politicization and advice on how the Liberals might reverse it. The Liberals further believed that beyond those with partisan ties to the government, an unhealthy number of deputy and assistant deputy ministers lacked competence. Accordingly, a wholesale reordering of the senior ranks of the OPS was high on the Liberal agenda.

McLeod took an early decision that neither she nor the transition team should talk with current senior bureaucrats (leading one team member to observe, as the election call neared, "It's killing some of the deputy ministers not to be able to talk to us"). One team member took on prime responsibility for gathering intelligence on current deputies from former bureaucrats and ministers, consultants, and others knowledgeable about the Ontario mandarinate. A "remarkable consensus" emerged on the deputies' capacity and characteristics, though it is possible that the similarity in assessments reflected an underlying homogeneity in the views and experiences among those approached for their opinions. Four distinct categories emerged from this review, each of which constituted roughly a quarter of the deputy minister cadre: the exceptionally able; the solid, competent "B team"; the highly partisan; and the politically neutral but possibly incompetent.

Those canvassed about deputy ministers also offered views as to abilities of assistant deputy ministers (ADMs). The Liberals gave some thought to removing for incompetence or partisan taint as many as fifteen or twenty (of roughly seventy) ADMs, but in the end this course was rejected as an inappropriate purge. Changes in the ADM ranks were to be left to the deputies.

One transition team member conceded that thinking about the nature and the extent of the Liberals' plans for changes in the upper reaches of the OPS were, at least in part, affected by pressure from the caucus, the party, and the business community, all of which were insisting on major changes in the senior ranks of the OPS. Key transition team figures indicated that a Liberal government would likely have fired about the same number of deputies as did the Tories, though their choices as to who should stay and who should go would not have precisely replicated the Conservatives' decisions.

In addition to the pros and cons of shifting or firing specific individuals, the transition team was cognizant of the systemic consequences of making extensive changes in the OPS. While they saw the need to signal their commitment to a professional, non-partisan public service, the Liberals understood that widespread change could prove disruptive to the organization. One transition team member commented, "We didn't want to make too many changes, but we didn't want the leader to be sabotaged by the bureaucracy."

The Liberals were also sensitive to the harm to OPS morale that could result from bringing in too many deputies from outside government. They did expect to appoint perhaps four or five deputies from the outside. Significantly, some of those the Liberals wanted to recruit were also high on the Tories' list. Michael Gourley, who was appointed deputy minister of finance by the Conservatives, was the Liberals' choice for that key post; they were also interested in pursuing Veronica Lacey, director of education for the North York School Board, to take on the deputy minister post in education – an appointment the Conservatives made some months after coming into power. Discreet, no-commitment discussions were held with a small number of prospective deputy appointees to sound out their interest in serving under a McLeod government.

Some thought was given to David Agnew's replacement as cabinet secretary, but no decision had been made. Several internal candidates were in the running, as were former Ontario deputies who had left for the private sector during the NDP regime. Press reports had tabbed Environment Deputy Minister Richard Dicerni as the Liberals' choice for cabinet secretary. Although Dicerni was among those under consideration, he did not enjoy any favoured status; neither McLeod nor many on the Liberal transition team even knew him (he had been appointed under the NDP). Indeed, since McLeod had had few if any dealings with most of the leading contenders, the transition team's advice was for her to meet with them immediately after the election and make her choice then.

Though it was a given that Agnew would be replaced because of his close association with Rae and the NDP, Liberal transition team members echoed the Conservatives' laudatory assessment of his role in the transition. The Liberals found him personally helpful and professional and also appreciated the thorough responses they received to their information requests from Cabinet Office. (These requests were mainly for publicly available information, but Cabinet Office provided more current data and did so far more quickly than the Liberals could have managed. Liberal inquiries about receiving information on "contentious issues" prior to the election went nowhere.) As well, the Liberals had lined up Cabinet Office assistance in identifying public servants for short-term secondments into new ministers' offices.

Senior personnel questions were of course highly sensitive, leading to concerns about possible leaks. It was thus decided that the lists of senior OPS officials proposed for firing or reassignment and of possible internal and external replacements would not be included in the main briefing book being prepared for McLeod. Instead she would be shown – not given – the lists by the person who had compiled them.

Overall, the transition team devoted substantial thought and attention to a Liberal government's relation with the OPS. This was evident, for example, in the material prepared for McLeod, which included a draft letter from the new premier to OPS staff. Without soft-pedalling the Liberals' commitment to reduce the public service by 12,000 and to bring about other fundamental restructuring, the letter emphasized McLeod's recognition of the professionalism and integrity of the Ontario bureaucracy and it promised sensitivity, fairness, and consultation. Even more telling was the template for the mandate letters to be given by the premier to deputies. These letters indicated that deputy ministers' performance would be evaluated not only on realizing the Red Book policy commitments but also on the government's corporate objectives. These were identified as corporate problem solving ("roadblocks arising from battles over ministry turf are unacceptable"); linkages between central agencies and line ministries (priorities to be centrally driven, managing implementation to be decentralized); a shift in emphasis from policy innovation to management and implementation; customer service; and continuous, wide-ranging government reform.[15]

Staffing

Though the selection of a Liberal cabinet was entirely up to McLeod (and was of course contingent on the composition of caucus), the personnel working group did offer her short lists of potential candidates for a few key portfolios. A more substantial task was sorting out and lining up ministerial staff. The Liberals' favourable situation rendered staffing issues more manageable for them than proved to be the case for the Conservatives. The Liberals' huge lead in the polls encouraged job seekers to make themselves and their credentials known well before the election. This allowed for an orderly, organized process for assessing and categorizing potential ministerial staff.

A small office, staffed by volunteers, was set up to review and process applicants' files. Accordingly, well before the election, a list of potential ministerial executive assistants and an extensive bank of candidates for other posts in ministers' offices had been established. The scope of the task was reduced by the recognition that the senior, experienced ministers would require little assistance in staffing their offices, and indeed "probably wouldn't have listened" had the centre tried to impose staffing decisions on them. New ministers, however, would generally have had executive assistants assigned to them from the centre. Staffing the Premier's Office was not much of a concern since most of the key spots were, as one Liberal put it, "pretty much locked up" by those already in McLeod's office.

The staffing process was sufficiently well under control that considerable attention could be devoted to ensuring that those rejected for political staff jobs were treated civilly and respectfully. Clear, timely communications with applicants were designed to avoid raising expectations unduly, to let unsuccessful candidates down gently and, ultimately, to keep them on good terms with the party even if they could not be offered jobs.

Structural/Policy Issues
The working group on government structure and policy implementation developed a number of ideas on restructuring government, both at macro (ministry structure) and micro (portfolio composition of cabinet committees) levels.[16] Having been told by McLeod that she wanted a cabinet of about twenty (tempered by the understanding that the precise number would depend to an extent on the size and nature of caucus), the group made extensive proposals for amalgamating and dividing ministries and reorganizing their mandates. Some were conventional, for example, consolidating the Solicitor General and Correctional Services ministries into a Ministry of Public Safety. Others were more innovative, such as the creation of a separate Ministry of Children's Services, or less conventional, such as subsuming most of the Ministry of Transportation, the Ministry of Tourism and Recreation, and responsibility for Ontario Hydro into the Economic Development ministry. Some decisions on ministry organization had yet to be finalized by the time the campaign ended.

Perhaps the most unusual idea broached the establishment of a powerful Ministry of Government Reform, to be responsible for a thorough restructuring of the OPS, fostering partnerships, customer service, and other key reform initiatives to revitalize the governmental machine. This major attempt at fomenting organizational and cultural change in the Ontario Government was the centrepiece of the Liberals' strategy for producing a government capable of responding effectively to the end-of-millennium challenges facing the province. An unusual feature of this entity was to be an active advisory committee of private sector CEOs and former cabinet secretaries (federal as well as provincial).

Among the other more noteworthy components of the Liberals' plans for structural reform were reduction in the size and scope of the Premier's Office and the Cabinet Office (modelled to some degree on similar changes in Ottawa) and creation of the post of associate minister. The role and duties of associate ministers were only vaguely sketched out, but they were to be more powerful than parliamentary assistants, who would continue to exist. Significantly, the office was discussed in the context of cabinet relations with caucus, which was the subject of a number of detailed recommendations (such as specific mandates for the first three of what were envisaged as influential caucus policy task forces – on sustainable development, the voluntary sector, and government reform).[17]

The cabinet decision-making system was to be streamlined. Although the number of cabinet committees would decline only slightly, a concerted attempt would be mounted to separate staff and structures engaged in crisis management from those setting priorities and developing policy. The Policy and Priorities Committee would be replaced with a Planning and Government Reform Committee and an Operations Committee. The Treasury Board would remain, with authority over expenditure allocations and management concerns. Two sectoral policy committees (on economic issues and social issues) would review substantive policy proposals.

Anticlimax

By the third week of the campaign, as the discouraging poll results emerged, it was becoming increasingly difficult to maintain the momentum of the transition work. Nonetheless, transition team members toiled diligently throughout the campaign, at least until the last few days, when the Liberals' fate was undeniably sealed.

During the initial stages of the exercise, little thought was given to the consequences for the transition of a minority government. One team member acknowledged that much of the planning for transition would be "totally off the table" in a minority setting. As the wheels began to fall off the Liberal campaign, a minority government began to seem a distinct possibility. Before the transition team could turn its attention to the prospect of a minority in any serious way, however, the Conservative surge had built to the point where, save some essentially pro forma gathering of briefing material for McLeod, the transition exercise effectively shut down.

In the end, beyond determining where various people with minority government experience would be on election night, nothing of substance was done to prepare for the possibility of a minority government.

Conclusion

In a few instances, the Conservatives differed from the Liberals in their approach to transition planning. For example, whereas the Liberals opted in a very limited way for paid, professional support, the Tories' efforts were undertaken entirely by volunteers. There was also a noticeable difference in the degree to which the Liberals engaged in significant planning for the recruitment and assignment of ministerial staff well before the election campaign began, and made early arrangements for vetting potential ministers for conflict of interest. Neither of these matters got much attention within the Tory camp until the election campaign was well under way. Finally, the Liberals were more inclined than the Tories to proceed by way of discussion papers and other documents; for example, they had prepared a detailed binder to be delivered to McLeod on election night.

The nature and extent of the respective leaders' involvement appears to have been quite similar. In both cases, the leader gave his or her approval to the general plans and directions that were to be followed, and received presentations from the transition people on key items as plans were firmed up. Beyond that, the leaders let their advisors get on with the job without interference or a great deal of direction. Once the campaign began, both parties created two distinct centres of activity, one for the campaign itself and the other for the transition, with informal liaison effected by senior staffers.

It can be seen that the Liberals put a good deal of effort and forethought into the question of how they would take power and the steps they would need to take to assume control of the Government of Ontario after a successful election campaign. Most of the conventional items – senior personnel assessment, relations with the senior bureaucracy, cabinet formation, the vetting of potential cabinet members, the cabinet committee system, the nomination of ministerial staff – were dealt with in advance and in a serious and thoughtful way. In truth, this should not be surprising, given that they were widely believed to be the heirs apparent; *not* to have engaged in transition planning would have been a surprise.

What is less in evidence in the case of the Liberals is a tight link between the transition work and the overall goals and strategies of the party. This is primarily because the overall goals and strategies of the party were not clearly determined or adhered to in a disciplined fashion. As the frontrunner, the Liberal Party appears to have opted to play it safe and to hedge its bets. Elements of its policy and program remained uncertain or undeveloped, or were firmed up more in response to political pressure than as a result of inherent conviction. The result was that the party's careful plans for taking power did not tie into or palpably advance its overall plans for governing Ontario.

Ironically, it was the party facing the longest odds that did the most extensive preparatory work, though the Liberals put a good deal of time and effort into their transition planning. More than anything else, what marks the Ontario Conservative Party's preparation for the transition was a thorough, highly professional, and comprehensive approach to planning. A governance mindset was established years before the election, which meant that all key elements of party activity had to be tested against the ultimate good-government goal. There needed to be solid, "implementable" policies, good candidates with an adequate regional distribution of potential cabinet ministers, a coherent election strategy, and effective transition plans to be put into effect should the party be successful in the pending election.

Despite the fact that the prospects for a Conservative victory were regarded as dim by almost everyone, the leadership of the party was able to develop a thoughtful, coherent approach to taking power. While they did not broadcast what they were doing, they were able to attract experienced people to their ranks, consult deeply if not widely on the matter, and fit their conclusions into an overall planning framework. Thus they came to power infinitely better prepared for its exercise than their predecessors had been.

Let us turn now to the act of taking power itself.

6
Cycling into Saigon: The Common Sense Revolutionaries Take Over

A Tory transition planner who had not accompanied the campaign team to North Bay for election night found himself alone in Toronto, without his campaign buddies, the morning after the election. Flushed with the excitement of victory and eager to get an early start, he entered the fourth floor of the Whitney Block, where the Cabinet Office is located. It seemed cavernous, but deserted. He had the eerie sense of apprehensive bureaucrats furtively watching him from behind the potted palms and filing cabinets. "I felt," he recalls, "like the first Viet Cong soldier cycling into Saigon after the Americans had left."

Such comments are a reminder that one of the most momentous and unremarked moments in a constitutional democracy occurs when one governing elite loses an election, and voluntarily – peacefully – gives up power to another. What in other political regimes can involve murder, a military coup, and occasionally civil war, in a constitutional order involves the peaceful, prosaic replacement of one group of rulers with another. We celebrate that accomplishment too little.

Traditionally in Canada, the people planning for a change of government carry on their work in almost complete isolation from one another until election day. The politicians and the staff in the competing political parties try to figure out the best way to take power, should they win the election. The bureaucrats in the government offices attempt to ready themselves for whatever new government the election might yield. The two previous chapters have offered an account of how these two quite different streams of activity played themselves out in the months leading up to the 1995 Ontario election.

On the political side, described in Chapter 5, the role of the governing New Democratic Party, given its gloomy electoral prospects, was confined to allowing the public service to do the necessary transition preparations without hindrance or complication. But the Liberals and the Conservatives, as we have seen, were both busy. As Liberal fortunes sank towards the end of the campaign, their plans for taking power came to a crashing halt. As Tory prospects rose, the challenge of having to grasp the reins of power efficiently and effectively assumed a stark reality.

Chapter 4 detailed the elaborate process that the Ontario public service (OPS) pursued both at the centre and in the line ministries. What contact took place between the bureaucratic and the political processes prior to the election – and there wasn't much – was tentative and indirect. The principal exceptions to this reality were the Public Policy Forum meetings between senior civil servants and representatives of the two opposition parties that, though tentative, were at least direct.

With the Conservative Party's electoral victory on 8 June 1995, the political and bureaucratic streams of activity joined, and both the Tories and the public service were confronted with the necessity of putting into practice what they had separately planned. The time pressures were formidable: the transition planners had two and a half weeks to put all the pieces in place for the new government since the Tories had settled on 26 June for the swearing-in. This date was premised more on symbolism than on logistics – it was ten years to the day since the Conservatives had turned the reins of power over to David Peterson's Liberals.

Things happened quickly at the centre. In most of the line ministries, however, a disquieting silence descended until the swearing-in, as Mike Harris and his colleagues focused on putting some of the central elements of the new government in place.

This chapter examines the actual transition from the perspective of both the centre and the line ministries. In terms of central activities, it looks particularly at the activities of the formal Conservative transition team, the construction of the cabinet, the staffing of political offices, and the new government's relations with the senior levels of the public service. The chapter then switches focus to gain "the view from the trenches" by discussing the transition experiences of three ministries: Environment and Energy, Attorney General, and Solicitor General. We conclude with a brief review of the nature and import of the treasurer's major financial statement of 21 July – which for us marks the effective end of the transition – and related developments in the summer and fall of 1995.

Taking Power at the Centre

First Days
A striking feature of the Tory takeover of power is the speed and surefootedness with which the incoming team acted. As Ernie Eves, Harris's minister of finance and closest caucus colleague, commented, "We were able

to hit the ground running on June 26. Some people are amazed that we were able to do what we did in the first four weeks. But there was a lot of hard slugging [sic] that went on behind the scenes in the weeks and months before June 26."[1]

Election day was Thursday, 8 June. On Friday, 9 June, Mike Harris, David Lindsay, and the balance of the premier-elect's entourage flew to Toronto and set to work. Lindsay called David Agnew and asked him to set the wheels in motion for the transition, which he did. Members of the Conservative team met with Agnew, who informed them of the arrangements that had been made for space and logistical support. At the Tories' request, Agnew called several deputy ministers and asked them to meet individually with Harris and his colleagues on Saturday at the Park Plaza Hotel near Queen's Park: Rita Burak, a career civil servant and the deputy at the Ministry of Agriculture and Food; Richard Dicerni, a former federal public servant who had been recruited by the outgoing premier, Bob Rae, and who was deputy at the Ministry of Environment and Energy; Larry Taman, a downtown lawyer who had served as an assistant deputy minister with Ian Scott in the Peterson government and had been brought back as deputy attorney general by Bob Rae; Deputy Health Minister Margaret Mottershead, a long-time public servant; Michelle Noble, the deputy at Solicitor General/Correctional Services; and Judith Wolfson, a lawyer who had joined the provincial government in the early 1980s and was deputy of Consumer and Commercial Relations.

None knew for certain the purpose of the meeting, nor who else was being contacted. But the purpose soon became clear: the Harris team regarded them as the key deputies, wanted them to know that, and wanted their advice on how to proceed. The meetings were also, at least for a couple of the deputy ministers, something of an interview for the top job of cabinet secretary. The deputies were brought to a suite in the hotel where they met first with members of the transition team; then they were taken to another room where they met with Mike Harris and David Lindsay. They were consulted both about matters within their specific area of responsibility and about some of the larger challenges the government would be facing. Several spoke afterwards of the sophistication and civility of these encounters. One deputy, who was invited to stay for lunch, realized that a new era was at hand: the food was actually decent and the sound of a cork popping was music to the ears.

News of these meetings spread through Queen's Park like wildfire, as the Tories must surely have known it would. This accomplished three purposes: first, it instantly identified the key officials in the Harris government; second, it made it clear that the incoming Conservatives knew what they wanted to do with the public service and would act with speed and determination; and third, it sent a message to the public service that the new government was prepared to work with officials and to respect their competence (though not everyone in government necessarily believed the message).

By the following Tuesday – five days after the election – arrangements had been made for the departure of David Agnew as cabinet secretary (to Massey College at the University of Toronto, with some part-time consulting for the government), and Rita Burak had been chosen as the new cabinet secretary. Another rapid change involved Jay Kaufman, the deputy minister of finance under the Rae government. Kaufman, who was widely perceived to be an NDP fellow traveller, had met with Harris and the Tory transition team, told them he assumed they weren't serious about the fiscal plan set out in *The Common Sense Revolution,* and inquired what they really wanted to do. By Wednesday, Kaufman had been released and his replacement (Michael Gourley, a vice-president at the University of Western Ontario and, before that, a senior public servant at Queen's Park) was at work.

It should be noted that these key moves were made before the Tories were even sworn in as the government on 26 June, prompting one central-agency official to remark: "The NDP assumed office, but they never took power. These guys are taking power even before they have assumed office." A small illustration of this point were the orders from Harris's office that Jeff Rose, the deputy minister of intergovernmental affairs and a close Rae confidant, should be effectively frozen out of the preparations the ministry was making for a meeting between Harris and Prime Minister Chrétien.

Once Rita Burak had been identified as the new cabinet secretary, she became a de facto member of the transition team, carrying responsibility for the public service dimension of the process (within, of course, the context of the transition team's previous work on the bureaucracy). The key personnel decisions were made by the cabinet secretary-designate and by the incoming premier. David Agnew, still formally in office until just before the swearing-in, performed a caretaker role as the official formally responsible, ensuring that the decisions and requests relayed to him by Rita Burak were carried out. One of the participants noted that the arrangement was awkward and cumbersome, given that the cabinet secretary-designate had to work indirectly through the incumbent, and that it would have been preferable had the outgoing government agreed to make the appointment official immediately, on behalf of the new government. Another participant made a rather different suggestion about how the Tories could have coped with the coordination and follow-through problem, namely, to have appointed David Agnew, who was after all the sitting cabinet secretary, to the transition team. Organizationally and logistically, such an arrangement would have made sense, but politically it surely would have been a non-starter.

The Functioning of the Transition Team

Clearly, the Tories' success in the taking of power owed a good deal to their very able and experienced transition team. As announced on 13 June 1995, the eleven-member team included David Lindsay and William Farlinger, Ernie Eves, four former Ontario deputy ministers, the director of administration for the Conservative caucus, and three people from the private sector, two of whom had extensive experience working in Tory ministers' offices in the 1970s and 1980s. (See Appendix D for a list.) In fact, several other people were as much a part of the transition team but were for various reasons not included in the official press release (for example, Stanley Hartt, who had been chief of staff to Prime Minister Brian Mulroney). The former deputies and political activists on the team brought a wealth of practical government experience. Significantly, private sector business types without extensive first-hand experience in government were a decided minority among the members of the transition team and, on matters relating to the public service, were inclined to defer to those with direct experience. A member of the team commented that its diversity was an important source of strength. The team included "policy wonks," "campaign street fighters," and former bureaucrats; moreover, in assembling the team "no segment of the party was left out ... Everyone [in the party] knew someone on the transition team." While this view was doubtless accurate in terms of Conservative Party dynamics, it is a telling comment that, in a 1990s Ontario context, an overwhelmingly male, middle-class, Anglo-Celtic group would be described as "diverse."

Members of the transition team we interviewed highlighted the crucial role played by co-chair William Farlinger. "Farlinger made it all tick," said one, pointing not only to his reputation in the business world but also to his close ties to Harris. This combination of attributes permitted Farlinger to bring credibility to the transition team that few others might have managed. Farlinger's effectiveness, another insider noted, was heightened by his dominating personality: "Farlinger is a very intimidating individual ... Both members of the transition team and ministers were intimidated by him."

After swearing a secrecy oath and signing a confidentiality agreement, the members of the transition team settled smoothly into offices prepared for them in the Whitney Block, across the street from the Legislative Building. Meanwhile, a small group of people, centred around Harris and Lindsay and who would form the embryo of the Premier's Office staff, saw to policy decisions that had to be made quickly and dealt with media and communications issues – in short, they handled the politics. Thus the division during the campaign between those with political responsibilities and those working on transition continued. To no one's surprise, the critical decisions were made primarily by Harris in consultation with Lindsay, Farlinger, and Eves. Although these three close advisors were all on the transition team, what counted was Harris's trust in their judgment rather than any influence of the transition team per se. Accordingly, the transition team didn't get directly involved in politics or policy; it concentrated on the nuts and bolts of taking over a government and trying to manage relations with the public service. As one member put it, "It became apparent early on that we didn't have the staff or the mandate to do anything on policy beyond organizing high-level briefings to search out the major issues." A central objective of their work was ensuring that the key political players were not distracted from their political tasks by mundane yet essential questions of management and organization.[2]

The transition team rapidly settled into a routine that persisted more or less until it went out of commission when the government was sworn in. The group would meet at 7:30 a.m. to sort out problems and ensure that nothing was falling between stools, then each person would go off to work on individual assignments. Members were given responsibility for specific tasks: for example, the organization of briefing sessions for incoming Tory MPPs and cabinet ministers; the formulation of a cabinet committee structure; the vetting of potential cabinet ministers; the political staffing of ministerial offices; and relations with the bureaucracy, including senior appointments. Dealing with such matters in a sure-handed way was important in fulfilling what one member of the team described as "the most important role played by the transition team ... its calming influence" on politicians and bureaucrats alike.

Central agency bureaucrats who dealt with the transition team reported that its members didn't ask a lot of questions and on matters of process (logistics of cabinet meetings, paper flow, and the like) were generally content to ask how things had been done before and retain the existing system. "On process issues, they [transition team members] asked and accepted the advice of the public service." Among other things, this gave them the advantage of seeming to be on top of things. It also meant that more time was available to deal with personnel concerns, which required more of the transition team's energies than the bureaucrats we interviewed had anticipated. For their part, members of the transition team took away from their experience a positive view of the central agency officials with whom they dealt, though one did comment that it was hard to take the measure of the bureaucrats since so many were so obviously concerned about being fired should they misstep.

The consistent message received from those we interviewed was that the system proved very effective. The planning process had prepared the group for most of the issues it would need to address. Members worked hard and worked well with one another; most found the experience enjoyable – one explicitly used the word "fun." Members were given ample latitude to complete their assignments; they did not indulge in game-playing, and egos were kept in check. This last may have been in part due to the fact that none of the members of the team was angling for future favour or employment with the government. Several did stay on in one role or another after the windup of the transition, but most of these individuals had been with the party in opposition; others had had no intention of staying and had to be persuaded. The operating principle, however, was that the transition work was a non-partisan, short-term assignment, not the start of a career in government.[3] Said one experienced member of the group: "It was the most businesslike of all the transitions I've seen. We stuck to our knitting and avoided political intrigue."

Cabinet and the Cabinet Office
The Tories' commitment to downsizing was applied to the central operations of the new government: a cut in the number of cabinet ministers and the consolidation of a number of ministries; a cut in the size of the Premier's Office; a cut in the size of the Cabinet Office; and a reduction in the number of cabinet committees.

As discussed in Chapter 5, Harris's advisors had prepared a number of cabinet models for the leader's consideration. They ranged in size from thirteen to twenty-two ministries with roughly equivalent numbers of ministers. The stripped-down model would have meant a cabinet smaller than any since the days of George Drew in the 1940s. Even the largest cabinet envisaged by the Tory planners was at the small end of the range of recent Ontario cabinets. Davis's final cabinet had thirty members and Frank Miller's first cabinet sported no fewer than thirty-three ministers; Peterson's cabinet initially had twenty-two but expanded to thirty by the end of his mandate and Rae's cabinet ranged between twenty-four and twenty-seven.

Mike Harris settled on a cabinet of nineteen. (As did his predecessors, Harris gradually expanded his cabinet; following the 1999 election it had grown to twenty-four.) Ultimately, as do all other first ministers, Harris made his choice based on his own best judgment, tempered by the views of his closest political advisors, but he did seek advice on prospective ministers from members of the transition team. Twelve of the nineteen ministers had served in the previous House, but nine experienced MPPs were left disappointed. Most of the returning MPPs not appointed to cabinet received consolation prizes in the form of parliamentary assistantships (one became Speaker of the House). Within the constraints imposed by the electors (Harris was the only Conservative elected in northern Ontario), the cabinet was reasonably representative of the province's regions, though ministers from Toronto and its suburban fringe were surprisingly numerous (five from Toronto proper; four from adjacent suburbs). According to Tory insiders, conscious efforts had been made to recruit high-quality candidates in various regions to serve as "geographic anchors" for cabinet, so as to avoid the problem that the NDP encountered of regional imperatives producing unknown and untested ministers. Harris's cabinet included four women, though not for the most part in influential posts, and one visible minority MPP. If a common thread could be divined among Harris's choices it was that the cabinet – like the caucus – was replete with "self-made men" and ministers from small business backgrounds. John Ibbitson contends that Harris "deliberately decided to appoint ministers to areas in which they had little or no previous experience."[4] Certainly this was true in several cases, but it was hardly a universal principle: in the previous parliament, five ministers had been official party critics for the portfolios they were given (and two other ministers had been critics in the more remote past); as well, Environment and Energy Minister Brenda Elliott had run an environmental products store and Bill Sanderson, the economic development minister, had extensive Bay Street experience.

The cabinet decision-making system in place from the NDP era featured an array of committees in addition to a full cabinet. A powerful Policy and Priorities Committee effectively served as an inner cabinet, while Treasury Board and Management Board (committees) oversaw the government's finances and its managerial responsibilities, respectively; a range of sectoral policy committees – on justice, economic development, social policy, and the like – also formed part of the cabinet structure. The memo from the former deputies on the transition team – which reviewed Ontario cabinet models from the Davis, Peterson, and Rae eras, and outlined the choices and decisions that had to be made – set the parameters for restructuring.

Given that the government would be focusing on a narrow, tough fiscal agenda and that such an agenda would have to be driven from the top, a streamlined cabinet process eliminating the policy committees seemed to make the most sense. This would reduce the opportunities for special pleading and stifle the inevitable spending proclivities of program ministries. Moreover, the policy committees' prime purpose was to generate and vet new policy proposals, but the incoming government already knew what it wanted to do and wasn't interested in new ideas or in being distracted from its fiscal priorities by opening up a series of internal policy debates. The goal, said one Harris advisor, was "implementation not debate." According to one Rae-era deputy, prior to the election some thought had been given at senior bureaucratic levels to reducing the number of cabinet committees and the complexity of the system, so that at least in some OPS circles, the streamlining idea was greeted positively. In presenting their arguments and conclusions to Harris and Eves, the three former deputies on the transition team also underlined the political complications of such a move. The ministers excluded from the powerful

Policy and Priorities Committee, who otherwise would have felt involved through chairing and participating in sectoral policy committees, would feel aggrieved at their lack of clout. Moreover, ministers would be more likely to get upset from time to time at not being consulted on major decisions affecting their ministries.

Despite these implications, Harris decided to proceed with the recommendation to eliminate the policy committees, on the understanding that adjustments could be made later should circumstances require. Just three standing committees of cabinet were confirmed: Policy and Priorities; Management Board (combining the previously separate functions of Management Board and Treasury Board); and Legislation and Regulations. Other cabinet committees would be established as needed on an ad hoc basis. However, it was the intention of the premier that they would focus on specific issues and that they would work within a limited time frame. (Some months later, central agency officials were of the view that the abolition of the sectoral committees resulted in palpably improved working relations among Cabinet Office, Ministry of Finance, and Management Board Secretariat on central policy issues.)

Both Cabinet Office and the Premier's Office echoed this stripped-down approach to governing. Their size was reduced substantially from what they had been under the Rae government. This was consistent with the central political message of having to do more with less; it also reflected, at least as far as Cabinet Office was concerned, the operating preferences of the incoming cabinet secretary, who wished to see line ministries and deputies take fuller responsibility for the informal coordination of overlapping activities and boundary problems. She also chose not to replace the deputy-level policy job in Cabinet Office, an inheritance from the previous regime, and instead established an assistant deputy minister-level "policy coordinator" position, reflecting the view that there was no great need to develop policy substantively but that there *was* a role in overseeing the implementation of policy. Two deputy minister-level positions were subsequently established in Cabinet Office, one to manage restructuring of the Ontario public service and the other to serve as associate secretary to cabinet and to oversee communications.

The Common Sense Revolution had said nothing about government structures and the Tories made relatively few changes to the existing ministry structure. This was a deliberate choice, made on the premise that the policy changes the government planned would be difficult enough without having to devote extensive time and energy to restructuring; as one Harris advisor put it, "Debate on how to reorganize government doesn't cut a goddamn thing." The oft-reconstructed Ministry of Culture, Tourism and Recreation was dismembered, with its cultural activities placed in the citizenship ministry and the other components absorbed into the Ministry of Economic

Development and Trade. In a reversal of an important central agency reform carried out by the NDP, Treasury Board, which was responsible for financial oversight, was merged with Management Board, whose remit included management and direction of the public service and related matters. Whether this change was, as some central agency figures averred, more important than the elimination of most cabinet committees is an open question. A little-noticed but significant realignment of bureaucratic power complemented the amalgamation of the two boards: the Programs and Estimates Division of the Ministry of Finance was shifted to the Management Board Secretariat (where it had been located prior to the NDP's reorganization of central agencies in the early 1990s). One deputy minister explained that the separation of fiscal policy from management issues had proved effective in the Davis era and that it was particularly important that a government fixated on fiscal concerns not dissipate its energies on management issues: "You don't want the deputy minister of finance worrying about purchasing procedures." A less sanguine view from other bureaucrats was that this restructuring fomented a debilitating turf war between the deputies at the Ministry of Finance and Management Board for control over crucial expenditure decisions and, paradoxically, abandoned the gains towards centralized financial decision making made during the NDP's time in office. Still others saw the change as less significant, since "to some extent it is just a name change," as one bureaucrat put it, with most people in the division continuing to do essentially the same things they had done prior to the reorganization.

The general proposition that guided the choices made in all of these areas was that it was easier to start out small and add strength incrementally if necessary than to start big and try to cut back later. In addition, it was thought to be important to set examples of restraint at the centre for the benefit of the government as a whole.

To ensure adequate administrative coordination, the cabinet secretary and the other deputy ministers brainstormed about what was required in the new circumstances. Expanding the existing system of deputy minister committees was one obvious alternative. Rita Burak adopted this approach, laid out a structure, and named the chairs. These committees included Justice, Social Policy, Business Climate, Major Transfers, Management Board (including Information Technology and Labour Relations), Executive Development, Audit, and Aboriginal Affairs. Some of these committees had existed under the NDP; others were new.

Setting Up the Premier's Office
As in any government, the arrangements for political support for the first minister – the Premier's Office – were critical. Two basic principles underpinned the establishment of Harris's office. For reasons of political

symbolism, the Tories simply had to reduce the number of political operatives in the Premier's Office; the whole philosophy of *The Common Sense Revolution* was cutting back on government and politicians. At the same time, the Premier's Office clearly would have to manage a large number of difficult political files; it therefore needed to be tough, decisive, and effective. The first objective was certainly achieved, but to the detriment, some argued, of the second.

The transition team talked to various people with experience in Ottawa, in other provinces, and in previous Tory regimes about the design of the Premier's Office. It took some time before recognition set in, however, that the particular tasks and constraints it faced were qualitatively different from those faced by earlier premier's offices: "We used to refer to 'the Ray MacNeil position' or 'the Gordon Ashworth job' until we realized that we were developing a different model."[5] The philosophy underlying the Premier's Office was entirely consistent with the overall thrust of the transition: "set up the office to allow David [Lindsay] to focus on the government's agenda as much as possible." This meant giving Lindsay direct control over policy, issue management, and communications while keeping everything else – correspondence, administration, scheduling, and the like – nearby but off Lindsay's desk. As principal secretary and as the government's prime strategic thinker, Lindsay was at the centre of all political activity; he was, in a very real sense, the premier's alter ego. Lindsay was the only official in the Premier's Office to report directly to Harris.

Those whom Lindsay gathered about him, from the campaign team and the Leader's Office from opposition days, were widely viewed – by both politicians and bureaucrats – as bright, highly competent, and tireless. The problem was that while they were very good, they were simply too few and therefore too stretched. In retrospect, several insiders (both from the Premier's Office and from ministers' offices) concluded that more staff should have been hired for the Premier's Office from the outset and that some of the government's political problems could be traced, at least in part, to the lack of capacity in the Premier's Office.[6] Bureaucrats from both central agencies and line departments recounted delays and problems resulting from their inability to secure answers and directions from the Premier's Office on key issues. In response, one senior Tory politico questioned this Premier's Office-as-bottleneck interpretation, noting that the government was rarely accused in its early days of moving too slowly. The issue, however, may have been less one of pace than of approach. One bureaucrat close to the centre observed several months after the election that some senior political staff were having trouble adjusting from the campaign trail to government, with its inherent complexities, bureaucratic necessities, and long timelines: to some extent, "they're still in campaign mode, where it's possible to rewrite the speech half an hour before the person steps up to the podium."

In designing the Premier's Office, the crucial link with Cabinet Office was a central concern. Thus the two were physically reunited on the fourth floor of the Whitney Block (traditionally, Cabinet Office and Premier's Office officials worked in adjacent offices in the Legislative Building, but Rae had moved Cabinet Office across the street, while he and his staff had remained in the Legislative Building). In keeping with the transition objectives of depoliticizing the public service and separating politics from administration, the Premier's Office was structured so as to avoid mirroring or duplicating the work of Cabinet Office. The policy unit, for example, initially comprised a solitary staff person.

MPPs and Cabinet Ministers: Orientation and Vetting

The non-partisan staff at the legislature provide regular briefings after each election for MPPs of all parties. Avoiding any overlap with that exercise, the Conservatives organized two orientation sessions, one for MPPs and the other for cabinet ministers. The party's orientation sessions were handled primarily by Pat Jacobsen. A former associate secretary of cabinet, she was seconded for three weeks from her job as vice-president, human resources, at Manulife Financial.

In fashioning the party's briefing session for MPPs, the transition team co-chairs explicitly took into account the two very different types of members composing the new caucus. The lion's share – some sixty-one of the eighty-two Tory members – were newly elected and thus had no legislative experience whatsoever.[7] A third of the returning MPPs had been at Queen's Park since the previous Tory regime, but at best their experience would be, by 1995, ten years old. Of the six MPPs who had previous ministerial experience, only one – Norm Sterling – had served in the Davis government; the balance, including Harris and Eves, were ministers for barely four months under Frank Miller. On the premise that a little knowledge might be a dangerous thing (the returning MPPs might believe they knew how government worked, but in fact be ignorant of the significance of some of the radical changes that had occurred in government during the last decade) all MPPs, the experienced as well as the novices, were required to attend the full orientation session. It dealt with such matters as values, public trust, and integrity; the public role of members; and the mechanics of setting up a member's office and choosing staff. A real effort was made to communicate to the members what the incoming premier wanted his government to be known for.

The one-day session was held at the University of Toronto ten days after the election and involved panel discussions. Ernie Eves and veteran MPP

Elizabeth Witmer spoke from their own experience about what it meant to be a member of the provincial parliament. Barbara Cowieson, director of administration in the Progressive Conservative Service Bureau, made a presentation about organizational issues, such as setting up an office and choosing staff.

William Farlinger oversaw the arrangements for vetting potential ministers. Planning for this activity did not begin until well into the election campaign. A committee of three was struck, composed of Darcy McKeough, a prominent Conservative and highly respected former provincial treasurer, Tory insider Jim Bailey, and Rob Prichard, president of the University of Toronto. Because of Prichard's associations with David Peterson and Peterson's attorney general, Ian Scott, there was some resistance in party circles to his participation. However, a case was made that he was a lawyer, he had done the same job for Peterson, he wanted to do it, and there was no reason not to trust him. Harris accepted the proposal, even speaking directly to an opponent of the idea to get him to agree. After that, all went smoothly. In addition to the committee itself, a team of about a dozen lawyers from major Toronto law firms volunteered their time to assist in the vetting process.

Harris and Farlinger decided to review every MPP, both because this was worthwhile in its own right and because it was a way of doing the necessary screening without tipping the premier-designate's hand about who was being considered for cabinet. Each MPP filled out an extensive questionnaire, which formed the basis for a searching interview. The team looked at business interests, possible conflicts of interest, and any personal history that might prove embarrassing. To overcome initial resistance to this process, Mike Harris and Ernie Eves were screened first, which stopped the grumbling. The process began with McKeough talking to each person; then the person would be sent to the lawyers for a full-scale vetting. If a problem arose, the three committee members would discuss whether the matter might be resolved. If it could not be, then the committee would talk to Harris and Farlinger. It appears to have been a smoothly operating and effective process: during the entire first mandate of the Harris government, no minister came under serious attack on conflict-of-interest grounds.

With the potential ministers vetted and the actual ministers appointed, a second orientation session was held for ministers a few days after the swearing-in. This session discussed the role of a minister; the need for balance in the constituency, ministry, and collective dimensions of their responsibilities; and their coordination functions. About a third of the seminar was spent on relations with the public service, involving a panel that included Tom Campbell and Rita Burak. Emphasis was placed on the distinction between the political and bureaucratic functions and on the value of a professional public service. Consistent with that emphasis, it was argued that a new government should get rid of the partisans in the bureaucracy early and then work professionally with those who remain. Mike Harris spoke at this session, saying much the same thing he would say subsequently to deputy ministers and to executive assistants to ministers.

One inexperienced minister, interviewed some considerable time later, professed no recollection whatsoever of the orientation session for ministers. She didn't doubt that the session had taken place, but concluded that in the blur of briefings and meetings, she was simply too new to appreciate the significance of the information presented.[8] Especially with regards to process issues and advice on "how to be a minister," these comments reflect a catch-22 dilemma. For ministers, particularly those setting out on their duties with little or no political experience, it may be difficult to absorb important advice and information in the abstract. Yet by the time they've been in office long enough to appreciate and benefit from that advice, they will already have encountered many occasions when they needed it and likely will be unwilling to take time from hectic schedules for meetings to tell them what they think they already know.

The transition team supplied all ministers with briefing documents tailored to their new responsibilities and setting out the policies and priorities of the new government. Detailed charts accompanied each document and outlined the nature of relevant party commitments, the source of the commitment (usually *The Common Sense Revolution*), and the proposed time frame for implementing the commitment. Ministers were also provided with comprehensive briefing notes on critical issues identified by the transition team.[9] The documents stated clearly that "only the new Cabinet has the power to decide how we will deal with commitments and statements made before the election. The Transition Team's job is merely to ensure that you are aware of them." (This document is included as Appendix E.)

Not surprisingly, one potential source of experienced advice and information that new ministers chose not to explore was the departing government. We were told that some very limited information exchanges took place at the staff level and that at least one outgoing NDP minister did have a serious policy discussion with his Tory successor, but these were very much exceptions. One Conservative minister discussed with her staff the pros and cons of contacting her NDP predecessor but in the end decided not to do so.

Dealing with the Deputies

As already noted, within days of being elected the Conservatives had replaced Cabinet Secretary David Agnew with Rita Burak, and Finance Deputy Minister Jay Kaufman with Michael Gourley. In addition, the Park

Plaza meetings with several deputy ministers two days after the election had made it clear who a number of the key bureaucratic players in the new regime would be.[10]

Early on, Harris attempted to assure a nervous public service that while some changes were in the offing, his government was not about to engage in a purge of officials who had been brought in during the Liberal and NDP regimes: "What we will truly rely on is who is the professional within the bureaucracy? Who are the best? Who are good? Who understands the agenda? ... That's more important than whether they were brought in under the Liberals or the NDP."[11]

Just before the swearing-in, seven more deputy ministers were fired: Thomas Brzustowski (Premier's Councils), Thea Herman (Ministry of Labour), Michael Mendelson (Cabinet Office), Rosemary Proctor (Community and Social Services), Jeff Rose (Intergovernmental Affairs), Jim Thomas (Management Board Secretariat), and Grant Wedge (Native Affairs Secretariat). One member of the transition team, who registered mild surprise at some of the names on the list of deputies to be dismissed and at some of the names not on the list, commented that "the choices very much bore the stamp of the premier and the cabinet secretary."

Although the Conservatives had stated that no further deputy minister firings would take place, Charles Pascal, the deputy minister of education, was dismissed a month after the new government took power.[12] Various rumours had Pascal as the loser of a struggle with his minister or as a victim of the Premier's Office, fired over his minister's objections; whatever the explanation, the Pascal firing sent shock waves through the system and undercut some of the positive messages the government was attempting to send to the public service.

Any thoughts that some Tories may have had about a purge of allegedly politicized bureaucrats below the deputy minister level were squelched by Farlinger, who insisted that the senior bureaucrats be entrusted to run their own shops and that it was their job, not the politicians', to fire those who deserved it. In our research we heard about less than a handful of bureaucrats other than the deputies who were said to have been fired because they were tainted by too close an association with the NDP. At the same time, several public servants whom we asked about this were unable to specify anyone who had been fired for political reasons but were also unprepared to accept that it had not happened, pointing out that the massive staff cutbacks made it easy to get rid of politically unpalatable employees under the cover of downsizing.

If overtly political firings below the deputy rank were very rare, it is clear that the Tories sanctioned a far-reaching restoration of an old bureaucratic guard at the senior levels of the OPS. Given the prominence in the transition team of such Davis-era deputies as Tom Campbell, Graham Scott, and Brock Smith, this was hardly surprising. As with any shift in power within a large organization, this entailed numerous consequent changes in personnel at the middle and senior levels of the public service as the bureaucratic fortunes of various players waxed and waned according to their links and experiences with the new bureaucratic elite and with the deposed deputies. Government bureaucracies may not be partisan but they are very political places, and the OPS is no exception; bureaucratic politics certainly played a role in the promotions and firings that occurred throughout the OPS in the months after the Tories came to power.

The Tories' strategy was to dismiss and replace quickly those who in their judgment had to go, and to do so in the name of re-establishing the foundations of a professional public service, allegedly compromised by five years of NDP rule. (Indeed, by playing to their prejudices and preferences, the Tories clearly exploited the bad blood between certain senior bureaucratic cadres and the NDP.) In keeping with this approach, the new appointments were all filled by serving or former public servants. The approach implied that those who were let go were partisan and incapable of working professionally with the new regime. Were they? Some had clear and obvious New Democratic affiliations, or were close friends of Bob Rae, but one could not contend that all who were let go were "tainted" by political associations with the former government. It is important to recall here that, as suggested in Chapter 3, the judgment about the degree to which the public service is neutral or politicized is in part a matter of perception. Some former deputies, and some deputies who survived the Tory purge, held the conviction that the Ontario public service had been politicized by the NDP and that the Conservatives were restoring its professional neutrality. To some extent, this interpretation confused centralization with politicization. The NDP had attempted, with mixed success, to enhance their capacity to implement their political agenda by imposing a greater degree of central bureaucratic coordination and control on the Ontario government than had any of its predecessors. The resentment in some bureaucratic circles of the NDP's efforts at shifting the system's balance of power towards the centre is significant here. David Wolfe has commented on the ease with which the desire to assert political control can be confused with attempts to politicize the bureaucracy: "The Ontario public service had long enjoyed an extraordinary tradition of bureaucratic decentralization, with far weaker control by central agencies than had been established at the federal level in the 1960s. Therefore, the old line bureaucrats who reacted negatively to the NDP's changes ... may have been reacting more to the NDP's assertion of central control over the policy system than to the making of an excessive number of political appointments at senior bureaucratic levels, since relatively few such appointments were actually made."[13]

Just as the NDP had offended bureaucratic traditionalists with their efforts to impose greater central control on the ministries, the Tories' sanctioning of Cabinet Secretary Rita Burak's reduction of Cabinet Office's influence in the policy-making process and the devolution of power back to the ministries was greeted favourably and interpreted as depoliticization.

The Conservatives adroitly took advantage of the perception that the OPS had been severely politicized by the NDP. But a salty comment by one of the fired deputies is worth noting: "I think that changing ten or so DMs [deputy ministers] – one-third of the senior cadre – as the Harris government has done is far more draconian than anything the NDP did, and a much more drastic intervention into the principle of the non-partisan public service. It's just not perceived as partisan by the main OPS players now." In at least a couple of firings, it is not clear – neither to us nor to many in the bureaucracy – in what sense the deputy failed to meet the criteria of professional competence and a willingness to work within the framework of *The Common Sense Revolution*.

Harris held his first meeting with deputies on 27 June, the day after the new government was sworn in. His remarks at the Deputy Ministers' Council paralleled a message he had given to his ministers and would subsequently give to Tory political staff. The text of his speech was distributed to senior managers throughout the public service. (See Appendix F for the full text of the speech.) Especially in the parts that address the principles of the public service and the appropriate working relationship between ministers and senior officials, Harris's speech draws heavily, in both vocabulary and concepts, from draft remarks that the Public Policy Forum had offered as a guide for an early meeting of the new premier with deputy ministers. (See Appendix A for the Public Policy Forum material.)

The most important feature of Harris's speech from our point of view is his statement of his conception of the public service and the proper relationship between bureaucrats and politicians. The new premier set the context with the following general statement: "I believe that Ontario is best served by a strong, healthy, and mutually respectful relationship between the government and the public service. I believe in a professional public service with appointments on the basis of merit. This means that the vast majority, but not all appointments to senior positions will be made from within the Ontario Public Service." He then proceeded to make five specific points, which can be paraphrased thus:

1 The traditional division of authority between the political and the departmental echelons of government must be respected. The cabinet

will make policy decisions after receiving advice from the public service; the public service will implement the decisions, once made.
2 A strong relationship between the minister and the deputy minister is essential. There must be regular, direct communication, not subject to the control of anyone else.
3 Beyond serving the minister, deputies have a second responsibility, which is serving the premier. This relationship will be expressed through the cabinet secretary, whose communications with the premier will be confidential.
4 While deputies and their ministers have line responsibility, they also have and must perform a corporate role with respect to the overall interests of the government.
5 "Parallel governments" should not exist, nor should political staff give orders to public servants. Ministers' offices will be much smaller than they have been. Political staff will manage the day-to-day political affairs of the minister and his or her communications with the public, the legislature, and the media.

This is an unvarnished but serviceable version of the conventional understanding of the relations between government and public service in a parliamentary democracy. Indeed, what is striking in the statement is the relative absence of business vocabulary and imagery and the relatively slight reliance on the private sector, either as a model or as a source of personnel and ideas.

It is simplicity itself to construe the Tories' Ontario project in classic business terms: a hostile takeover of a wealthy but foundering corporation; the arrival of no-nonsense, aggressive new management; a ruthless turnaround operation, where failing product lines are terminated and uncompromising cost-cutting measures are introduced to staunch the flow of red ink. Yet, while that describes much of the substance of the new government's mandate, in this speech, at least, Mike Harris makes little explicit appeal to business and business culture.

Several other parts of the speech are worth noting in passing. There is a stark outline of the mess that the premier sees confronting Ontario and a strong statement of determination to fix it. Declaring that "the problems ahead are massive, mistakes unavoidable and vigorous and sometimes destructive criticism inevitable," Harris speaks of the "gut-wrenching changes both inside and outside government" that will be called for during his mandate. He outlines the key elements of the Common Sense Revolution and states that he is "unconditionally committed" to reaching those goals. It was a sobering message for the members of the Deputy Ministers' Council and a clear declaration of what would be expected of them under the new regime, but it was also consistent with what Harris and his Tory colleagues had been saying during the campaign and would say later – for example, at the time of the July economic statement.

In the senior ranks of the Ontario mandarinate, the removal of the "partisan" deputies and the return to a decentralized model of policy making contributed to a positive view of the new government. So too did the Tories' more "civilized" behaviour. Said one deputy, "It was important that they were respectful; there was an assumption that we were professionals and that we would do the right thing"; another observed, "It's so nice to have ministers say 'thank you'"; yet another gushed, "God, they have good manners compared to the other bunch [the NDP]." Bad manners is not politicization but it can be an important factor in shaping critical political-bureaucratic linkages. One central agency official noted on this point that "with much of the bureaucracy the clash of class cultures [with the NDP] was immediate and visceral ... [whereas] the Tory and Liberal cadres do come from the professional middle classes. Senior bureaucrats are far more comfortable with Tories and Libs: they come from the same class and share similar world views." Whatever its roots, the NDP's human relations with the senior ranks of the OPS were little short of disastrous; one deputy, who professed to be closer ideologically to the NDP than to the Tories (but who survived the purge) argued that the NDP's inner group seemed to have taken its cue from Rae's weak social skills with senior officials and came across as rude, uncaring, and dismissive, with no respect for the public servants whose job it was to support them. Both by design and by inclination, the Tories played on their "better manners" to build a positive working relationship with the deputy ministers.

If the Tories were appropriately polite and respectful, apparently public servants were sometimes found lacking in the requisite social graces. In one ministry, a memo came down from senior management castigating staff for not treating the minister appropriately and setting out proper rules of conduct for dealing with him. Staff were enjoined not to lecture the minister with slides in boardroom settings but to sit beside him on the couch to explain issues and problems and to observe strict limits as to the number of officials taking part in ministerial meetings.

Manners aside, the senior officials' favourable view of the Tories was by no means universal in the OPS. The respect and appreciation shown to the top public servants were often notably absent in the Tories' dealings with the middle ranks of the bureaucracy. A common sentiment among middle managers in the OPS was that the Conservatives proved every bit as contemptuous of civil servants as the NDP had been, albeit for different reasons. The Tories were certainly adroit at winning the support of the upper reaches of the public service, but it is very much an open question whether this reflects simply an astute strategic decision aimed at taking control of the bureaucracy or a genuine belief in the values and importance of the public service.[14]

The Staffing of Political Offices

Staffing of political offices was generally agreed, among those interviewed, to be the most problematic component of the transition process. Part of the problem was structural. Unlike the Liberal Party, which, as the odds-on favourite to win, had started early and developed a substantial roster of possible political staff, the Tories, as a party regarded as having little chance to win, did not attract a large number of able and ambitious people to its ranks. As the person responsible for the staffing function stated, "We were after a particularly narrow market, mainly people who had a meaningful involvement in the Progressive Conservative Party and preferably those who had direct hands-on experience in the recent election and a thorough understanding of the policy platform. As well, candidates had to have the energy and enthusiasm to work extremely long hours for relatively low pay."[15]

Caucus staff from opposition days were far too few to fill many of the gaps (moreover, key opposition staff moved with David Lindsay into the Premier's Office), though some accepted the critical "executive assistant" positions – the top staff posts. The party engaged in an informal process to attract qualified people by putting the word out through party headquarters, through the central campaign organization, through the fundraising organization, and through the campaign itself. In addition, the provincial party used the federal party network to let people know about its personnel needs, though there was evident wariness about taking on what one senior figure termed "Mulroney retreads." Individual members of the transition team also encouraged people in consulting firms and law firms to think about taking on staff positions. Much of this took place rather late in the game, however, and we heard comments that a greater effort might have been made more quickly to seek out potential staff through individuals and organizations friendly to the party. An important barrier to successful recruitment, though, was that, particularly for the executive assistant positions, the pay rates could not compete with the salaries that high-quality potential recruits were earning in the private sector.

If not enough top-notch candidates came forward or were recruited, too many résumés poured in from those the team did not particularly want. Some unsolicited applications turned up quality candidates, so that between sifting through the résumé pile for good prospects and ensuring that everyone was treated civilly, so as not to sour them on the party, a good deal of time and effort was spent on recruiting and reviewing potential staffers.

Not only was the pool of known, experienced candidates far too small, but also the physical capacity of the team assigned to vet the thousand applications for staff positions – received within days of the election – proved quite inadequate. One senior transition planner supervised the process, with assistance from another party official, an OPS human resources specialist, and public service clerical support. Would-be political staffers who wrote in seeking posts received a brief acknowledgment letter that noted, "We originally intended to interview everyone who contacted us, but the volume of applicants and the tight time frame required us to change our approach to a résumé screening process."[16] The team reviewed résumés, interviewed candidates, and produced a book of recommended candidates from which ministers could draw their top staff.

One member of the transition team, who had been involved in the Mulroney transition in Ottawa, advised against centrally assigning political staff to ministers. The critical question of personal compatibility between a minister and senior political staff, the thinking was, could only be judged by those directly involved; moreover, the signal to ministers implicit in imposing staff from the centre – that the premier and his top advisors did not trust them to make important decisions – was hardly the message that the government wanted to send. Thus for the most part ministers were left to choose their own staff. In many instances, this meant choosing one or two top people and then delegating much of the remaining hiring to the executive assistant. Harris went out of his way at an early cabinet meeting to emphasize the importance of good staff and to encourage ministers to pick staff from the book prepared by the transition team. Most did, though some experienced MPPs brought their own staff with them. Ministers who chose staff not listed in the book of recommended candidates were asked to clear them with the Premier's Office. At least one minister's proposed appointee was vetoed by the Premier's Office. One insider commented that "they [the Premier's Office] watched pretty carefully," but looking back, others thought the process too laissez-faire.

A transition insider thought in retrospect that a serious error had been made in not insisting that political staff be hired from "the terrific book [of candidates] that was passed on to ministers." Allowing ministers – particularly first-time MPPs who didn't always appreciate the importance of good staff – to pick staff not listed in the book resulted in some very bad hiring decisions, and some staff who were simply not up to the job: "Some [ministerial] staff are clearly overwhelmed; they may be true believers but they've never run anything beyond a campus youth club ... [This] continues to be a problem to this very day [September 1996]; ministers have suffered for it." Another member of the transition team observed, with the benefit of hindsight, that too much of the staffing exercise was driven by a "spoils of office" dynamic and that insufficient attention was paid to the question of what qualities and abilities ministers needed in their staff.

Most of the veteran MPPs appointed to cabinet had filled at least a few key staff positions very quickly, but delays in hiring staff did prove to be problematic for some ministers. One consequence of not having essential staff positions (notably the executive assistant and the communications and policy advisors) on board quickly was that for some ministers many of their briefings took the form of extended meetings between themselves and the bureaucrats, with no political allies or advisors present. Neophyte Environment and Energy Minister Brenda Elliott, who had little familiarity with Queen's Park and its players, took a month to make her first staff appointments. Elliott does not believe that any significant problems occurred because of this delay, but this view is not shared by bureaucrats or politicos.[17] The heavy emphasis in the first few weeks on fiscal issues – which meant that prime attention focused on overall government direction rather than on individual ministers – may have mitigated the adverse effects of staffing delays.

At the outset a directive was issued limiting each minister to ten political staff. The objectives, of course, were to keep the government "lean and mean" and to avoid what Harris had called "parallel governments," by keeping ministers' offices much smaller than they had been under the NDP. Almost immediately, though, the "penny-wise and pound foolish" nature of this approach became evident – "You just can't run the Ministry of Health or the Ministry of Education with ten staff," said one executive assistant – and political staff complements in the larger, more complex portfolios began to increase. Even in the smaller ministries, however, bureaucrats reported bottlenecks in obtaining ministerial decisions on various issues because their ministers relied on single policy advisors. A number of ministers' offices functioned with well below the centrally imposed level of ten staff for some months, though within a year of the election, virtually all ministers' offices had between nine and twelve political staff.

David Lindsay and others from the Premier's Office held an initial session for political staff on issues such as dealing with the bureaucracy, and they subsequently convened regular meetings to brief ministerial staff on political and policy developments and to encourage networking. However, political staff and bureaucrats alike told us that more was needed to educate the ministerial staff about the workings of government.

Conclusion

Beyond the staffing of political offices, there were a few other minor problems in the transition operation at the centre. Occasionally, for example, the Conservatives, having taken the briefing books, called for information that was already contained in them, not having had the time to go through them properly. Also, the fact that most of the transition team members were temporary sometimes created bottlenecks, as too many things had to be cleared directly through David Lindsay. Particularly as the swearing-in drew near, bureaucrats who approached transition team members seeking directions or decisions would be told: "I won't be here next week; you'd better ask David Lindsay."

All told, however, these were little more than hiccups in a strikingly successful operation. Very quickly and very effectively, the Tories found themselves in a position to carry out their political agenda. This is especially noteworthy in view of the very limited experience among the new ministers. Only a few had cabinet experience, and even those, including Premier Mike Harris and Finance Minister Ernie Eves, had generally held only minor portfolios for brief periods in 1985 under Frank Miller.

Taking Power in the Line Ministries

An experience common to most of the line ministries we studied was the strange period of suspended animation into which they lapsed after the 8 June election. Typically, this lasted until the cabinet was named and sworn in on 26 June. Perhaps naïvely, many senior officials in line departments assumed there would be a good deal of activity created by demands from the centre, but, in fact, the work of the incoming government, the transition team, and Cabinet Office was highly inward looking in the first few weeks, as MPPs were vetted, ministers were selected, the cabinet structures and processes were decided upon, the fiscal position of the government was reviewed, and so on. Clearly, the early dismissal of several deputy ministers sent tremors through the OPS and jolted the ministries directly concerned, but it affected them more as recipients of decisions taken elsewhere than as active participants in support of central decision-making processes.

Within a few days of the election the ministry contact group assembled by Cabinet Office had effectively shut down. Partly this reflected the inherently greater difficulty communicating and coordinating on matters of substance, which became more important after the election, than on process. Partly, line bureaucrats found the changes in the status and personnel of Cabinet Office to be unsettling (one official commented on the air of unreality suffusing Cabinet Office in the early going, reminiscent of the Avignon papacy).

A few ministries were marked by frenzied activity in the days following the election. This occurred in ministries that had not prepared themselves adequately for a Conservative government. Officials pored over *The Common Sense Revolution* and other Conservative documents, retooled briefing material, and scanned the incoming Tory caucus for potential cabinet ministers. This activity was self-generated, however, and was a matter of making up for lost time.

The Transition in Three Ministries
A good deal of variety was evident in the transition processes experienced in various ministries, deriving from the kinds of preparations the individual department had made; whether a new deputy was arriving at the same time as the new minister; the experiences, personalities, and preferences of the minister and the deputy; and the nature and responsibilities of the ministry itself. Two illustrations of such variations are useful. First, whereas some ministries encountered significant continuity/corporate memory problems in gearing up their transition exercises, in one ministry at least two members of the ministry transition team had been involved in the 1990 transition and one had also participated in the 1985 transition. Second, in the Ministry of Natural Resources, the bureaucrats' briefing plans had to be modified by a unique set of exigencies: forest fires were unusually severe in the summer of 1995 and accordingly many of the minister's briefings took place in planes and helicopters flying to and around fires. How this may have affected the transmission of information and advice is hard to judge, but it was said to have hastened the bonding process between the minister and his deputy and assistant deputy ministers.

To illuminate the ground transition experiences, in the next pages we briefly describe what took place in three ministries: the Ministry of the Environment and Energy, the Ministry of the Attorney General, and the Ministry of the Solicitor General and Correctional Services. We make no claim that these three are in any formal sense representative of the entire range of ministries (they do not include, for example, any big-spending social ministries), nor that our short accounts have done full justice to their transition preparations and experiences. We chose to highlight them because all had features of interest and because we had unusually good access in all of them to key people involved in the transition.

The Ministry of the Environment and Energy
The Ministry of the Environment and Energy (MOEE) performs a range of functions aimed at protecting and enhancing the province's natural environment. Its energy-related activities are very limited; even before the small Ministry of Energy was folded into the Ministry of the Environment, for most practical purposes the Ontario Government's energy policy was effectively set by its mammoth problem child, Ontario Hydro. A defining characteristic of the ministry is its literal distance from the centre of power; the ministry's head office on St. Clair Avenue, two kilometres north of Queen's Park, is the only ministry headquarters farther than a few minutes' walk from the Legislative Building.

Officials at the ministry had been expecting a hectic time after the election, but what they experienced in fact was almost total "radio silence." The ministry felt cut off from the centre, partly because the Tory transition team clearly had other priorities than dealing with line ministries, and partly because changes in Cabinet Office personnel and in the role of Cabinet Office meant that communications became weak and sporadic. The normal range of contact points with Cabinet Office was reduced to two – the deputy minister and one other MOEE official. The ministry found this hiatus particularly unexpected, because staff had worked up approaches to two issues the Tories had made top priorities, namely, the freezing of Ontario Hydro rates and arrangements for the Interim Waste Authority.

The new minister was Brenda Elliott, a first-time MPP from Guelph. As the former proprietor of an environmental products store, she was well informed about a range of environmental issues but had limited background in politics and, what she subsequently came to regard as a more serious shortcoming, no experience in managing large organizations. She did bring with her some familiarity with government, but observes that "no one really knows how it works until you're there."

After the initial cabinet meeting on the morning after the swearing-in, she arrived, unannounced and by herself, at the ministry headquarters. She noticed that her name was already on the sign outside the building, checked in with the security guard, and took the elevator to the floor where the minister's office is located. Stepping off the elevator she encountered a sea of dead plants, ratty furniture, and a generally forlorn atmosphere. The deputy minister appeared shortly, showed her around, and introduced her to the ministry staff who were to be seconded to her office.

The next day the briefings began. An assistant deputy minister typically ran briefings with support from a handful of staff; for the most part Elliott had no political advisors or staff with her at these sessions. She found the briefings to be well organized and informative, but the question of whether there were other things she should know was constantly in the back of her mind: "The key thing as minister is to figure out what you're not being told." (Elliott for some time toyed with the possibility of meeting with the previous NDP minister but in the end abandoned the idea.)

Complicating Elliott's task of learning to be a minister and the bureaucracy's efforts to prepare her was the fact that she was not only new to government but also a first-time MPP. She therefore felt that it was important to spend a good deal of time in her constituency, leaving her only a few days a week in Toronto. She had been warned about it but only truly appreciated the workload of being an MPP and a minister once she had experienced it first hand. Elliott also made a very deliberate decision to take "great pains to keep my personal life intact"; keeping her family a high priority meant returning to Guelph every evening and limiting weekend engagements. This too reduced her availability at Queen's Park.

Overall, Elliott spoke of having developed a positive and trusting relationship with the bureaucracy, though one unhappy incident brought home to her how different are the world views of politicians and officials. Very early in her tenure a television reporter's request for an interview with Elliott was turned down without her knowledge; the reporter filed an embarrassing item about the minister's refusal to speak to the press, which Elliott only learned about several days later. "There wasn't any malice in this," she recalls. "It was simply the bureaucrats trying to protect a new minister ... Bureaucrats really don't understand politics."

Elliott hit it off well with her deputy minister, Richard Dicerni, and was distressed to learn that he had been chosen to replace Charles Pascal, who had been fired as deputy minister of education a few weeks after the initial purge of deputies. She asked Harris not to move Dicerni, arguing that she needed his advice and expertise and that assigning her a deputy without experience in the MOEE could prove problematic, as indeed it turned out to be when her entreaties failed.

The minister's first political staff person, her executive assistant, was not hired until Elliott had been in office for a month, with the rest of the staff coming on board soon after that. Until the political staff were in place, ministry officials looked after running the minister's office, a task they were not entirely comfortable handling. Even when the political staff were in place, they required a fair bit of support from the bureaucracy at the beginning, in part because they had missed the orientation sessions held earlier for other political staff. "They were pretty green; they needed a lot of coaching," was one official's assessment.

The department gave the minister an overview memorandum and two binders; the first binder dealt with four key policy issues (for example, Ontario Hydro and the Interim Waste Authority, which dealt with garbage), while the second contained information on less pressing issues and material on departmental organization and procedures. While the plan had been to concentrate on the issues binder, interspersed with meetings with assistant deputy ministers to review different parts of the ministry and go through the second binder, in reality almost all of the time was spent on the overview document and the key issues contained in the first binder. As political staff were hired, they were given both binders, but officials at MOEE concluded that they did not use them much, since they were frequently asking for information already contained in the binders. They appeared to have a sense that the briefing material had been prepared at the direction of the former government, and therefore did not feel any ownership of it.

In the early going, Elliott spent most of her time at the ministry; the "centre" made few demands on her time. Some minor items required her signature or her attention but, with the two big MOEE issues — Ontario Hydro rates and the fate of the Interim Waste Authority – having apparently lost their urgency for the premier and his top advisors, little in the way of important ministry policy issues came across Elliott's desk. What did prove enormously time-consuming was the need to find huge expenditure cuts and staff reductions in order to meet the centre's demand for savings. The two principal problems that Elliott identified in her first few months in office stemmed from the need to identify and realize substantial cuts. The first problem was "the sheer volume and speed of all the changes ... We were all going flat out ... Everything was new for all of us and the very heavy agenda made things especially tough"; the need to deal with the urgent left little time or energy to reflect on a wide range of policy issues. The second problem was the extent to which ministers laboured at their tasks in isolation; the press of business meant that ministers "weren't making time for each other" so that they had insufficient opportunities for informal exchange of ideas and experiences. MOEE's physical isolation exacerbated Elliott's difficulties, but the fundamental issue as she saw it was the lack of time for ministers to spend with other ministers.

The Ministry of the Attorney General
The Ministry of the Attorney General (MAG) serves as the government's central repository of legal expertise and advice, administers the provincial court system, and delivers a small number of programs such as those provided by Public Guardian and Trustee and the Family Responsibility Office (which attempts to ensure that court-ordered family support payments are made).

MAG was one of the departments characterized by a high level of activity after the election, once the abstract prospect of a Tory win had become very real. The assistant deputy ministers met daily between the election and the swearing-in to oversee the transition arrangements. A project team, with representatives from each ministry division and important subgroup, had been at work for some time, but had been concentrating more on nuts and bolts issues than on matters of substantive policy or politics. An indication that process took pride of place over policy among the ministry transition planners was the lack of interest in gathering and analyzing the speeches and legislative questions of the opposition party critics.

The deputy attorney general, Larry Taman, was one of those interviewed in the first days by Harris and the transition team. This caused widespread concern in the ministry about what that might mean. Was it the prelude to a sweeping reorganization? Would they have a change of deputy? Did Taman possess some special inside knowledge about what the government intended? There were widespread rumours about the possible restructuring of the government – for example, that MAG might be asked to absorb the small Ministry of Intergovernmental Affairs, the Ontario Native Affairs

Secretariat, or the Ontario Women's Directorate. The rumours and insecurity rife in the department were counterbalanced by the expectation that the new minister would almost certainly be one of two experienced MPPs, Norm Sterling or Charles Harnick. Given Harris's predilection for unconventional ministerial appointments, together with the fact that the Tory caucus contained a surfeit of lawyers, this was a questionable presumption. In the event, however, Harnick, the member from Willowdale and former critic of the ministry, was named minister.

Partly because of the distinctive, quasi-autonomous prosecutorial role of the department and partly because of its unique lawyers' culture, in which the legal professionals see themselves as their own bosses, the organization of a coherent, corporate briefing process was a challenge. Much substantive information, with extensive detail, had been prepared, but the deputy and his transition planners had to work hard to get members of the ministry to think about what was needed from the perspective of the ultimate recipients of the information, namely, the new minister and his political staff. For example, procedures that bureaucrats know and take for granted, such as the cabinet cycle and the process for receiving and dealing with cabinet documents, needed to be explained as part of the briefings.

The deputy minister cribbed an idea from an article by Gordon Osbaldeston, a retired clerk of the Privy Council in Ottawa.[18] Osbaldeston had suggested that a useful first step was for a deputy to write a letter to a new minister. The MAG deputy did this, and the letter became the centrepiece of the written briefing. It contained an introduction to the senior people in the department; it noted the things to do in the first days in office (e.g., a courtesy call to the chief justice); it noted the things not to do (e.g., state an opinion about an accused's guilt or innocence while a trial is ongoing); and it pointed out some of the key issues that would require attention in the next little while. The letter was accompanied by a binder of briefing material, some of which duplicated the information requested by the Cabinet Office for the central process. This binder was not finished until the day of the swearing-in.

The deputy also had information prepared as working notes for him on the campaign commitments of the political parties insofar as they related to the Ministry of the Attorney General. For example, during the campaign the Tories undertook to get rid of "photo radar," and in fact abolished it soon after the election. The deputy needed to be in a position to point out that this would also eliminate an estimated $250 million in revenues over the next three years, money that had been designated to improve aspects of the justice and policing system, such as the purchase of computers for police cars. That expenditure pressure would continue, even if the source of funds was cut off.

A good deal of effort went into anticipating and covering the small details that would shape the first encounter of the minister and the department. The idea was to make the new minister and his staff feel welcome and well supported from the very beginning. The transition group made these arrangements by imagining the minister arriving on the first day. What would he or she want, need to know, and call for, by way of support? How would the minister and the political staff be provided with cellphones, security passes, credit cards, and parking access?

The deputy minister advanced the principle of same-day service for these items. Take cellphones, for example. What does same-day service mean? Someone suggested that it meant talking to the minister about what kind of phone he or she wants. No, came the reply; it doesn't mean an interview about a telephone, it means the provision of a telephone. Eventually the staff decided to do a mock run-through of the arrival of the minister to test their arrangements and get the bugs out of the system. These preparations appeared to have paid off; the minister was clearly touched, for example, by the fact that his name was already on the door upon his arrival at MAG after the swearing-in.

The minister brought two political staffers with him; neither had prior experience in the matters within MAG's ambit. The ministry seconded a scheduler and a policy advisor to the minister's office; the latter in fact did more coordination and office management than policy work. Positions in the minister's office were then filled over the next several months. The minister went to most of the initial briefing sessions on his own, and apparently found the written material very useful. The deputy minister insisted on attending all briefings and since his heavy corporate responsibilities required him to be away from the ministry a good deal, occasions arose when the minister was ready to be briefed but the deputy was unavailable and so the briefing was postponed. Given the deputy's view that the briefings should be sharp, focused, and done by very senior officials, most of the sessions were restricted to the deputy and his assistant deputy ministers. One ministry official argued that whatever the benefits in terms of the briefing process, this approach had the unhappy consequence of giving the minister the sense that only a few key people are needed – that they know everything and can do everything – when in fact it is important, especially when cuts loom, that the minister understand the complexity of the process, the wide range of staff involved in supporting him, and the value to the organization of those below the assistant deputy minister level. The notion that involving more staff in the briefing process might have been justified as a general morale booster is supported by a comment we heard from a middle manager at MAG about the poor morale in the ministry at the time, to the effect that a common view was, "I guess we have to do this transition even though they're going to lay us all off."

Part of the briefing plan was to bring several related issues together into "policy forums," but the minister, to the initial consternation of some, asked to be briefed on particular issues out of the order that the bureaucrats had planned for him. Staff had to remind themselves that this, after all, was his prerogative. The minister also suggested that he embark on a series of "meet the division" tours; these apparently proved to be little more than pro forma walkabouts – possibly because they had not been anticipated and organized in advance by the ministry, possibly because the bureaucrats failed to appreciate the importance to politicians of meeting people and "pressing the flesh."

Finally, the new people at the centre of government, as well as the new cabinet structure and process, caused some confusion and difficulty at MAG in the first months. It was not clear to officials at MAG how to route cabinet documents, what the roles of the various deputies' committees were, whom they should be dealing with at the centre and on what issues, and how they were to go about getting things on the government's agenda. There were also complaints about being asked for legal opinions on complex policy issues on impossibly short notice. Much of this is probably part of the inevitable working-in period of any new government.

The Ministry of the Solicitor General and Correctional Services
The NDP had amalgamated two separate ministries, Solicitor General and Correctional Services, and the Tories were not about to expand the number of ministries by undoing this change. The Ministry of the Solicitor General and Correctional Services (SolGen) is responsible for policing and public safety and for management of the province's jails, reform schools, and other correctional institutions.

By election day everything was in place and ready at SolGen but, as at MOEE, until the cabinet was sworn in and the new minister was named, officials were in limbo, with almost nothing to do. During this period they had effectively no contact with the Conservative transition team.

Officials were surprised, and a bit taken aback, when Bob Runciman, the MPP from Leeds Grenville in eastern Ontario, was named minister, because he had been the Tory SolGen critic and they had assumed that critics would not be named to the portfolios they had shadowed. They were concerned because of his criticisms of the ministry in opposition and because he was known to have very firm opinions about a wide range of police and correctional issues. On the other hand, there was an advantage in that he was an experienced politician and he and his staff were far more up to speed on the ministry's issues than others might have been. In addition, it was unusual, and helpful, that – unlike most solicitors general – Runciman was actually pleased to get the post. Once he was named minister, transition officials at SolGen began an intensive review of his statements in opposition, paying particular attention to those with clear time commitments, such as his promise to issue hollow-point ammunition to police within 100 days of taking office.

Runciman arrived on the day after the swearing-in with two political staff to check out the office and meet the officials. His name was on the building's sign by the time he got there. Unlike many other ministers, Runciman had his key staff either with him from the outset or on board soon after becoming minister; his executive assistant was in place by the first week of July and his policy advisor arrived soon after. Accordingly, apart from secretarial help, the temporary staff that the ministry had lined up to work in the minister's office were not needed. Very rapidly, the minister's staff were included in the frequent ongoing briefings and readiness meetings that are necessary in a crisis-driven ministry like SolGen. This reassured the political staff that the structures were in place to respond to tough issues and unexpected events.

For the first two weeks or so the centre put relatively few demands on the minister's time, though as a non-Toronto MPP he did spend time away from the ministry in his constituency. The minister and his staff were generally available, however, so that the department was able to proceed with its briefing routine more or less as planned. Runciman and his staff agreed to the form and content of the briefings and seemed pleased with the general approach, although they did ask for some alterations in the sequence in which the items were addressed and the amount of time spent on each item. Initially Runciman found that he was being inundated with information, some of which he neither needed nor wanted, and he directed that briefings be limited to one or two a day; Runciman picked the items that he wanted to be briefed on from a menu offered by the bureaucrats.

SolGen had acquired a new deputy minister just a few days before the swearing-in, and thus found itself preparing a set of briefings for her as well, chiefly by adapting the ministerial material already in hand. The deputy was present for most of Runciman's briefings, but these were not primarily designed as joint briefings; she had received some briefings prior to the minister's arrival and continued to have her own briefings separate from Runciman. Still, it was an unusual situation, with the deputy minister, who was entirely new to the ministry, knowing less about various issues than did the minister.

Not surprisingly, "everybody wanted to be in the room when the minister [and the deputy] were being briefed." After some initial crowded meetings, the numbers attending briefing sessions were quickly reduced. Typically, Runciman was accompanied by his executive assistant and, subsequently, by his policy advisor; in addition to the deputy minister and the responsible assistant deputy minister, five to eight ministry officials would be present. "There were always too many people at briefings," complained one participant.

Beyond the briefings, some time was devoted to meeting important "stakeholders" with whom Runciman would regularly deal as minister. To an extent, competing political and bureaucratic agendas contended for the minister's time; for the bureaucrats the briefings were central, but Runciman placed a higher priority on starting to implement the policy agenda and on finding financial and staff cuts – as in other ministries, SolGen's activities were substantially driven by preparations for the July economic statement. As well, the decision made at the first cabinet meeting – to do away with photo radar – commanded extensive time and attention at SolGen, at both political and bureaucratic levels.

Runciman and his staff made it clear that, on policy matters, they did not want to be presented with options, but wanted to be told how and when the ministry would implement the Tory commitments. It simplified the ministry's job that Runciman and his staff were familiar with the issues and had adopted clear-cut positions; although there was some pressure resulting from the desire to implement a large number of changes quickly, there was no need for extensive policy work-ups or lengthy discussion of options, and, as an experienced politician, Runciman had realistic expectations about what could and could not be done within a given time frame.

Overall, though some personality conflicts emerged subsequently, Runciman quickly developed good relations with the bureaucrats. He was pleased with the preparation the officials had done and with the way they moved quickly and effectively to implement what he wanted done: "The bureaucrats were very professional; they were ready; they had taken the trouble to know me and my history and they knew our platform."[19] Ministry officials presented Runciman with position papers that allowed him to attend right away to issues where quick decisions were needed, and they had worked up cost estimates of various initiatives that he wanted to pursue.

Isolated instances occurred that suggested to the minister and his staff that some resistance to their agenda was present among officials; in one briefing, for example, the clear thrust of the presentation was to dissuade Runciman from going ahead on a matter on which the Tories had made a strong, public commitment. Not all bureaucrats had immediately understood that the exercise was to implement a blueprint, not to mull it over. Most did understand this, however, and a good many were energized by a minister willing to develop projects and to take the time to look carefully at aspects of the ministry that no minister had shown any interest in for years. It may also be, as one figure at the ministry suggested, that the nature of SolGen's work and mandate fosters a conservative culture well attuned to someone like Runciman.

The transition process rapidly transformed itself into "business as usual" as the normal conduct of the department's affairs proceeded. Law enforcement was one of the few areas for which *The Common Sense Revolution* promised stable funding, so that SolGen was faced with substantially fewer budget and staff cuts than most ministries. However, some cutbacks were necessary, and they required care and attention, particularly the politically sensitive staff reductions in the ministry's large office in the premier's constituency of North Bay (the headquarters of the Ministry of Correctional Services prior to the amalgamation), but overall they were not so substantial as to require a major reorganization, as in other ministries.

Transition to Governing
The Tories weren't interested in taking firm, quick control of the levers of governmental power as an abstract exercise; they had an extensive, far-reaching policy agenda to implement as expeditiously as possible. The transition exercise was closely tied to the Tories' top political priorities: putting *The Common Sense Revolution* into practice and imposing the budgetary and staff cuts that it entailed. Accordingly the government's main energies during its first month were directed towards a major economic statement on 21 July 1995. If the swearing-in on 26 June marked the end of a key phase of the transition, the 21 July economic statement can be seen to be the culmination of the transition. To be sure, transitional activities such as staff hiring continued for some time, but the 21 July statement clearly demonstrated that the government was well in place and moving forward on its agenda. In short, the transition was over.

During the campaign, Harris had mused about calling the legislature into session soon after the election. Once faced with the realities of governing, though, the Tories quickly abandoned this idea as impractical and potentially dangerous. In the event, the House opened on 27 September, some three months after the Harris government took office. This timing was in line with the "parliamentary calendar" set out in the Assembly's *Standing Orders*.

The NDP had not introduced a budget in 1995; instead, Finance Minister Floyd Laughren had released what he termed "The Ontario Budget Plan" shortly before the election call in the spring. This document was for all intents and purposes the NDP's final budget, and the fact that it had been neither formally brought before the legislature nor approved by it was of little practical or legal consequence. The Tories' 21 July economic statement set out some early policy decisions and budget cuts but lacked the detail of a budget. In November, Finance Minister Ernie Eves made what he called the "1995 Fiscal and Economic Statement," which in presentation, level of detail, and degree of media hype looked very much like a budget, though strictly speaking the first Conservative budget did not appear until May 1996.[20] In a sense, the 21 July statement was a preview of some the key elements of the November statement. Internally, the centre's demands of the line ministries for information on which to base staff and dollar cuts continued steadily through the July and November exercises.

Indeed, a principal reason why the line ministries heard little from the centre during the first few weeks was that the attention of the key political players and senior central agency bureaucrats was firmly focused on matters fiscal, which crowded almost everything else off the agenda. According to some bureaucratic observers the Tory transition team and the political advisors around the premier were unprepared for the amount of time and attention that the economic statements in July and November would require and for the extent to which they would pre-empt work on non-fiscal issues. The Tories certainly planned to keep the fiscal situation front and centre but underestimated how all consuming it would become.

Michael Gourley's early de facto installation as deputy minister of finance was crucial to spearheading the efforts that culminated in the July economic statement. Bureaucrats close to the budget-cutting exercise contend that the Cabinet Office-driven preparation of detailed briefing data on a ministry-by-ministry basis was also an important factor in the successful delivery of the July statement. With the essential information packaged and ready for review, "the public service," as one put it, "was freed up to launch into the fiscal frenzy leading to the 21 July statement."

Line ministries' communications with the centre were largely confined to responding to requests for data on potential savings from various cutbacks and program cancellations and receiving marching orders setting out the number of public service positions to be eliminated. (In at least some ministries, these directives were issued prior to the swearing-in of the new government.) For one neophyte minister, lack of communication from the centre proved troubling: for the first few weeks after the swearing-in, she recalled, "we were pretty much left on our own ... That was a pattern that didn't change ... There were times when we were actually pleading for advice and direction from the Premier's Office and we didn't get it ... It wasn't that they didn't care, they were just so overloaded themselves."

Bureaucrats also found themselves at something of a loss for want of clear, consistent channels to the centre. Personnel changes at Cabinet Office along with its more laissez-faire role meant that some ministries had, beyond the deputy's link to the cabinet secretary, only one contact point at Cabinet Office. Given the tumultuous policy environment, this was inadequate. One line bureaucrat commented that through the summer of 1995, "we had to figure out for ourselves what to do," citing a policy issue relating to a prominent Tory campaign pledge on which the ministry was ready to act but lacked information on what the process should be, who should be involved, and just what was expected of the ministry. Ultimately, "we were called on Friday to bring [proposals for implementing the policy] in on Monday." This person added that several months later, "there is still confusion over the roles and communication with Cabinet Office and the Premier's Office." A middle manager in another ministry also pointed to a lack of clarity and direction from the centre that was still causing problems months after the swearing-in; the role of the deputies' committees and the informal power relations with the centre, for example, remained ambiguous. Overall, the situation was bothersome but by no means debilitating: "People are generally confused about the process, though they are muddling along."

None of this is to suggest that the ministries were left with little to do; far from it. Ministries were in fact hard pressed during the first months of the Tory regime, identifying staff, programs, and services to be cut and working up policies to implement *The Common Sense Revolution*. In ministries such as Natural Resources, Education and Training, and Environment and Energy, which were hit by particularly large staff reductions, the task wasn't limited to making extensive, painful cuts; it quickly became evident that so many gaps had emerged and resources for important functions were so strained that substantial reorganization would be necessary to put the remaining pieces together in a coherent, effective manner. Reorganizations, especially those entailing consolidation and downsizing, consume substantial amounts of time and energy on the part of senior officials. Related to this, the high rate of staff turnover and the attendant loss of experience and corporate memory significantly complicated the tasks facing ministers and ministries in delivering programs and in responding to policy demands and budget cuts from the centre.

For the Tories, getting on with the "CSR" – a term that rapidly entered the jargon – was their central reason for being. This critical task was not to be left to chance. Between the election and the swearing-in, staff in the proto-Premier's Office worked at consolidating the commitments from *The Common Sense Revolution* and from the election campaign (many campaign promises, such as the elimination of photo radar, did not appear in the CSR) into a coherent package that was then parcelled out to ministers as part of their "marching orders" – customized sets of instructions to all ministers detailing their responsibilities in implementing the agenda. Indirectly, of course, these were also instructions to the bureaucrats. One Tory figure observed that in terms of the transition, "the real value of the CSR was to give the public service a sense of direction ... It allowed us to hit the ground running, which in turn gave us both internal and external credibility." The political work of assigning responsibility for discrete components of the agenda was done in concert with Cabinet Office staff, who set in motion the necessary bureaucratic processes: designating lead ministries on specific projects, scheduling discussion time at the Policy and Priorities Committee and the like. Roughly a year into the mandate, a figure in the Premier's Office admitted to mixed feelings about how effectively the bureaucrats had implemented the agenda. While they had done an admirable job in realizing the specific goals they had been assigned, he was "surprised at how some of the civil service are great literalists," looking for specific policy direction rather than thinking in terms of the overall philosophy of *The Common Sense Revolution,* and assuming that the CSR and the election promises constituted the sum of the Tories' program.

Conclusion

The Tories had campaigned, won, and taken office on a commitment to make sweeping changes to Ontario and its government. A successful transition was the key to realizing this commitment, and successful it was. The transition planning exercise and the work of the formal and informal transition teams – strongly assisted by a high level of bureaucratic readiness – had accomplished the necessary groundwork to permit the new government to take swift and sure control of the levers of power. Harris and his advisors had engendered among the senior civil service an effective combination of love and fear through firing allegedly politically tainted deputies, emphasizing the ideals of a neutral, professional bureaucracy, and ruthlessly cutting staff throughout the OPS. They also had established a cabinet decision-making system well attuned to their political priorities. If staffing of ministers' offices had been uneven, a strong, albeit overburdened Premier's Office was in place to take command.

The Conservatives moved quickly, making and implementing important policy decisions. Almost instantaneous were such moves as the elimination of photo radar, a 22 percent cut in welfare rates, and a moratorium on non-profit housing; extensive staffing and funding cuts followed in the July economic statement – itself a major accomplishment for a government in office less than a month. Good transition planning and execution were not the only factors at work; the Tories' unshakeable political will and Harris's domination of the political process were also critical. The premier was, in the words of one of his staff, "very hands-on" in directing the cabinet through its initial decisions: "The circumstances [of inexperienced ministers] coincided with Harris's style and instincts," which manifested themselves in the belief that for a government with a tough, clear agenda, "there has to be strong centralization of decision making at first." If this meant, as it did in at least one instance, taking a politically controversial initiative away from a ministry with a neophyte minister and assigning it to an experienced minister, this was done. If it entailed Harris and Eves focusing the entire government on the need for cuts in the July and November economic statements, then this was done. A corollary of the concentration of decision-making authority in Harris and the Premier's Office was setting aside routine or low-priority issues, particularly those coming from the line ministries. A few months after the Tories took power, a central agency bureaucrat commented on Harris and Lindsay's recognition that not everything could be done at once and that realistic priorities had to be established: "They may not be very familiar with the system yet, but they have good intuition for what's manageable."

7
Not Politics but Good Government: Making Transitions Better

Transitions are about government, and are thus best evaluated according to whether they do or do not contribute to the achievement of good government.

This may seem blindingly obvious, but much of the difficulty in achieving effective transitions, and therefore in contributing to good government, arises from the fact that transitions are actually experienced quite differently by the participants. For them, transitions feel like politics, and too often they wind up *being* about politics, and not much else.

This is not surprising, given that transitions by definition come at the end of an election campaign and involve a defeated political party leaving office and a victorious political party taking the reins of power from it. In addition, public servants are frequently (and often justifiably) in a state of high anxiety, recognizing that the incoming party may misunderstand their role and mistrust their motives, and that it may choose to assert its control over the public service in ways inconsistent with its understanding of itself. Fear and insecurity, victory, defeat – it is a highly charged, emotional moment.

A transition, then, can be misapprehended as the last stage of an election campaign, the most aggressively competitive moment in the democratic cycle, rather than as the first stage in the life of a new government. This ambiguity between governing and politicking leads to transition tensions, not only between the major actors but *within* their ranks as well. Parties are primarily understood as electoral machines, doing battle against other political formations to secure popular support and win elections. But they also perform an equally indispensable second role; they are actual or potential governing agents. For a party taking power after a successful election, the transition is the hinge between these two critically important functions. A political party that has eyes only for the electoral contest is unlikely to make a good transition. (On the other hand, a party with an exclusively governmental focus may not find it easy to win an election.) As citizens know all too well, electoral success and good government are two very different things; the first is a necessary, but by no means sufficient, condition for delivering the second.

This concluding chapter begins with a very brief summary of developments after the 1995 transition, including a review of the transition planning done as the 1999 election approached. We then summarize and consider the factors behind the success of the 1995 Ontario transition. Next we offer some general observations on what we have learned from this study of the Tory transition, followed by some thoughts on our findings as they relate to political parties and to the public service. Finally, we look to practical lessons emerging from recent Ontario transition experience.

After the Transition

To describe Ontario politics after the Conservative electoral victory in 1995 as tumultuous scarcely seems adequate. Within days of taking office, the Common Sense Revolutionaries had taken decisive action on several fronts, such as the abolition of photo radar and a 22 percent reduction in basic welfare rates. Less than a month after being sworn in, the Conservatives made a major economic statement detailing the myriad cutbacks and program reductions they would be implementing. In the following months and years, hardly any aspect of Ontario public policy escaped major change. Far-reaching restructuring in health, education, and the municipal sector (all giving rise to widespread, angry protest), major labour legislation, a bitter strike by the main public service union, extensive layoffs in the Ontario public service (OPS), and attendant service reductions were only some of the controversial policy departures of the initial Tory years. The government adopted a conscious and largely successful strategy of confounding its opponents by moving quickly on a wide range of fronts simultaneously while making few concessions on even the most controversial policies. We have no intention of enumerating, let alone evaluating, these sweeping changes, but we do want to suggest that without the solid foundation provided by their very successful transition, which put them in such a strong position to take and implement decisions quickly, the Conservatives could not have done as much as they did in such a short time. Drawing a direct causal link between specific facets of the transition and the unfolding of particular policy initiatives would be well nigh impossible and we make no attempt to do so. However, the effective control over the machinery and the personnel of government provided by the transition surely stands as an essential condition for bringing about the policy changes that the Tories intended.

At the same time, we do not mean to imply that a programmatic party with a tough agenda for change needs only good transition preparation and execution. Governing and preparing to govern are fundamentally different enterprises. It is even possible that unless this distinction is clearly understood and appreciated, a successful transition may, paradoxically, lead to difficulties in governing. Though we cannot develop the topic here, it could be argued that the ease and success of the transition gave the Tories an exaggerated sense of their ability to control the political agenda and to implement their program easily. In turn, this may have led to significant political problems for the Tories to the extent that they seriously underestimated the opposition they would encounter in pushing ahead with some of their more controversial policies. For example, in the donnybrook over Bill 26, the so-called "omnibus bill" introduced in the fall of 1995, the Tories' plans for sweeping and rapid change to a wide number of statutes encountered political and procedural obstacles far more formidable than they had anticipated. Be that as it may, the importance of a good transition is beyond doubt – or, looking at it the other way around, the adverse effects of a bad transition can be debilitating.

Given how central to the transition were the placement and replacement of deputy ministers and the hiring of political staff, a brief review of their tenure (and for the deputies, their origins) is warranted. Confining our attention to line ministries and central agencies, fourteen of twenty-three deputies in place at the end of the Rae government were retained by the Conservatives, most in the same positions.[1] All but two of the replacements for the deposed deputies were promoted from within the OPS and those two had both recently held senior bureaucratic positions in it. Two and a half years later, eight Rae-era deputies were left, only three of whom remained in the positions they had held under the NDP. Their replacements were, with one exception, career bureaucrats (mostly in the Ontario government, though two came from the municipal sector); the exception was a private sector CEO. No comprehensive data exist on career paths of Ontario deputy ministers, so precise comparisons with previous regimes as to turnover and tenure are not possible. Nonetheless it does appear that, aside from the initial purge, the high rate of deputy turnover in the first years of the Harris government did not differ dramatically from the rate that had characterized the preceding decade and more. It was certainly in line with the extent of changes to the deputy cadre that characterized the initial years of the Liberal and NDP governments, as described in Chapter 2. Most of the deputy ministers who left did so voluntarily, choosing to explore more attractive opportunities, particularly in the private sector where far better salaries were on offer.

Political staff proved even more mobile. This is scarcely surprising in view of the nature of the positions and the uncertainties surrounding the suitability of those recruited to serve in ministers' offices. (The skills required in a political-governmental post are not easily found in non-governmental settings; the need to mesh well on a personal level with the minister is essential but not predictable; top positions in ministers' offices are classic "burnout" jobs, calling for a level of energy and commitment that is difficult to maintain over an extended time; the attractions, especially financial, in the consulting and other worlds are significant for experienced political staff.) Looking at the three top political staff positions in ministers' offices, just over a year into the mandate, fourteen of the eighteen original executive assistants were still in place, as were thirteen of the nineteen original policy advisors and eleven of the fifteen original communications assistants.[2] This is a substantial, if not remarkable, rate of change. Over the next fourteen months, however, the turnover rate accelerated: although sixteen of the original eighteen ministers remained in cabinet, only eight of the original executive assistants, five of the policy advisors, and three of the communications assistants remained (and not all of them were still with their original ministers). Put differently, after two and a half years only sixteen of the original fifty-two top ministerial staff – 32 percent – still held positions in ministerial offices. Again, comparative data are lacking, but this is by any standard a high rate of turnover. We have no basis for judging how, or indeed if, this pervasive transiency of Conservative political staff is linked to the transition exercise, though it certainly underlines both the difficulty and the importance of careful selection of ministerial staff.

Transition Planning in 1999

In the summer of 1999, the Harris Conservatives accomplished what no one had managed in Ontario since the days of John Robarts in the 1960s. They won a second consecutive majority government. The factors underlying the Tories' 1999 electoral victory need not concern us here,[3] but we *are* interested in the question of institutionalizing transition planning: Were there serious efforts at preparing for a possible change of government as the election approached? Had the fine work in 1995 been a one-time-only exercise or had the importance of thorough transition planning come to be accepted by the parties and the bureaucrats? Overall, the answers are positive and encouraging.

The NDP did no transition planning whatsoever prior to the 1999 election. Although one of our prime recommendations, set out later in this chapter, is that parties take seriously their responsibility to govern by engaging in transition exercises well in advance of elections, it is hard to fault the NDP on this score. Unlike the Conservatives in 1995, who saw themselves as genuine contenders for power (even if the pundits and their political opponents did not), the NDP in 1999 was preoccupied with political survival. Remarkably, throughout the first Harris mandate the NDP's standing in the polls was routinely well below the 21 percent they had attracted in the 1995 election, and the party faced the very real possibility of losing all but a handful of its seats (in the event, they won only nine, on just less than 13 percent of the vote). Faced with such a situation, the party's failure to engage in transition planning is at once unsurprising and defensible.

Going into the 1999 election, the Liberals clearly faced an uphill battle, but nonetheless had some reasonable prospect of deposing the Tories. Accordingly, they mounted a comprehensive formal transition planning exercise, modelled generally on what had been done in 1995. As in 1995, Karen Pitre was the central figure; none of the others involved in transition planning in 1999 had played a role in the 1995 transition. Beginning in the spring of 1999, two or three months before the election was expected, half a dozen Liberals met weekly to assign tasks, compare notes, and measure progress. Their task was not nearly the same sort of extensive, from-the-ground-up exercise that it had been four years earlier because they were able to build on the work and the material prepared for the 1995 transition. Substantial updating and revision was necessary, but the framework developed in 1995 – the questions to be addressed and possible answers in terms of setting priorities, modifying or retaining structures, making decisions on political and bureaucratic personnel, and the like – seemed to serve well in 1999.

As in 1995, the principal product of the transition group was a comprehensive briefing book for party leader Dalton McGuinty. The overall format closely resembled that used in 1995, but, in addition to updates necessitated by changes in government structure, finance, and policy, as well as in the political environment, the book was written and compiled with greater attention to basics and detail, reflecting the fact that McGuinty (unlike Lyn McLeod) had never served in government. An illustration of the type of new concern that generated thought and research was the possibility, mooted by NDP Leader Howard Hampton midway through the campaign, of a Liberal-NDP coalition should the voters not return a majority government.

One of McGuinty's staff attended the weekly transition planning meetings and the group met once or twice with a senior campaign figure as election day neared. Considerable attention and energy were devoted to developing a process for recruiting and screening political staff. A review of the senior ranks of the OPS was conducted with a view to possible changes, but it was a far less extensive exercise than had been the case in 1995. The lower priority attached to vetting senior bureaucrats for acceptability doubtless owed a good deal to Liberal comfort with the changes wrought by the Tories among deputy ministers during the 1995 transition. (It also signalled a similar attitude as to what constituted a neutral, non-political public service.)

Bureaucratic preparation for a possible change in government was far more extensive, suggesting that the notion of transition planning as a routine component of good government may be taking firm root in the Ontario public service. We found clear indications that bureaucratic transition planning is becoming more professional and more routine and is perceived as less politicized. Our interviews with officials in line ministries and in the Cabinet Office demonstrated that the OPS prepared for a possible transition in 1999 carefully and professionally. Planning was built on the experience of 1995, with adaptations made as necessary to meet changed circumstances and concerns.

The central plan for a possible transition was developed and driven by Cabinet Office at the behest of Cabinet Secretary Rita Burak with Premier Harris's approval. As in 1995, individual line ministries also prepared customized transition plans for potential new ministers. Though ministries differed in their approach and in the thoroughness of their plans, our sense was that the overall level of preparedness varied less across ministries than had been the case in 1995. Cabinet Office staff assessed the strong and weak points of the 1995 transition. In principle, this would have been done shortly after the 1995 transition was complete, but with the press of business at that time, the review did not occur until the next election loomed. Those in charge of the central exercise conferred with some of the bureaucrats (both in Cabinet Office and in line ministries) who had been involved in previous transitions. Informal discussions were held with members of the 1995 Conservative transition team, and with colleagues in other provinces and in the Machinery of Government unit in Ottawa's Privy Council Office. Once the plans were developed, Burak presented them to the premier, who accepted and agreed with the approach.

Among the aspects of the transition plan put to Harris and sanctioned by him were meetings between Cabinet Office staff and representatives of both opposition parties. Held early in the election campaign, these meetings, while not involving as many top echelon officials as those organized by the Public Policy Forum in 1995, were rather more routine. The cabinet secretary simply issued invitations to the opposition party leaders, without apparent need for assistance from an intermediary organization.

The 1995 transition arrangements proved a good foundation on which to build. No fundamental changes were made in that process, though a number of significant refinements were introduced. Cabinet Office gathered information via a ministry contact team similar to that used in 1995. Ministries were asked to submit material according to templates similar to those developed in 1995, permitting information from the ministries to be presented uniformly and consistently. The 1999 process involved deputy ministers as well as lower-level contacts in each of the ministries. Finally, as in 1995, Cabinet Office asked ministries to identify "hot" issues that government would have to address within days of taking power, but it set the bar high with the implicit question: Is this an issue the premier will have to address before the minister is in place? As a result, very few issues submitted by the ministries were deemed to be truly urgent.

Once the election writ was dropped, the plans were laid out at a meeting of deputy ministers, so as to ensure their support and to render the process transparent, at least within the senior ranks of the bureaucracy. The desire to operate transparently was tempered with a decision not to advertise what was under way too openly throughout the system due to concern that a perception might develop that Cabinet Office and the deputies were making assumptions about the election outcome. The centre seems not to have encountered any serious reservations or concerns on the part of the line ministries about the transition exercise or about the nature and the purpose of the information sought from them. More so than in 1995, transition planning appears to have been well accepted as an exercise in good government. The process benefited from the cabinet secretary's credibility with the OPS, as a career bureaucrat, and with the premier, with whom she had developed a strong working relationship.

As in 1995, at the centre the principal transition preparations were seen primarily as an information-gathering exercise. What information about a wide range of machinery and process issues would the premier-designate and his transition team need to get their government up and running? But some things were added, primarily in the area of policy analysis and implementation. Cabinet Office framed advice on the possible reorganization of government (ministry realignments, for example) and cabinet decision-making structures. Certain policy issues were drawn from the business plans of the line ministries. Policy papers were put together on several big issues (for example, homelessness) that any government, regardless of party, would need to address in some fashion, however different their policy responses might be. These papers neither proposed nor analyzed solutions but rather were designed to be base point analyses, having "the same currency with all parties," on which any government could fashion its particular solutions or responses. One of the papers displayed an inventory of the accomplishments of the OPS in major restructuring initiatives in the last few years.

Some of the government-restructuring ideas developed in this context were reflected in the cabinet making after the election, for example, the consolidation of health and long-term care under a single minister. In addition, towards the end of the Tories' first mandate, a series of sectoral cabinet committees had been set up to aid in the policy-development process, and this matter was put on the agenda for the post-election government.

Senior staff throughout the bureaucracy made themselves familiar with the election platforms of the various parties, but because of the sensitivity of the matter Cabinet Office did no organized costing out or evaluation of the plans of the various parties, nor did it gather information from ministries about what they were tracking and whether or how they were analyzing party platforms. As in 1995, the view was that this kind of work simply could not be done effectively in a neutral way, and it was recognized that the existence of a public service document mapping out the costs and implications of party electoral commitments could prove highly problematic.

With the Conservatives returned to power, the transition preparations were not fully tested, but there appear to have been several improvements over the 1995 process. The line ministries provided better, more concise information. This reflected lessons learned from the previous transition as well as discipline instilled by the practice of requiring ministries to prepare annual "business plans" that was introduced during the first Harris government. The 1995 experience had focused very much on implementation; in 1999 the issues that all parties were interested in required a stronger bureaucratic policy-development capacity, and this need was reflected in the transition preparations. Perhaps most important, it is clear that the transition process is becoming routinized and accepted as a necessary component of good governance, and is being accepted as such by the OPS. Cabinet Office staff spoke with pride of having been asked for advice and documents by other provinces facing possible transitions. Across Canada, transition is becoming a matter that cabinet secretaries discuss with one another, as they would any other dimension of their work and responsibilities.

Explaining the Success of the Tory Transition

We asked several of the people that we interviewed why the Conservatives were so effective in taking power after the election of 8 June 1995. With few exceptions, the factors they mentioned are those that an attentive reader will have divined from the foregoing chapters. The cooperation of Bob Rae and the leadership of David Agnew made it possible for the public service to ready itself effectively for a change of government. The public service knew that a change was coming and was well prepared. Conservative Leader Mike Harris attached great importance to an effective transition. The Conservatives – displaying a clear governing mindset – engaged in extremely thorough planning. The Conservatives sought the advice and counsel of experienced former deputy ministers in preparing their transition planning. The Tory policy goals were clear, thereby reducing the confusion and ambiguity of the transition and also aligning the expectations of the public service with the intentions of the incoming government. The Conservatives knew that they had to work effectively with the public service to succeed; they realized that they could radically reorganize the public service or pursue their policy agenda, but not do both, and they chose the latter. William Farlinger's authority and weight as co-chair of the transition team helped ensure that people on both sides – political and bureaucratic – would do what was expected of them. The transition team functioned in a non-partisan, businesslike, collegial manner. The Tories took power in the summer, when things were quiet. The media gave the Conservatives the benefit of the doubt at the beginning of their mandate. Each of these factors clearly played a role.

The Conservatives, as we have seen, had planned and for the most part had planned well. That they had planned at all is especially noteworthy; with all of the political work facing a party with such apparently dismal prospects, it would have been very easy to lose sight entirely of the need for serious transition planning. However, plan they did; the Tories' approach to transition was sophisticated and gave them a good road map in the early days. They had assessed the mood of the public service correctly; their early behaviour and their strategic appointments and firings in the senior ranks of the public service seemed to confirm, for many of the senior civil servants who remained, the Tories' intention to re-establish a mutually respectful relationship between the politicians and the bureaucracy.

The clarity of the policies in *The Common Sense Revolution* meant that policy implementation, not the development or exploration of policy options, was to be the order of the day. Therefore, it was a matter of cranking up the machinery of government to make it possible for the Conservatives to achieve what they said they wished to achieve.

The Conservatives were also lucky to be inheriting power from the NDP, which felt that it had been badly served during its assumption of power in 1990. Bob Rae made it clear that everything possible should be done to ensure a smooth, professional transfer of the reins of government to the election victors. A different attitude on Rae's part could have complicated the process greatly.

The Ontario public service for its part was anticipating a change of government – though not, for most of the preparation period before the election, the change of government that ultimately occurred. Led by Cabinet Secretary David Agnew, the bureaucracy systematically prepared itself for the transition, both at the centre and in the line ministries. A great deal of thought went into the planning, the result being the most sophisticated and professional transition arrangements ever assembled by an Ontario public service.

For a large part of the senior public service, the departure of the NDP and its replacement by either the Liberals or the Conservatives was seen as an opportunity to re-establish the neutral, non-partisan bureaucracy that, it was believed, had been the hallmark of Ontario public life until 1990. These officials were thus desperately anxious to start things off on the right foot with the incoming government, and spared no effort to ensure that the premier-elect and his colleagues received the support they wanted.

Thus, because of the confluence of several forces, the people of Ontario were witness to a remarkably efficient, and in fact surprisingly serene, takeover of political power by a party that many would not have thought capable of such a performance. If the Tories' policy intentions were revolutionary, the way in which they took power exuded common sense.

Observations

We begin with four general observations about transitions. First, while transitions are important – indeed, crucial in the operation of constitutional government – they have elicited little interest among Canadian academics, bureaucrats, and political activists. Certainly, as we noted in Chapter 1, the scholarly literature on this topic is most notable for its paucity. Even among those most directly affected – Canadian politicians and senior bureaucrats – relatively little attention is paid to transitions. Particularly for political parties, this is surprising since transitions are not just about nuts-and-bolts issues (though these must be attended to) but are essential for parties wishing to take power and to implement their programs quickly and effectively; successes and failures in transitions can set the tone for a party's time in office. More often than not, however, what is seen as the technical matter of taking power after a successful election is treated very much as an afterthought, despite the impact it can have on public opinion and on the successful launching of a new government. This may be in part owing to the structural factors cited in the first paragraphs of this chapter. It may also be due to the fact that Canadian political parties tend to be electoral coalitions with weakly articulated policy platforms and a strong focus on winning elections. For many opposition parties, then, research and strategic planning is devoted almost exclusively to developing a winning electoral campaign, with little thought given to the tasks a new government will confront.

A second observation flows from the low priority accorded transitions within the Canadian political system. Few rules or constraints, and relatively little in the way of institutional memory, shape how transitions are done. The shallowness of the grooves of established practice in this field means that a heavy planning burden is placed on the newly victorious political party, which is often only poorly equipped for the task. In turn the lack of institutional memory and established routines makes for a good deal of reinvention of the wheel. Ottawa, which has gone some way towards institutionalizing this process, stands as a partial exception to this observation. To some extent, the situation is subject to the vagaries of the party system in the given jurisdiction. It is hardly surprising that there was not much transition thinking in Ontario until 1985, because there had been no transition for forty-three years. Since 1985, however, the frequency of change appears ultimately to have encouraged a more professional approach to this matter, although it took ten years and two elections before that began to emerge.

Expectations are clearly relevant in shaping the approach to the taking of power. In 1990, neither opposition party in Ontario expected to win, and neither was prepared to take power. The Ontario public service was equally unprepared. When the NDP came unexpectedly into office, the result, as we have seen, was not pretty. In 1995, both opposition parties believed that they were going to win, and the public service anticipated a change of government; the result was impressive planning and preparation all around.

Third, depoliticizing the transition process is probably a condition of doing it better. In the 1995 transition, the sitting premier supported the transition preparations of the bureaucracy, and the incoming Tories rapidly developed a respect for the professionalism and helpfulness of the cabinet secretary whom they were about to fire on the grounds of his partisan past. One central transition figure remarked to us during the election campaign that "if we all act like grown-ups, things will be fine." If open-hearted trust is more than one can expect at the outset of the transition process, recognition by all parties of the transition process as a non-partisan exercise need not be beyond reach. A better understanding of what transition is and a fuller comprehension of the different roles of the political and bureaucratic players would help in the achievement of this happy state.

Finally, the alignment or misalignment of the party and public service cultures defines much about the nature of the transition. It is worth noting that both the NDP and the Harris Conservatives are conviction parties. Harris's 1995 revolution, however, was only indirectly designed to be visited on the public service, and it is clear that, despite the inherently different positions and responsibilities of the politicians and the senior bureaucrats, the two groups spoke the same language. Indeed, the Tories decided early on that they would not pick a fight with the leaders of the OPS, but would instead secure their cooperation. The mandarinate, for its part, was anxious to please. The New Democratic Party, on the other hand, assuming office in 1990 with an unmanageable program but a fairly clear ideology, appears to have been deeply suspicious of the public service as part of the governing elite; significant elements within the public service returned the compliment, at times acting as if the NDP were illegitimate interlopers who had unaccountably laid hold on political office. The cultural and attitudinal compatibility in the case of the Tories, and the incompatibility in the case of the NDP, help to explain the way in which the two transitions unfolded.

Political Parties

We asked the co-chairs of the Conservative transition team what would be the most crucial advice they could offer those facing transitions, based on their highly successful experience. William Farlinger's thoughts relate to the public service and are presented in the next section. David Lindsay's advice goes to the heart of the transition imperative for opposition parties; our observations take his reflections as a starting point:

> In our Parliamentary system, the focus for opposition parties and the media is Question Period. In this adversarial system, there is daily pressure on the opposition to embarrass the government and gain media attention.
>
> To achieve a successful transition, an opposition party must look beyond the bright lights of Question Period and focus on how it plans to govern. This thinking will shift the focus from one of merely criticizing to one of developing alternatives, not only for an election campaign but throughout the daily routine of opposition.
>
> In thinking ahead to forming the government, an opposition party should consider the obvious issues of policy development and implementation in addition to the administrative necessities of decision-making structures and staffing.
>
> In short, developing a transition plan and implementation plan should not occur after the election, but must be an integral part of a political party's and leader's strategic plan.[4]

Our first observation with respect to political parties is that – as Lindsay's comments confirm – effective transition preparations generally arise within political parties that possess a "governing mindset." However effective it may be on the hustings, a political party that is thinking seriously about what it will do if it forms the government will almost as a matter of course think about how to take power. The Liberals' extensive and impressive transition preparations in 1995 and the NDP's complete lack of transition planning in 1990 are obvious illustrations. The Tories, with their *Mission '97* plan, took transition preparation a step further than most parties do, even those that have a governing mindset; this serves merely to dramatize the point. The party as a whole need not be thinking about transition, but the leader needs to support this part of the planning process and people need to be assigned to develop plans and a timetable.

Second, to echo a point made more generally above, the clearer the platform and the policy intentions of the party, the easier transition will be. The sense of confusion and drift will be reduced; the attention of public servants will be focused clearly on helping the government to achieve its goals; by working together on what is now a common enterprise, mutual trust will be established more rapidly. The nature of a transition, as something necessary but instrumental, will be kept clearly in focus. A party that wins power but is not clear what it wants to do with it will have difficulty assuming control of the public service and determining the direction of government machinery.

Third, prior experience of government, or access to such experience, greatly assists a party taking power. The provincial Liberals under David Peterson were approaching provincial office for the first time in four decades in 1985, but they were able to call on the experience of governments in other jurisdictions possessed by many party activists. The NDP, as a third party with relatively limited government experience in its stock of political capital, had a much smaller pool of experienced people on which to draw for assistance. The Harris Tories, too, had very limited practical experience, but they compensated for this by relying heavily on experienced public servants who had left government and were now free to participate in active politics. This was particularly helpful in the transition, which centrally involves taking control of the public service.

Finally, the party in power that is going down to defeat has the capacity to shape decisively the transition planning exercise. It can have only a very limited impact on the preparations for taking power being made by the parties running against it in the election. Its control over the public service, however, is substantial, even in the months prior to an electoral defeat, and – should it choose – the party in power can make it difficult or impossible for the public service, whatever its preferences, to mount an effective transition planning exercise. The premier, for whom the cabinet secretary works, can license the bureaucracy to make ready for a possible change of government or he or she can make it very difficult for the bureaucracy to do so, raising mistaken but powerful questions of loyalty to block initiative. In 1995, then Premier Bob Rae, to his credit, strongly supported the public service in its transition preparations.

The Public Service
The reason why an obstructive premier is so difficult for the public service to deal with goes back to the distinction between the party as government and the party as electoral competitor. The tension between these two roles becomes most evident at and around election time. It is the public service's duty to serve the government of the day loyally and responsibly, whatever party is in office. The continuing, professional public administration supports the system and the government, not any particular political formation. How can it properly support the system prior to an election if the government, acting in an obviously partisan fashion, forbids the

actions necessary to offer proper system support? At times like these, there is no arbiter of correct behaviour except the government itself, and it is the government that is the problem. There are no easy answers here; public servants wriggle on the hook and operate as best they can.

Another observation about the public service follows from William Farlinger's central piece of advice for those charged with mounting a transition: "The single most important responsibility the transition team has is to recommend a Secretary of the Cabinet to the Premier elect. With a newly elected government that has been out of office for some time, this is probably not something that the Premier elect has spent a lot of time considering. The choice, once made, is very important to the ongoing functioning of the government, and has a serious impact on the appointments of other Deputy ministers since the Secretary of Cabinet will have strong recommendations to make to the Premier on that score."[5] Despite the pervasiveness of approaches rooted in the "new public management," with its emphasis on "de-layering" and rendering government more client oriented, public administration in Canada still operates very much on the hierarchical, command-and-control model. Civil servants see themselves as operating in a tiered structure of interlocking offices, with responsibility running up a chain of command to the deputy minister and minister. Deputy ministers regard themselves as responsible, not only to their particular minister but to the cabinet secretary as the senior civil servant and to the premier himself or herself. To carry out an effective transition, a political party and its leader need to keep this reality very much in mind. Either confirming in office or replacing the cabinet secretary quickly is the key to much that follows. The machinery of public administration can begin to respond efficiently to the requirements of the incoming government once this appointment is clear. The next tier is the deputy minister cadre more generally; it is not necessary that all steps contemplated be taken at once, but a party leader needs to be acutely aware of the messages to the public service that will be sent by action or inaction on this front. Informal communication in a public service is remarkably efficient, and impressions about the intentions of the incoming government will circulate very rapidly in the first few days of a transition.

A related observation reiterates both the importance and the imprecision of the distinction discussed in Chapter 3 between politics and administration. Given that the essential validity of the distinction is more than a little problematic, it is not surprising that precise lines of demarcation are by no means clear, and that operational boundaries in a given situation are shaped in large measure by previous practice and by the expectations and assumptions that have grown up around a given order of things. All of that is brought into play at the time of a transition. It is helpful for an incoming government to be conscious of that fact and to redefine the operational boundary, should it choose to do so, consciously rather than inadvertently and without being aware of the effects that such a shift may have. It is clear, too, that public servants will use the distinction between politics and administration to protect the things they value; this is perhaps almost inevitable, given that there is no formulaic model that divides the two.

Our final point about the public service grows out of the previous one. While it is the case that in the Canadian system the public service is regarded as neutral and professional and is not deemed to have a political character, this does not mean that the public service and the persons who hold the offices in the bureaucracy lack interests. They seek recognition, status, and security, as do other professionals. They want to be appreciated. They want politicians to understand and respect the role of the public service as they themselves understand it. They want the line between public administration and political action to be acknowledged and adhered to. While none of this is political in any partisan sense, it nevertheless constitutes a framework of values and practices that the bureaucracy will seek to protect and advance. Yet because it is clothed in claims of neutrality and professionalism, it is sometimes difficult for politicians hot from a very different world – to comprehend.

Practical Lessons and Recommendations

Any number of specific nuts-and-bolts ideas and recommendations for mounting a transition may be gleaned from our account of the 1995 Ontario transition. Our purpose here, however, is to highlight lessons to be drawn from that experience, lessons of overarching concern that transcend the particular circumstances facing transition planners in different jurisdictions. To that end, we make four general sets of observations:

1. *Institutionalize transition planning.* The central practical lesson to be drawn from this case study of a Canadian political transition is the following: a significant improvement in our constitutional democracy could be achieved if the act of taking power was "institutionalized" and "normalized." Too often a transition is regarded as a kind of post-election afterthought and little preparation has been made for it; too often it is perceived to be a "one-off" event with no relevant precedents; too often those engaged in the taking of power have had little prior experience in the matter and can look to few institutional supports or traditions on which to rely.

Despite the politically charged nature of the event, the taking of power could be handled in a much more routine and professional fashion without in any way compromising the principles of parliamentary government. Certainly the public service has long been accustomed to and has developed routines to accommodate changes of ministers within the same governing party; of course, the wholesale change of ministers in a transition differs in important ways from a cabinet shuffle, yet many of the essential elements are similar. More generally, the value and the legitimacy of explicit, detailed transition planning needs to be firmly established both within the bureaucratic culture and among the top priorities of political parties.

A key element in fostering acceptance and understanding of transitions as part of routine political and governmental planning is the recognition that transition planning is not a variation on the hurly-burly of partisan politics but is quite simply about good government.

2. Foster a more open relationship between opposition and bureaucracy. Opposition parties need to know more about government; bureaucrats can share information without being disloyal. In thinking through a better and more institutionalized approach to transition, it is useful to start with the period well before the election is called, because a portion of the difficulties attendant on the taking of power derive from the way in which Canadians are inclined to operate their parliamentary system. Consider, for starters, the following pithy observation by a political activist who has experienced life on both sides of the legislature: "There is a curiously Manichaean view of the relationship between government and opposition that may not help governance. The government has all the information and all the power and is supposed to know the answer to everything and not make mistakes. The opposition is supposed to oppose whatever the government is doing, no matter what its quality, and offer alternatives which are preferable. Little in the way of a cooperative relationship is possible. It is a tough transition from opposition to government – and vice versa. There is nothing in opposition that prepares you for being the government."[6]

One of the major impediments to effective action by political parties fresh to power is sheer, honest ignorance of government operations and the public service. We see no reason why substantial briefings of opposition politicians by civil servants about the organization and processes of government could not be mounted well before the start of a campaign, and, indeed, throughout the life of a given parliament or legislature. Understanding how structures and processes of government work is distinguishable from knowing what the government of the day is doing or is considering. Educating opposition parties about public administration does not undermine parliamentary government, nor is it incompatible with party politics in a democratic system. The barriers to reform in this area have more to do with the inevitable friction generated between contending political parties battling one another for political power, as well as the highly developed survival instincts of civil servants.

We think, then, that it would be a marked improvement in parliamentary practice if opposition party representatives – elected members as well as staff – were, as a matter of course, given regular briefings by civil servants on government operations. The distinction between basic information about a ministry's mandate and programs on the one hand and political and policy-sensitive matters on the other would clearly have to be respected. While discriminating one from the other requires careful judgment, it is by no means impossible, and would be the condition on which such a practice would have to be founded.

The barriers to doing this are obvious. The government of the day will not want opposition party members nosing around its operations, getting to know the civil servants, and becoming better informed and better equipped to criticize the government. Why give the opposition any help at all? The civil servants, for their part, will resist being made the monkey in the middle. Why would they want contact with the opposition if it will complicate their lives? It is fraught with risk; it could foster suspicions of disloyalty in the government they serve. All of this is perfectly human and understandable, and it no doubt explains the opposition's isolation from the governing process, but none of it poses an impediment in principle to reform. Things *could* be done differently if the will were there.

In Ontario, some approximation of this practice has occurred, to our knowledge, in only one field, namely, national unity and the constitution. The government, whether Conservative, Liberal, or NDP, has typically briefed the opposition and allowed opposition spokespersons to be present at critical points in the process of constitutional negotiations. This has gone much further than the arranging of neutral information sessions; it has in fact entailed detailed briefings on sensitive policy matters still under negotiation. Significantly, however, this unusual practice has been possible because there is a strong inclination in Ontario to treat national-unity and constitutional matters in a non-partisan fashion. Nevertheless, the absence of serious breaches of confidence or partisan game-playing in this area does suggest that more is possible than might be imagined at first.

If opposition contact with the civil service were a more normal feature of parliamentary government, then the briefings of opposition representatives by bureaucrats just before or during the election would not be regarded as such a tricky business. It would be very helpful for the opposition parties to be able to determine how their plans and initiatives, should they win the election, line up with the government reality as the civil servants experience it. This kind of encounter would serve not only as an information exchange but also as a get-acquainted session, in which the foundations of mutual trust and respect could begin to be established and in which each side could develop some appreciation of the role of the other. The encounters organized by the Public Policy Forum during the 1995 campaign were a first, timid step in the right direction. A second significant step occurred in 1999 when an (admittedly limited) election-time encounter between key bureaucrats and opposition representatives took place without the necessity of a legitimizing organization such as the Public Policy Forum.

3. *Accept that transition planning is an essential responsibility for political parties.* Surely the most obvious lesson to emerge from the Conservatives' highly successful transition in 1995 (and what would likely have been a similarly successful Liberal transition, had the voters seen things differently) is the importance of thorough transition planning well in advance of an anticipated election. Moreover, considering the dividends that a good transition can pay for a party assuming office, the costs are low. Few resources are required: little by way of funds and only a small number of people (some of whom may not be party activists and thus do not represent a redirection of personnel from the political agenda).

One of the reasons that political parties find it so difficult to commit to transition planning is that they do not wish to assume – or more accurately, be seen to assume – an outcome before it is determined. The party in office cannot be seen to be permitting contingency planning on the part of the bureaucracy; if word leaks out, it will be interpreted as the rankest defeatism. The opposition parties cannot make known their plans for taking over the government, since they will be criticized for counting their chickens before they are hatched. It is unseemly for a political party to spend its time thinking about what it will do after it is elected, when the voters have not yet spoken. In the case we examined, it was certainly understandable that a party with such apparently remote prospects of victory as the Conservatives would not wish to draw attention to its transition planning. It was striking, however, that even the Liberals, who were widely seen as virtual shoo-ins in the impending election, were almost equally as reticent about their transition planning as the Conservatives. We are not naïve; we understand that, given the circumstances, the politically astute choice was to avoid drawing attention to transition preparations.

Yet if the conventions were slightly different, if the implications of free elections in a multi-party system were understood and accepted, it would be regarded as a dereliction of duty for a party seriously competing for political office *not* to be planning how it would take over the reins of power should it be elected. It would be seen as a failure in the discharge of its responsibilities for a sitting government *not* to ensure that every opportunity was afforded other parties to prepare themselves to take office should the wisdom of the electorate so require.

As Chapter 5 indicates, a number of commonalities marked the Conservatives' and the Liberals' transition planning exercises, yet their organizational models and the processes they followed also differed in important ways. The lesson we draw from this and from other transitions, both successful and unsuccessful, is that no single best model of transition planning exists. What's important is not so much the specific model and approach to transition preparation as the commitment to a serious, thorough transition plan.

Having said that, let us commend three specific organizational choices to would-be transition planners. These recommendations reflect a notable success in the 1995 transition, a somewhat problematic aspect of that transition, and a problem common to both the 1990 and the 1995 transitions. First, because of the difficulty of combining electioneering and transition planning within the same structure, it would appear to be useful for a party to make an organizational division between transition and election planning before the election and between transition implementation and political decision making after the election. This functional specialization seems helpful in not blurring the focus and confusing the mandate of either group. Certainly, it worked well for the Ontario Tories in 1995. A second key recommendation, suggested by what was arguably the weakest aspect of the Tory transition, is the importance of a party having a substantial pool of candidates for political staff positions vetted in advance of an election. Finally, it is significant, though not surprising, that both neophyte and experienced Tory ministers reported that they were just not knowledgeable enough to gain much value from the orientation sessions held for them shortly after they took office. And by the time they knew enough to benefit substantially from structured seminars featuring advice and information exchange about the curious business of being a minister, they were too busy to partake of such an exercise. While we would not want to see initial orientation sessions abandoned, we believe that mandating a day perhaps three or four months after taking power for a cabinet retreat to review what ministers have learned and what they need to learn would be a good investment of time. A formal, mandatory session would have to be slotted into each minister's timetable from the outset; if the premier made it clear that he or she saw it as a valuable undertaking (and ensured that policy issues did not intrude), so too would ministers.

4. *Encourage public service transition planning.* As for the public service, the first and most important point is that the party in office allow it to serve the system, rather than the party, in the period prior to an election. The bureaucracy should be understood as having a professional responsibility to consider how it would assist a new government in taking office. This should not be regarded as evidence of disloyalty or of unprincipled, mercenary

behaviour, but as an expression of the constitutional obligations of the public service to the continuing support of the political system. Obviously, the most crucial cues and permissions here come from the premier and the cabinet, but bureaucrats should not simply be passive recipients of government directives and approvals. The leaders of the public service have a responsibility to remind the government of the day of the importance and legitimacy of transition planning within the bureaucracy and to advance the cause of serious transition preparations. Lower-echelon bureaucrats should come to understand transition planning as an exercise in good government, without partisan overtones. Again, of course, senior figures in the government, political as well as bureaucratic, must set the tone.

Transition planning should be a normal and inevitable part of the ongoing administrative cycle of public administration, in no way extraordinary or anomalous but in every way a conventional part of the civil service routine. It might not, in a particular case, be needed, but, as we have seen, the exercise brings substantial benefits to the system in other ways, even if it is not called on because of a change of government. It can and should be treated as a periodic opportunity for stock-taking and a chance to assess certain aspects of the political-administrative interface, making whatever mid-course corrections may be necessary.

Indeed, we would go further. Having reviewed the basic materials prepared by the public service during the 1995 campaign, we cannot honestly see any reason why almost all of it could not be posted on a government Web site, there to be available not only to politicians but to journalists, citizens, and anyone else who cares to review it. It is difficult to see what genuine problems this initiative would create.

Such dissemination of basic data on government would require formal government sanction. Other recommendations for public service transition planning fall entirely within the rubric of bureaucratic officials. We have three such middle-range proposals to put forward. First, special care is required to ensure that the very different circumstances and needs of the central agencies, especially Cabinet Office, and of the line ministries are given adequate attention. Among other things, this entails establishing and observing the fine line between essential coordination and standardization from the centre and scope for individual line ministries to engage in preparations best suited to their unique constellations of issues, organization, interests, and personnel. Second, while bureaucratic transition planning must necessarily be non-partisan, it is imperative that public servants called upon to prepare and implement transitions have a good understanding of and feel for politics and an appreciation of the perspectives and needs of politicians. Third, though bureaucrats involved in transitions must be prepared with information and advice, they must expect and accept that the politicians and their staff won't necessarily want to do things in the way that the bureaucrats had planned. To be sure, all of these admonitions are part of the normal kit baggage of experienced, astute bureaucrats and apply to much of the work of the senior public service; they become especially crucial, we suggest, in transitions.

Conclusion

Let us, by way of conclusion, return to some of the themes set out in the opening chapters. Even in an established liberal democracy such as Canada, in which all participants accept the legitimacy of the electoral process for determining who gains and who loses political power, the transition from one set of rulers to another can be problematic. The issue is not, as in dictatorships or unsettled democracies, the identity of the new political masters and the question of whether their claim to power will be accepted by political opponents and by the governed. Rather, the issue is ensuring good governance. The skills and resources that win elections are not necessarily the ones needed to run a large government; moreover, as we have seen, opposition politicians can be woefully ignorant of government, both its structures and processes and its substantive policies.

A smooth, effective transition is essential to the prospects of any newly elected political party wishing to bring about change and to implement its policies. As was evident in the months and years following the 1995 transition, a good transition is no guarantee of untroubled implementation of a party's agenda. Yet by the same token, the politics of imposing major policy change are sufficiently difficult even when the government party is firmly in control of the levers of power thanks to an effective transition; a party whose capacity to govern is not fully developed because of a poor transition faces all the more formidable obstacles in realizing its policy goals. It would be simplistic to attribute all of the problems that the Ontario NDP faced in implementing its agenda to the failures in the 1990 transition, but so too it would be wrong to ignore its negative effects on the party's subsequent capacity to govern effectively.

As we have seen, transitions are multi-dimensional, but many of their key elements – certainly those with the greatest potential to generate serious problems – relate to the interface between the political and the bureaucratic. The very definitions of the political and the administrative may be contested. Developing a good working relationship between senior officials and elected politicians (and their staff) is essential for all concerned, but it is especially important for the politicians. And while it is very easy – and indeed correct – to state that such relations must be built on trust and professionalism, the practice is far more difficult. As Leslie Pal has written, "Becoming a minister is much like becoming a colonial governor: one must cultivate the loyalty and support of the natives who have their own folkways and who seem to be deeply suspicious of outsiders."[7]

Both politicians and bureaucrats have a responsibility to plan thoroughly for transition and, as part of that planning, to ensure that each group understands and values the roles and constraints that the other faces. Bureaucrats are of course accustomed to adapting to differing approaches, priorities, and levels of understanding as their political masters change, though they must take care to avoid the easy assumption that all politicians and parties are of a piece in their needs and experiences. Politicians, quite naturally, are principally concerned with substantive policies and outcomes and are generally uninterested in governmental structures and processes; this can incline them to regard as mere "plumbing" crucial administrative issues central to bureaucrats. In short, the possibilities for bureaucrats and politicians to undervalue and misperceive one another are legion. This is of course part of the natural order of governmental life in Canada, but it can prove especially problematic during transitions.

Although we were favourably impressed with how both the public servants and the political partisans handled the 1995 Ontario transition, we do not wish to suggest that the Ontario Conservatives and the senior Ontario bureaucrats found some magic formula and that any successful transition must follow the approaches and techniques that they employed. No single "best way" exists for conducting transitions; clearly, though, solid planning is essential (tied in, for political parties, to what we have termed a "governing mindset"). Certainly, much of value can be learned by examining the experiences of the 1995 Ontario transition and its immediate predecessors. We hope that this book has contributed both to the understanding of transitions past and to the success of transitions yet to take place as others cycle into their Saigons.

Appendix A:
Two Public Policy Forum Documents Given to Opposition Parties

Public Service Reform in Ontario: Messages for Party Leaders

Good Government Is Good Politics
Whomever Ontarians elect to Queen's Park this year – the NDP, Conservatives or Liberals – the new government will rely heavily on the Ontario Public Service to implement its agenda. It makes good political sense for the OPS to have the capacity to deliver the results which have been promised during the election campaign.

To one degree or another, all parties have advocated smaller, less costly government. However, even if programs are cut and the workplace trimmed, smaller government will still have a large and important job to do in Ontario. There will still be laws and regulations to enforce. Ministers will still need policy advice. And there will be a growing demand for vital services in areas such as education, health care, transportation and public security. The public service must be organized and equipped to do all these jobs well at a price taxpayers can afford. The status quo cannot simply be replaced with a smaller status quo.

In areas such as education and health care, Ontario is among the world's highest per capita spenders. The challenge is to translate these dollars more effectively into results. To make government work better, systematic reform of the public service is essential.

The OPS has already absorbed a great deal of change under difficult circumstances. In recent years, Ministries have been amalgamated, and whole layers of management have been eliminated, while salaries and benefits have been frozen. Across the system, innovative managers and employees have been able to improve service quality and, at the same time, substantially reduce the overall cost of operating the government.

Despite impressive success in doing more with less in the public sector, Ontario's deficit remains unsustainably high. The role of government in Ontario must be redefined and the public service restructured to execute this new role in the most effective way.

Making Change Happen

The Need for Political Leadership
Casting a new vision for government in Ontario will take political acumen and courage. Implementing it will require sustained political leadership. The government must put reform of the bureaucracy at the centre of its agenda and not allow competing priorities to push it aside.

Around the world, determined political leadership is the common thread running through all successful public service restructuring efforts. Without leadership from the highest office, reform will fall victim to inertia. Ministers must be concerned not only with developing policy, but with developing the capacity of their Ministries to implement policy.

The Private Sector Can Help
Some suggest that the public and private sectors are so intrinsically different that management models and approaches developed in one arena have little in the other. This is wrong. Government can learn a lot from the private sector. Effective human resource management, more than anything else, drives quality and productivity in a service industry such as public administration. People are people, whether they work in or outside of government. They have the same needs and respond to the same incentives.

The business community has a great deal of experience with strategic organizational restructuring. Many, if not most, of the problems the OPS will encounter in restructuring its operations have already been faced by large companies. Experience in the service sector may be particularly relevant since public administration is essentially a service activity.

If invited to play a meaningful role in helping the OPS to restructure, CEOs and other private sector leaders will respond positively.

Directions for Reform
The organization and management of the public service must be shaped by the roles and responsibilities it will undertake. However, it is safe to assume that many of today's approaches to managing people and programs in the OPS will have to change. Until future roles are determined, it will be premature to prescribe a detailed course of restructuring. Still, a new government must signal the priority which it places on reform. Immediately following the election, it should consider:

1 Launching a government wide, zero-base program review posing questions such as: What are the provincial government's core responsibilities? Are there areas in which services could be delivered better or at lower cost by municipalities or the non-profit sector? Are there functions which could be carried out more effectively through licensing arrangements or joint ventures with the private sector? Are some activities simply not affordable in today's fiscal climate? Are there areas in which government involvement should increase?

   This review should be launched in the very early stages of the mandate, before the government becomes the prisoner of existing structures and of the electoral timetable.
2 Appointing a special commission, once the program review is completed, to develop an action plan for public service restructuring and to monitor the pace of reform. The commission should involve senior officials and CEOs who have past experience in government. Labour leaders should also take part.
3 Clarifying the roles of Ministers and senior officials and their responsibilities toward each other.
4 Establishing its philosophy and intentions regarding the appointment of outsiders to senior positions in the public service.
5 Creating a new senior cabinet position – Minister Responsible For the Public Service and Reform of Government – and assign a respected, *senior* Deputy Minister to support the Minister.
6 Articulating a new philosophy for public sector management stressing:

   - the need to attract and retain good people
   - the need for Ministries to draw up formal business plans and to benchmark best practices
   - the need to measure performance by customer-driven standards
   - the need to hold people (e.g., Ministers and Deputy Ministers) accountable for results.

Establishing the Right Relationship between the Premier and the Ontario Public Service

Rationale
The Premier will find, with some marked exceptions, a public service executive corps willing and able to serve the government in a professional, non-partisan fashion, as most senior public servants recognize the need to overhaul the mission and structure of government in Ontario, and are prepared to get on with the job.

The OPS has undergone a great deal of change over the past several years. Public servants have had to do more with less, and most have responded within the impossible guidelines provided them. Some Ministries have been merged and reduced in size while operational budgets have been trimmed. It is clear, however, that the expenditure reductions needed to balance the provincial budget will not be realized by continuing to chip away at existing programs. Indeed, the key to effective downsizing rests in identifying programs that can be dropped, transferred to other jurisdictions, or privatized in whole or part.

Success in reforming and revitalizing the public sector will require concerted leadership from the Premier and Cabinet, the establishment of a trusting relationship between Ministers and senior officials, the need for officials to clearly understand the vision of the government, and they must have the flexibility and tools for achieving that vision.

Strategy
The Premier should meet with the Deputy Ministers shortly after Cabinet is sworn in. The Premier's remarks might be structured as follows.

Introduction
The election campaign is over. The business of the new government is now the priority. It is no secret to you and to all the members of the legislature that the government of Ontario faces the greatest challenge in our lifetime. I have been elected on a platform of real change. Not just the old concept of replacing a tired administration with a fresh team, but more essentially, on changing the role of government and the way it does business. This means gut-wrenching changes, as the Premier and Cabinet must establish a blueprint for smaller, more affordable government in Ontario.

I wish to address a number of matters relating to the management of government and the roles we must execute together if we are to be successful.

1. The structure and organization of government
2. The fiscal situation
3. My attitude toward the public service
4. The working relationship I envisage between Ministers and the public service
5. The developing and implementing [of] a strategy for public service reform and restructuring

1. The Organization of Decision Making
- Structure of Cabinet Committees
- Role and organization of the Premier's office
- Introduction to key staff
- The rationale and timetable for Deputy Ministerial appointments

2. The Fiscal Situation and Role of Government in Ontario
- The fiscal crisis is real and requires a substantial reduction in government spending, made all the more challenging by the need for tax reductions, to give the public more hope and confidence in the future. We must also contemplate that a recession may not be too far away.
- Across-the-board cuts will not do the job. Instead, we must rethink government,

determine what businesses we will be in, then organize the public service to transact that business with maximum efficiency.
- We will explore new models for delivering services, including privatization and joint ventures with the private and not-for-profit sectors; however, we recognize there are limitations on these options. We are not "disinventing" government, but repositioning it.
- Even though government will be smaller, public policy development and service delivery will still play a vital role in Ontario – it is crucial to change, and to ensure a government that works well.
- I want Ontario to be recognized as a leader and innovator in public sector management, both in Canada and internationally, and I intend to give the tools and machinery to those who are prepared to do the job.

It is critical that we develop, implement and communicate a coherent fiscal and public service management agenda. The first step must involve a comprehensive review of programs and activities. The Minister of Finance will establish cost reduction targets, and every Ministry will conduct a zero-based review of its spending programs, and present expenditure reduction plans to Cabinet. The review process will be concluded in three to four months.

We must determine which businesses the government will be in, and which ones it will not be in. Then, we must ensure that the public service is organized and equipped to implement this new vision in the most effective way. The management agenda will flow directly from the fiscal agenda.

3. *Principles about the Public Service*
   - I believe in a professional public service, with appointments based upon merit.
   - The vast majority, but not all appointments to senior positions, will be made from within the OPS. However, there will always be a need to bring new blood into the system and, in some cases, specialized skills and experience not available within the OPS.
   - The process of change in our society, and the challenge of repositioning government, dictates that we must bring people into government from the private sector on an assignment/volunteer basis to handle specific projects concerned with policy, service delivery, or restructuring. In most cases, it will be possible to simply borrow them.
   - I believe it is vital to step up the quality and quantity of exchange between the OPS, the broader public service and, particularly, the private sector. Greater cross-fertilization will not only improve understanding, but open the doors to both in a way that should encourage a more effective and responsive economy.
   - If government is to work well, Deputy Ministers must have the tools to manage effectively – we recognize that our success as a government depends on your performance. Notwithstanding the imperative to reduce the size of the public service, Ministers and Deputies must work together to
     - focus on efficiency, not just head count;
     - measure, recognize and reward performance;
     - set clear performance targets for Ministries, and give the public service leadership the instruments and flexibility they need to meet those targets;
     - ensure that flexibility given with one hand is not taken away with the other – we need to develop a consistent approach to downsizing and cost reduction; and,
     - develop a people-centred management culture which values employees and customers, and demonstrates these values through tangible action.

4. *The Working Relationship between Ministers and Senior Officials*
   - Deputy Ministers are appointed by the Premier. They are responsible to me through the Secretary of Cabinet. That must signal first and foremost your corporate duty to

the government as a whole – obviously for the government to succeed at implementing its agenda, Deputies and Ministers must work collectively as a team at both the corporate and the ministry level. Ministers and Deputies must have mutual confidence and there should be no barriers between them.
- I appreciate that there were some tensions between Ministers and Deputies under the previous government due, in part it would seem, to confusion over respective roles and responsibilities. Ministers' political offices will be leaner, and political staff are not to be a parallel bureaucracy. Senior public servants will be expected to assist them in an appropriate way. However, political staff will understand and respect that managing the public service and implementing public policy is the responsibility of Deputy Ministers.
- I respect the traditional division of authority between the political and departmental echelons of government and I want you and my Ministers to work on the basis of that assumption. My Ministers and I are the elected representatives, and we will make the decisions. That is our job. Your job is to provide us with the best advice and to implement the decisions as effectively as possible.
- I want you to speak your minds, challenge our assumptions, and advise us on the implications of various policy options. There is nothing wrong with constructive disagreement behind closed doors. It is vital that you understand our policy intent and that we are fully aware of the implications of various policy options. In the management of the difficult times that lie ahead, I need the best advice – not cheerleading.
- I am prepared to meet regularly with this group, primarily to deal with structural and management issues to help ensure you are aware of the corporate vision of the government, and to be certain that relations between Ministers and senior officials continue to evolve in an atmosphere of trust and understanding.
- That said, we must recognize that the new emphasis will be on accountability – the focus of this government will be on achieving results; as senior executives you will be held accountable for achieving results and will have the appropriate authority to achieve them.
- I recognize the connection between authority, accountability and compensation. The compensation freeze is a particular problem, not just in recruiting and retaining top-flight people, but in limiting your ability to reward performance. This is a political hot potato, but we will have to move on it – the link between performance and reward must be direct and visible to the public service and to the public at large.

5. *Developing and Implementing a Strategy for Public Service Restructuring*
- I recognize that the OPS has already absorbed a great deal of change in recent years – change that involved imperatives of fiscal restraint with mixed signals on flexibility to manage the changes. I have many concerns about the atmosphere in which you have had to manage, and I hope to develop accountability systems that are needed to make a flatter, more decentralized, empowered organization work better. This, however, will take time and much of the form will have to be developed in relation to change. The new government will not embark upon a major re-organization of the OPS until a new vision of government is clarified – form will follow function.
- I don't want to speculate on what the government or the public service will ultimately look like, save that we will make good on our campaign promise to reduce the number of employees by (date).
- I want to make program cuts and accompanying staff cuts as quickly and humanely as possible. I recognize that what happens to the people who are let go will affect the morale and performance of those who stay and whose dedication and cooperation we need.
- The responsibility for public sector reform must be shared among the Cabinet and the public service and must be carried out with the support of the private sector.
- I have already announced that Treasury Board and Management Board will be merged and form a single portfolio under the Minister of Finance.

- I will establish an independent Advisory Committee to assist in the public service reform process. The Committee will be co-chaired by the Secretary of the Cabinet and a private sector CEO who has a good understanding of government in Ontario. Members will include present and former public servants and business leaders. The Committee will report directly to me, and comprise eight people, four from the government and four from the private sector.
- Among other issues, the Committee will advise on:
  - executive compensation, reward and accountability;
  - measures to increase the exchange of people and ideas between government and the private sector;
  - building new, value-added relationships between the government and public sector unions with a view to resuming collective bargaining;
  - new models for policy development and service delivery;
  - restructuring processes; and,
  - recruitment of private sector expertise into the public service.
- I will take the Committee's advice very seriously and use it to help navigate the political mine fields of public sector reform.

You have my full support. The reality is that good government is good politics and, unless you and your colleagues are well equipped and motivated, we are not going to achieve our political agenda. That link is the most critical aspect of good government.

Appendix B:
Excerpts from *Mission '97*

[*Mission '97* was a booklet given to those attending the Progressive Conservative Party of Ontario General Meeting in Windsor, 16-18 October 1992. Its purpose was to give party members an idea of the work already done and to encourage their participation in the next phases of the work.]

What Is It?
As Progressive Conservatives, what do we stand for? What are our principles, values, and beliefs? And how do we make sure we translate them into policies and actions when we form the next government?

To answer these important questions, Mike Harris made the decision this past spring to develop a mission statement ... a simple and concise expression of what we stand for and how we will act as the government of Ontario. This is not an election slogan. It is a framework for how we will govern.

How Was It Developed?
In keeping with the open and democratic nature of the party and its constitution, all aspects of the party were involved in this process from the very beginning.

Input sessions were held with caucus members, riding presidents, the party executive (including the five regional vice-presidents), and the PC Women's, Youth, and Campus Associations through May and June.

Representatives from all those groups formed a steering committee, which met in June to develop a draft mission statement based on input from the various constituencies across the party and the province.

That draft statement formed the basis for another round of consultations in July resulting in the development of a series of strategic objectives. This input gave final shape to the mission statement being presented to you at this convention.

Why Mission 1997?
Mike Harris and the steering committee, based on input from the party, decided they didn't want a statement that focused simply on the short term goal of getting elected, but one which reflected the longer term goal of governing Ontario. The action plans flowing from this mission statement should focus not only on getting elected but on how we will govern after that election.

What Is the Statement Used For?
This mission statement will serve as our guideline as we form policies, build our organizations, choose candidates, raise funds, and make all the other necessary preparations for becoming the next government of Ontario.

What Happens Next?
To be effective, a mission statement must include a plan for translating your beliefs, values, and principles into reality. There must be a time line, measurable results, and a list of actions to be taken. Our mission statement can be broken into four main elements:

- building a safe and prosperous Ontario
- adhering to shared values
- governing with leadership
- implementing policies.

The steering committee outlined a series of strategic objectives from these four elements ... We must now translate those strategic objectives into action plans.

[A two-page diagram set out the mission statement and under each of its three components ("Strategic Elements") set out "Strategic Objectives."]

Mission 1997
We will build a safe and prosperous Ontario by:

- adhering to shared values based on individual rights and responsibilities, fairness, and equality of opportunity
- governing with responsive, competent, and principled leadership
- implementing innovative, consistent, and responsible policies.

[Under the second strategic element were the following strategic objectives.]

Election Strategy	In order to implement our agenda, we will develop and implement a detailed campaign strategy which will result in our forming the government after the next election.
Recruitment	Recruit the best team (volunteers, staff, candidates) according to established criteria in each category, commencing January 1, 1993.
Transition Strategy	Complete the development of a detailed, integrated transition strategy 6 months prior to the next election.
Direct Involvement	Implement innovative methods for directly involving the public in governing themselves.

[Under the third strategic element were the following strategic objectives.]

Policy Framework	Develop a comprehensive policy framework, including the principles upon which policies will be built by January 1, 1993.
Policy Development Process	Implement a direct involvement policy development process to delineate specific policies in major strategic areas beginning spring 1993.
Policy Implementation Plan	Develop a policy implementation plan and schedule 6 months prior to the next election.

Appendix C: The Liberal Approach to Organization, Management, and Decision-Making in the Government of Ontario

6 June 1995, draft

The Liberal View of Government

An Overview
Governments in the 1990s face an unenviable set of circumstances:

- the fiscal strain brought on by high public deficit and growing public debt;
- an economic climate characterized by global competition, structural market transformations, uncertainties brought on by the pace and nature of technological change, and high unemployment;
- on-going public cynicism and distrust of political institutions, politicians, and public servants; and
- a belief that government has lost its way, in terms of what its role is, as well as its ability to carry out its functions.

The Liberal vision of Ontario is a province where individuals have real opportunity and where people and communities work together to achieve common goals; an Ontario in which people are secure – through a strong economy, universal health care, high-quality education, safety from crime, and a healthy environment.
    The Ontario Liberal Plan is built on five themes:

OPPORTUNITY – Ontarians want the opportunity to work, to get a good education, and to build a secure future.
SECURITY – Ontarians must be able to feel safe in their homes, on their streets, and in their schools.
COMMUNITY – Government must realize that not every problem can be resolved by a "one-size-fits-all" policy. The focus of problem-solving must be at the community level.
AFFORDABILITY – Government must plan smartly, spend wisely, and live within its fiscal means.
ACCOUNTABILITY – People, businesses, and institutions must be accountable for their actions.

The Liberal approach to government aims to create a government which is more effective, more efficient, more flexible (while still accountable), costs less and is more responsive (through decentralization, devolution, citizen participation, and consultation).

The Liberal Approach to Government
The central policy question for the nineties is: What is the role of government?

- What must government do?
- What should government not do?
- What is desirable for government to do, but cannot be afforded?
- How should government do the things it must do?

Liberals believe that government needs to be reformed, not destroyed; that government needs to rethink what its core business should be, and concentrate its effort on running that business efficiently, effectively, with an increased focus on meeting the needs of the people it was elected to serve, and with an emphasis on fairness and social justice.

Liberals believe that the primary role of government is to set the policy framework within which other parts of society – other governments, the private sector, the voluntary sector, and individual citizens – can act. The provincial government should focus more on establishing the correct set of policies, and become less program and service delivery oriented.

The Liberal view of the role of government reflects the belief that these other parts of society – other governments, the private sector, the voluntary sector, and individual citizens – have a role to play in reaching and fulfilling mutually agreed goals and responsibilities. A key purpose of government is to build partnerships with these other parts of society by creating opportunities for their participation, establishing the operating rules and, in general, ensuring that these players are able to take on the increased responsibilities inherent in this evolving role of government.

It also means that government must move away from the traditional control mentality toward conducting policy making and program delivery. Government must be more oriented to responding to citizen concerns, more sensitive to a customer-focused approach to service delivery, and more attuned to taxpayer desires for value for money. Government must be supportive of the marketplace and entrepreneurship, setting boundaries which enhance the public interest, while avoiding barriers to innovation, productivity, and job creation. Government must bring governance closer to the people, through meaningful consultation, and by strengthening the capacity and facilitating the ability of communities to address their own concerns.

Getting Our Own House in Order

The first steps must involve reforming the nature of the provincial government by:

- restructuring the organization of government, to reduce the size and the scope of its activities;
- reviewing the functions of government, to streamline its operations and heighten its ability to respond to citizens and to serve its customers in an effective manner;
- reinvigorating the operations of government, by decentralizing the delivery of services, empowering employees, promoting public service, listening to citizens, and adopting a greater customer orientation; and
- focusing the decision-making processes of government, to concentrate on priority concerns and the capacity for long-term planning.

In all this, the government must be guided by its operating principles (more effective, more efficient, more flexible, less costly and more responsive), as well as by its priority policy agenda, in particular, fulfilling the commitments of the election platform.

To ensure more responsiveness and greater input into government decision-making, and better use of elected representatives, government caucus members will have more opportunities to participate in the development of government policies, thereby better reflecting the views of their constituencies in the legislature. As well, the position of Associate Minister will carry more responsibilities, in dealings with the relevant ministry, in participating in the decision-making process of government, and in its interaction with the public at large.

The Liberal Approach to Policy Preparation and Decision-Making in the Government of Ontario

1. Objectives
There are a number of objectives which inform a Liberal Government approach to policy-making:

- to provide a clear set of directions to government policy activities;
- to ensure focused attention is given to issues of high priority to the government;
- to heighten the capacity for a government-wide approach to policy development;
- to strengthen the government's ability to address complex, interrelated issues;
- to clarify the policy mandates of individual ministries;
- to focus equal policy attention on immediate, developing, and long-term issues;
- to build stronger feedback mechanisms for decision-makers, through monitoring and evaluating initiatives;
- to broaden partnerships with policy communities, to broaden the scope of policy inputs.

2. Ministries
The ministries under a Liberal government are:

Agriculture, Food and Rural Affairs
Children's Services
Community Services
Consumer Protection and Services
Culture
Economic Development and Infrastructure
Education
Employment
Environment and Conservation
Finance
Government Reform
Health
Justice
Local and Regional Development
Natural Resources and Northern Development
Public Safety
Trade
Treasury Board

3. Structure
There are a few structural circumstances which bear noting:

- There will be two Cabinet policy committees, the Committee on Economic Policy and the Committee on Human Services Policy.
- There will be several coordinating or review committees of Cabinet, comprising a Planning and Government Reform Committee, an Operating Committee, and a Legislation and Regulations Committee.
- The Treasury Board of Cabinet will review policy decisions having regard for their fiscal and personnel consequences and government operations consequences. (It will combine the functions of the earlier Treasury Board and Management Board).
- From time to time, ad hoc committees of Cabinet will be created, for a limited term, to deal with specific issues of concern to the government.

4. Responsibilities
Cabinet committees will have the following responsibilities:

Planning and Government Reform Committee The Planning and Government Reform Committee will:

- serve as the government's medium- to long-term think-tank;
- determine the government's major plans for a rolling six- to twelve-month period;
- monitor government progress on implementing its election platform;
- in particular, monitor progress with respect to the government's reforming government agenda;
- decide what can, and should, be done during the mandate;
- generate the agenda framework under which the Operating Committee will operate;
- have responsibility for all Throne Speeches;
- play a major role in the annual budget preparation process;
- receive all reports of inquiries, Royal Commissions, and the Premier's Council;
- control the research agenda of the government;
- monitor the results of academic research relevant to the government;
- keep abreast of changing public values, as well as changing public attitudes on major policy issues;
- coordinate interdepartmental initiatives.

Operating Committee The Operating Committee will:

- manage the agenda of Cabinet and set priorities for the use of Cabinet time;
- develop a strategy, and monitor the implementation of the strategy, for dealing with any crisis;
- manage the government's media and communications strategy;
- oversee the government's strategy for the Legislature;
- monitor the perception of the government's activities among the citizens of the province;
- act as a forum to resolve impasses in Cabinet Committee or Cabinet deliberations.

Policy Committees review and make recommendations to Cabinet. Their jurisdiction is defined by the policy field, not simply by the ministry from which the item emanates.

Cabinet Committee on Economic Policy The Cabinet Committee on Economic Policy will review Cabinet proposals relating to policy topics which fall under the following ministries:

Agriculture, Food and Rural Affairs
Consumer Protection and Services (issues relating to economic policy)
Economic Development and Infrastructure
Employment
Environment and Conservation
Finance
Local and Regional Development
Natural Resources and Northern Development
Trade

Cabinet Committee on Human Services Policy The Cabinet Committee on Human Services Policy will review Cabinet proposals relating to policy topics which fall under the following ministries:

Children's Services
Community Services

Consumer Protection and Services (issues relating to consumer protection)
Culture
Education
Employment
Health
Justice
Public Safety

Cabinet Legislation and Regulations Committee The Cabinet Legislation and Regulations Committee will review proposed bills and regulations to ensure they accord with government intentions.

Treasury Board of Cabinet The Treasury Board of Cabinet will review:

- the impact of policy proposals on government spending, operations and/or personnel requirements;
- program evaluation reports;
- ministry requests for accommodation or reallocation of existing resources;
- the management of issues between the government as employer and its public sector employees;
- human resources management and administration policies;
- applications for approval relating to information technology acquisitions, below market value disposition of real assets, and related items.

The Ministries of Government Reform, Consumer Protection and Services, and Treasury Board will sit on the Treasury Board of Cabinet, otherwise, membership is not based on portfolio.

Ad Hoc Committees of Cabinet Ad hoc committees of Cabinet will exercise those functions for such periods of time as are directed by the Planning Committee of Cabinet.

Cabinet Cabinet as a whole will perform the following functions:

- receive and review recommendations of the policy committee of Cabinet, after they have been reviewed by Planning Committee or Operating Committee, and where relevant, Treasury Board;
- receive and review those decisions of the Planning Committee and Operating Committee which require Cabinet endorsement;
- make those decisions it is required to make with respect to regulations and orders-in-council.

5. Process

The proposed structure for policy development and decision-making is predicated on distinguishing different types of policy work and different levels of policy endorsement. Policies can be defined along a number of continuums, from single ministry issue to cross-government concerns, from short-term solutions to long-term reforms, from program adjustments to wholesale policy overhauls, and so on. While it may not always be possible to describe with precision where a given policy proposal should fall, the following division of labour anticipates a distinction between issues of government-wide importance (and which require central review and direction), and those matters which are refinements of previously agreed-upon policies and which are largely within the purview of one ministry.

The Planning and Government Reform Committee The Planning Committee sits at the apex of the policy development process. Its function is to provide the framework for government policy-making, and to direct medium and long-term planning. Its purpose is not to conduct actual policy development, except in those cases where it specifically undertakes that responsibility.

The Planning Committee's functions could best be described as follows:

TO COMMUNICATE the government's broad policy objectives, primarily through its preparation of the Throne Speech and its participation in the preparation of the Budget;

TO ANTICIPATE the need for government policy initiatives, in response to public trends and policy developments, through its review of changing public attitudes, its overview of ministry policy work, its receipt of all government inquiries, royal commissions and Premier's Council reports, and its review of policy discussions occurring in other jurisdictions and among policy communities;

TO PROVIDE DIRECTION for the development of policy by a specific ministry or group of ministries, by offering a framework for the policy initiative;

TO COORDINATE policy development by several ministries, either directly led by the Policy Committee, or by a Cabinet committee or ministry mandated by the Committee;

TO MONITOR the development of mandated policy initiatives, as well as the implementation of government agenda items, including election platform items, the reform of government, and such other items as it identifies.

Policy Development Directive A principal means by which the Planning Committee performs its function is the use of a Policy Development Directive, which provides a framework for policy development to take place. In most cases, a Policy Development Directive would identify the issue to be addressed, the principles which should guide the policy, an itemization of concerns and interests to be balanced, and, in some cases, some of the options which should be considered. A Policy Development Directive does not seek to prejudge the policy decision, only to give authority and set boundaries for the exercise. The impetus for a Policy Development Directive may be at the direction of the Planning Committee or at the request of a ministry or set of ministries.

A Policy Development Directive is required:

- for major policy initiatives;
- where there is a notable departure from existing policy or practice; and/or
- where the issue is complex and/or involves considerable interministerial coordination.

A Policy Development Directive is likely unnecessary where an initiative is straightforward, involves routine policy maintenance, falls largely within the jurisdiction of one ministry, and/or reflects a continuation of existing policy or practice. It is also more unlikely where there are no fiscal or legislative implications. (Ministries contemplating an initiative must notify Cabinet Office to determine whether a Policy Development Initiative is required.)

A Policy Development Directive made by the Planning Committee should be reported to the full Cabinet and be minuted as a Cabinet decision.

Once a Policy Development Mandate is issued, the actual work of preparing the subsequent Cabinet Submission occurs, either through a particular ministry, an interministerial team, or at the direction of Cabinet Office. The review of the Cabinet Submission is conducted by either a Cabinet Policy Committee, the Operating Committee or the Planning Committee. The choice of which options forms part of the Planning Committee's Policy Development Directive decision.

Operating Committee The Operating Committee exercises political control over the activities of government, in terms of the day-to-day agenda (both of the Cabinet system and of the Legislature), and tactically, in terms of the messages the government communicates, dealing with political "crises," and resolving policy disputes within the government. In terms of functions, the significant items to note would be that the Operating Committee:

- sets the agenda for the full Cabinet;
- seeks to resolve impasses arising from Cabinet and Cabinet policy committee discussions;
- receives reports from the various policy committees (except those items mandated to go to the Planning Committee) before they advance to the full Cabinet;
- reviews the media plan for major policy announcements;
- monitors developments in the Legislature;
- develops the strategy for any current issue which is attracting substantial attention.

Because of the immediacy of much of their work, the Operating Committee should meet weekly.

6. Implications for Staff and Staff Work

The nature of the Cabinet committee process has a number of implications for the work of staff, primarily relating to Cabinet Office and the various policy activities of the ministries.

In order to describe the primary functions of the various policy bodies within government, it would be useful to review the generic types of policy work done by policy analysts of all sorts (i.e. central agency, line ministry, political staff) within government. This is outlined in the following:

Functional Activities of Policy Units
1. Policy Agenda Development: defining government goals, objectives, policies, and conducting priority reviews
2. Policy Development: preparing specific policy papers, identifying options and potential programs to be considered
3. Program Design: designing concrete courses of action, or programs, to achieve policy objectives
4. Program Evaluation: examining proposed or actual programs to determine if they will achieve, or have achieved, their objectives
5. Policy Firefighting: doing rush assignments, short-term work under pressure, and studies of "hot" issues of the moment demanding a "quick study"
6. Coordinating and Liaison: coordinating operational and long-term plans, or the programs of various branches, and providing liaison with other ministry groups, other ministries, other governments, and/or groups outside government
7. Socio-Economic Research and Forecasting: doing research projects, long-term forecasting, scenario writing, and extrapolations
8. External Scanning of the Environment: identifying external threats and opportunities, and conducting inquiries into the nature, causes, and possible solutions of new and existing policy issues
9. Needs Assessment: determining the need for new policies, programs, and services
10. Legislation: providing advice on legislation, and assisting program staff to work with legislative counsel to draft new legislation and/or amendments to existing legislation
11. Executive Assistant Support: preparing speeches for the Minister and senior officials, preparing correspondence, hosting visitors, compiling data from line divisions, and arranging meetings, workshops, and conferences
12. Policy Advice: preparing policy papers, having input into priority-setting, and assisting in defining overall objectives and strategic plans (adapted from M. Hollander and M. Prince, "Analytical Units in Federal and Provincial Governments," *Canadian Public Administration* 36, 2 [1993]: 190).

In broad-brush terms, the following characterizations should apply:

Cabinet Office staff would take a lead role in defining the policy framework (i.e., Policy Agenda Development), in coordinating major government interministerial policy development work (i.e., Coordination and Liaison), sometimes directing specific Policy Development, and in conducting major policy reviews. This would include directing broader external scanning exercises.

Finance and Treasury Board would take lead roles in major or significant Program Evaluation, and Socio-Economic Research and Forecasting.

Line ministries would concentrate their efforts on Policy Development, Program Design, Policy Firefighting, Needs Assessment, Legislation and Executive Assistant Support, with secondary roles in Program Evaluation and External Scanning, and where relevant, Socio-Economic Research and Forecasting. They would also undertake lower level coordination and liaison.

Ministry political staff should be capable of monitoring line ministry policy work, and, in particular, undertake Policy Firefighting and Executive Assistant Support, and provide Policy Advice to the Minister as a member of the Executive Council.

7. Sequence of Decisions

In essence, one can anticipate two types of Cabinet decisions, for convenience sake, Tier I and Tier II decisions.

A Tier I decision is a higher order government decision, requiring a Policy Development Directive from the Planning Committee, and probably involving some degree of involvement from Cabinet Office.

A Tier I item, once prepared under the direction of a ministry, set of ministries, or Cabinet Office, then gets reviewed by the appropriate Cabinet policy committee, then the Operating Committee, before it proceeds to Cabinet. (Planning Committee may indicate that the item should return to Planning Committee, rather than proceed through this process.)

A Tier II decision, while ultimately going to Cabinet, evolves from and is directed by the relevant ministry, and proceeds to the relevant Cabinet policy committee, then the Operating Committee, before it proceeds to Cabinet.

A Tier I process may be initiated by a ministry or Cabinet Office. A Tier II process will almost always be initiated by a ministry. A Tier II process may be bumped up to the Tier I level by Cabinet Office.

Treasury Board performs its review after the item is considered by either Planning Committee or Operating Committee, prior to proceeding to the full Cabinet. The item may also be discussed in Caucus before the full Cabinet deliberation.

After Planning Committee issues a Policy Development Directive, disputes concerning the policy should be resolved in the relevant Cabinet policy committee or, if necessary, the Operating Committee, unless the Planning Committee specifically designates that the policy recommendation return to that committee.

Appendix 1: Elaboration of principles underlying the Liberal approach to government
Appendix 2: List of functions associated with new ministries [not reproduced]
Appendix 3: Examples of types of functions which will be undertaken by Ministry of Government Reform

Appendix 1: Elaboration of Principles Underlying the Liberal Approach to Government

Principles Underlying the Liberal Approach to Government

The key principles underlying the Liberal approach to government are the following:

Focus on Consultation
- Government should be more open and more consultative than it has been in the past, while still recognizing that consultation cannot go on forever, and that decisions must be made within a reasonable time frame.
- Consultation must become more of a bottom-up than a top-down process because problem identification ought to be primarily a front-line issue.

Focus on the Individual Citizen
- Increased responsibility must accompany increased citizen influence.
- Individuals should be treated as customers, rather than captives.
- As much as possible, government should reduce its role to setting the policy framework within which individual citizens and communities will make their own decisions with respect to which services they will use.

Focus on Effectiveness
- The operation of government should be streamlined, simplified, and modernized.
- Government should match private sector delivery standards, for those programs and services it continues to deliver itself.
- Government should establish and publish performance standards for services, so that citizens know what they can expect, in terms of time, cost, and access to public services.
- Maximizing customer value and the public good derived for each tax dollar spent should be the measure of the effectiveness of a government program or service.
- Government should substantially reduce the amount of money it spends on providing services to itself.
- The overlap and duplication which now exists between the provincial government and local governments should be reduced.

Focus on Local Needs
- Government should reduce its level of interference with local government, especially in areas where funding from the provincial government is not involved.
- Program and service delivery methods should be sufficiently flexible to reflect local conditions.

Focus on Enhancing the Role of the MPP
- Individual MPPs should be much freer than in the past to have their votes in the legislature reflect what the MPP believes is best for the people the MPP represents.
- Legislative committees should have more ability to influence policy and legislation.
- Government MPPs should have more input into decisions of Cabinet.

Implications of these Principles for the Way Government Operates

The following illustrate some of the implications of these principles:

Government Which Is Closer to Citizens
- Citizen consultation on an issue should begin earlier than it does now.
- Citizens should be encouraged to contribute their time and talents on a voluntary basis to many provincial government agencies, boards, and commissions.
- Customers should be given opportunities to provide input into the design of programs and services intended for use by them.
- Within government administrative units, authority should be decentralized so that decisions are made closer to the customer.

Government Which Is More Flexible and Accountable
- Administrative units of government should be subjected to less rules and regulations, and have greater flexibility in how they operate on a day-to-day basis, as long as they fulfill their mandate.
- Customer satisfaction measures, best practices, and the bottom line should be used to drive improvements in government services.
- The roles, responsibilities and, equally important, the accountability of the provincial government, local governments, private sector service providers and customers should be clearly defined and understood by citizens.
- The amount of red tape and government paperwork hampering business from operating efficiently should be substantially reduced.

Government Which Is More Efficient
- Competition should be promoted among service providers in order to improve efficiency; thus, there should be considerably expanded use of market control mechanisms, rather than bureaucratic control mechanisms.
- Measures of customer service and value for money, frequently used in the private sector, should be applied to measure the effectiveness of government programs and services.
- The number of provincial government agencies, boards, and commissions should be substantially reduced.
- The provincial government approval process, for business, local governments and individuals, should be streamlined.
- The speed with which government responds to a problem should be enhanced.
- The percentage of government expenditures which are spent providing services to government itself should be reduced, so that a larger percentage of expenditures will be spent external to the government, providing services to people.

Government in Which the MPP's Role Is Enhanced
- A more open budget process should be developed, including allowing certain budget proposals to be debated in public before a legislative committee, before the government finalizes the budget.
- While individual government MPPs would be expected to support government legislation which reflects commitments made in the Liberal Party's election platform, and to support legislation arising from a Liberal government's budget, for most other bills MPPs should be free to vote according to what they believe to be best for the citizens they represent and for the people of Ontario as a whole; thus MPPs should be free to vote against government bills without defeating the government.
- Legislative committees should have their usefulness and importance increased by allowing them to initiate legislation, to allow for more public input and more varied forms of input, and by reducing the enforcement of party discipline within committees.

...

Appendix 3: Examples of Types of Functions Which Will Be Undertaken by Ministry of Government Reform

The structural changes put in place by the new government are only part of the reform process. The reduction in the number of ministries and rationalization of ministry tasks is only a first step toward a more effective and more responsive organization. The major responsibility for effecting the broad corporate transformation which needs to take place falls with the Ministry of Government Reform, and the Cabinet committee charged with overseeing this process is the Planning Committee.

Among the activities which the Ministry of Government Reform will be undertaking is a review of the many generic support functions currently being performed in almost every ministry. These include functions such as legal services, human resources services, information technology support, policy development and analysis, and so on. The Ministry will head this broad review, which will be divided into a number of task forces, each with its own chair and support secretariat. These reviews would involve:

Legal Services Review, chaired by the Ministry of Justice
Human Resources Services Review, chaired by Ministry of Government Reform, with secretariat support by the Human Resources Council
Financial Services Review, chaired by Ministry of Government Reform, with secretariat support by Financial Officers' Council
Policy Services Review, chaired by Cabinet Office, with secretariat support by Policy Executives' Council
Accommodation and Asset Management Review, chaired by Ministry of Government Reform, with secretariat support by Accommodation Directors' Council

Information Technology Review, chaired by Ministry of Government Reform, chaired by Information Technology Education Council
Customer Services Review, chaired by Ministry of Consumer Protection and Services
Regional Offices Review, chaired by Ministry of Government Reform
Administration Review, chaired by Ministry of Government Reform, with secretariat support by Chief Administrative Officers' Forum
Other possibilities: investigation and enforcement; libraries; analytical laboratories

Appendix D: The Conservative Transition Team

Co-chairs
David Lindsay   Principal Secretary to Mike Harris
William Farlinger   Former Chairman, Ernst and Young

Members
George Boddington   President, Policy Concepts; former Executive Assistant to Davis-era minister Dennis Timbrell
Thomas Campbell   Former Deputy Treasurer; former Chair, Ontario Hydro
Barbara Cowieson   Director of Administration, PC Service Bureau
Ernie Eves   Veteran MPP; Finance Minister-designate
Patricia Jacobsen   Senior VP of Human Resources and Corporate Services, Manulife Financial; former DM of Transportation; former Associate Secretary of Cabinet for Executive Resources
Mitch Patten   Vice President of Marketing, Municipal Gas Corporation; former Special Assistant to Premiers Davis and Miller
Graham Scott   Partner, McMillan Binch; former DM of Health; former DM of Environment
Brock Smith   Special Advisor, Public Perspectives Inc.; former Deputy Treasurer
Bill Young   President, Westborne Management Group

Source: "The Transition Team," Ontario Progressive Conservative Caucus News Release, 12 June 1995.

Appendix E:
Political Briefing Material Given to Conservative Ministers

Confidential Briefing on Issues Coming before Cabinet

Introduction
In the days ahead, each Minister will begin the briefing process with his or her Ministry staff. This introduction and the tabs which follow are designed to provide a quick political overview and context for those briefings.

Where We Were; Where We Are
At the start of the campaign, and for a considerable period of time leading up to the election call, the Ontario PCs were supported by about one-quarter of the electorate. At the end of the campaign, support had risen to just under half.
Let's look at some of the factors which contributed to that rise.

Issues
In terms of the issues which mattered to Ontarians, when the election started we were competitive in a few but trailed in virtually every category.
At the end, we were leading in every category with particular strength in the areas of reforming <u>welfare</u>, ending <u>quotas,</u> and cutting <u>taxes</u> to create good jobs.

How Did This Come About?
It wasn't just that people agreed with our policies and thought we knew what we were talking about. In the end, two very important factors resulted in victory:

- Our communications were incredibly focused and disciplined. From a communications perspective, we ran virtually a textbook campaign. One message stood in stark contrast to the cacophony of messages which were heard from the other side.
- We had one team, which spoke with a united voice and stayed right on our policies. No contradictions. No deviations.

In addition to this, the Liberals came apart at the seams and ran an unfocused, undisciplined campaign which careened from crisis to crisis.
Without both occurrences, we would not have been able to be successful in the way that we were.

Political Challenge
The political challenge now faced by a Harris government is to convert success we achieved on the campaign trail into success in government.
We have been authorized by the people to <u>do what we said we would do</u> and to <u>keep</u>

our promises. Many Ontarians still don't like us (as they don't like all politicians), but they have decided to give us an opportunity to prove to them that we are different.

They want to believe we will keep our promises, but are waiting for the first sign we will break them.

If we do, the survey data is clear – retribution will be swift. The voters' expectations of us are high and it will be a challenge to deliver.

The Mike Harris Political Style

The style which Mike Harris projected during the campaign is very much part of the government that voters elected us to deliver. Open, honest, approachable, down-to-earth and united are some of the words which could be used to describe our style.

We must remember that our style was as much a factor in our election success as the list of policies enunciated during the campaign.

Summary

There is no question but that in historical terms the trust conferred by voters on the new government is impressive: they gave us eighty-two seats and almost half of the popular vote.

There is also no question but that success was achieved in the context of the three leaders who "applied for the job." In terms of political communications, the job has just begun.

We got here by having a plan and sticking to it. To continue to earn the confidence of the electorate, we will need not only to stick to that plan but stick together as a team which communicates in a disciplined manner.

Briefing to Minister on Issues Coming before Cabinet

Commitments We Have Made

During the past five years, the Party has taken a number of positions and made several commitments affecting your Ministry.

Some were made by Mike Harris during the recent election campaign, others appear in the *Common Sense Revolution,* and still others were made directly to persons and organizations concerned about particular issues.

Only the new Cabinet has the power to decide how we will deal with commitments and statements made before the election. The Transition Team's job is merely to ensure that you are aware of them.

Consequently, we have prepared the attached chart of commitments affecting your portfolio. It shows what was said, where we said it, and how soon we promised to do it.

(Except where the name of a particular caucus member appears on the chart, all commitments were made by Mike Harris, or were attached to correspondence bearing his signature. Note that the former caucus critic for your portfolio also may have made statements or taken positions of which you may wish to be aware.)

Appendix F:
Speech by Premier Harris to Deputy Ministers, 27 June 1995

[The following is an unofficial transcript of the speech, as records in the Premier's Office do not include a confirmed version of the Premier's remarks on this date.]

The task of undertaking major change has begun. Your crucial role in this change is of the utmost importance to me in addressing my undertakings to the people of Ontario.

I put before the electorate a program of real change ... a program that will demand difficult decisions, tough calls, and will at times be painful to implement. Many of the initiatives will require substantial creativity, energy, and imagination from you in guiding and implementing the changes.

Together we must meet the greatest challenge faced by Ontario in half a century. I will expect a great deal from you. While I do not have all the answers to the perplexing challenges facing us, I do have the confidence that we can succeed together.

One of my key commitments is to change the way government does business. This means gut-wrenching changes both inside and outside government, supported by a focused and determined public service. Small and more affordable government in Ontario is not just a philosophy – it is a necessity.

In establishing our new relationship there are a few things that I wish to share with you that I have already outlined to the Cabinet.

I believe in a professional public service with appointments on the basis of merit. This means that the vast majority, but not all appointments to senior positions will be made from within the Ontario Public Service. This does not, of course, eliminate the need to inject new blood into the system from time to time and to seek out skills and experience not found within. *The changes I have made reflect this philosophy.*

Today, the public image of politicians is negative and that of the public service is not much better. To refurbish the public image it will be essential for both elected and professional public servants to re earn public respect through performance.

I regard the senior public service as the key to ensuring that we can effectively deliver our undertakings to the Province. Let me share with you the foundations of the relationship.

First, the traditional division of authority between the political and departmental echelons of government must be respected. The Cabinet will determine the policy decisions and set the direction. That is our job.

Your job is to provide us with the best advice in reaching and implementing the decisions as effectively as possible. It is therefore vital that you understand our policy intent and that your experience is brought to bear on the impact of various policy options.

I have told the Ministers that there is nothing wrong with constructive disagreement behind closed doors. In the management of the difficult times that lie ahead, we need the best advice – not cheerleading. One former colleague used to tell his senior departmental staff: I welcome challenge to my policy ideas or those of the government as we work together to develop our policy options. Indeed, I will be poorly served by you if you do not advise me of external opposition or other pitfalls I might encounter, in pursuit of government policy.

That said I do require your absolute commitment to the final policy determination of the government.

Second, a strong direct relationship between the Minister and the Deputy Minister is essential. Your access to the Minister is not subject to the control of anyone else. You have a right and duty to communicate regularly.

Third, I have acknowledged the difficulties inherent in a reporting arrangement that demands your direct loyalty to the Premier while meeting your responsibilities to the Minister.

The key to success rests in the nature of your relationship with the Secretary of Cabinet. I chose Rita Burak because I value the importance of the confidence that you and I must mutually share in the Secretary.

Rita is well known to you and through her you will communicate with me on a routine basis. Your reports to her will be for me only and will be dealt with in confidence.

Fourth, while you and your Minister have a crucial departmental role to play I fully expect that your departmental demands will not blind you to the overall corporate interests of the government. To that end, I am prepared to meet regularly with you to ensure you are aware of the corporate vision of the government.

Fifth, Ministers' offices will be much smaller than they have been. They will concentrate on managing the day-to-day political affairs of the Minister and his communications with the public, the legislature, and the media.

I do not believe in parallel government, and I do not approve of political staff giving orders to public servants. That said, the role of the political staffer is extremely important to good government, to political communications, and to the ability of the Minister to cope with the unending pressures of government. I therefore expect Deputies to ensure that reasonable political staff requests are addressed quickly and effectively.

I have given the same message to Cabinet and I will discuss it later with the political staff. It is crucial that my remarks are not interpreted solely as recognizing the need to respect each other's role ... the Minister as Minister, the Deputy as Deputy, and the political staff as political staff.

What I am underlining is the need for teamwork between all the key players. All must work in an atmosphere of trust and respect if the Province is to be served.

You are my executive management team. We have made some obvious changes in some senior positions to reflect the new priorities. I see no reason in principle why each of you cannot serve me effectively. I harbour no resentment to those who professionally served my predecessor – indeed I would have expected no less of you.

That said, the agenda of the common sense revolution constitutes a sharp departure from business as usual.

I have many concerns about the atmosphere in which you have had to manage. You have had to cope with restraint, but often without the tools. The demands that lie ahead are unprecedented, and will call for an enormous effort and while I will endeavour to provide the tools to do the job, that will not always be possible.

Now I wish to address some realities and expectations. The Common Sense Revolution Plan is founded on three fundamental objectives:

- To Cut Taxes and Create Jobs
- To Cut Spending and Balance the Budget, and
- To Provide Ontario with a Real Plan.

I don't need to tell you that perhaps the greatest challenge comes in the form of the need to cut spending. We do indeed have a fiscal crisis and we must respond with substantial reduction in government spending.

This situation is made all the more challenging by the need for tax reductions, to give the public more hope and confidence in the future. We know that across the board spending cuts will not do the job. Instead, we must rethink government, challenge old assumptions about what can be done, and develop proposals to change policies in the radical ways needed to meet the spending reduction targets we will set for the Government.

We must also ask what business we will be in and then ensure that we organize to carry out that service in the most efficient way.

It is critical that we develop, implement, and communicate a coherent fiscal and public service management agenda. The three objectives of the Common Sense Revolution Plan will act as guideposts along the way. The Minister of Finance will be announcing spending targets for each Ministry for this year as a start. We must take action now if we are to get public expenditures under control.

These targets will be announced shortly so that you and your Minister can work together to implement them.

We will be working with you and your Minister over the coming months to develop a second phase of spending reduction plans for 1996-97. Those spending reduction plans will have to be real and they will cut deep to support the tax reductions that we have promised in the Common Sense Revolution Plan.

While this is a short time frame we must have a rational fiscal strategy as Government that reflects the commitments made in the Common Sense Revolution Plan.

You and I both know there is an unforgiving nature to the fiscal plan we must put in place to guide Ontario's finances over the next five years. It is unforgiving in both the political and the practical sense.

If we do not meet the expectations we will suffer the consequences and if we do not achieve what we have set out to achieve Ontario will enter a deficit debt spiral that will make even the most hardy abandon hope of turning the economy around. And we will all pay dearly for that failure.

I am unconditionally committed to reaching our goals, but very open to discussing how we get there. If there are better ideas out there about how to cut spending, reduce waste, and improve efficiency, we want to hear them.

The management agenda must flow directly from the unforgiving nature of the fiscal agenda. This will involve a new emphasis on accountability – on achieving results; I want Ontario to be recognized as a leader and innovator in public sector management, both in Canada and internationally, and I intend to support those who are prepared to do the job.

I expect you to energetically pursue the potential for new models for delivering services, including the creation of special operating agencies, privatization and joint ventures with the private and not-for-profit sectors; I want you to look at them as real opportunities to both limit expenditures and provide better service either within or outside government.

The name of the game is getting our house in order, not simply moving expenditures off the balance sheet.

The role of Government remains substantial but it will be provided by a small and more focused public service. We are repositioning Government.

We will reduce public service employment by 13,000. I understand that many of you believe that with the right moves that number could reach 15-20,000 and indeed those numbers may eventually prove necessary

It is clear, however, that we must make program cuts and accompanying staff cuts as quickly and humanely as possible. This will require a strategy to address public service employment issues.

I recognize that what happens to the people who are let go will affect the morale and performance of those who stay and whose dedication and cooperation we need. Consequently, a layoff, severances and early retirement policy strategy is also an immediate requirement.

As part of my commitment to downsizing I have cut the number of Cabinet ministers and consequently grouped some Ministries under certain Ministers. To further demonstrate my commitment to downsizing I will be cutting the size of the Premier's office and the Secretary of Cabinet is cutting Cabinet office.

I have established a new Cabinet Committee structure designed to serve a government that must emphasize downsizing as an absolute priority.

There will be three standing committees – Policy and Priorities Board, Management Board, and Legislation and Regulations. Management Board will reflect the combination of the previously separate functions of The Management Board and The Treasury Board into one central agency. There will be other Cabinet Committees established on an ad hoc basis usually to address a major issue or initiative. They will involve the Ministers and Deputies relevant to that issue or initiative.

I do not wish to have too many committees or to have them last too long. Consequently, they will be focused and have a specific time frame.

The challenge ahead will require all our energies if we are to accomplish the goals we have undertaken.

I am confident in your support but I am also aware that we are undertaking changes that stretch our experience.

It would be a mistake not to engage experienced resources in the private sector that are ready and willing to assist on a voluntary or loan basis. I will utilize that experience in government on an assignment/volunteer basis to help us develop specific projects concerned with policy, service and delivery, and restructuring.

This poses opportunities – not threats – to the public service as it provides access to a wider experience base.

I respect the political independence of the public service and I want to protect it as it has served Ontario well. Denial of partisanship is not, however, a denial of teamwork. I need, and Ontarians would expect nothing less than, effective teamwork from the key elements that constitute democratic government.

Teamwork that combines the political and policy direction of the legislature with the management skills of its public service.

The problems ahead are massive, mistakes unavoidable, and vigorous and sometimes destructive criticism inevitable.

If we work together we can overcome these barriers and turn around the economic and social problems that have limited our province. I believe that we are up to the challenge and together we can rebuild Ontario.

Appendix G:
On the Record:
Ensuring a Place in History
Peter DeLottinville and Ian E. Wilson,
National Archives of Canada

Between election day on 15 June 1944 and the swearing-in of a new Saskatchewan government on 10 July, the outgoing government of Premier William Patterson destroyed all of its records in huge bonfires behind the Legislative Building in Regina. Less than a year after assuming office, the first social democrat government elected in Canada passed an archives act. It was progressive and far-ranging legislation and reserved the decision as to which official records were to be kept and which were to be destroyed to the professional judgment of a provincial archivist. Decades later, when asked why his new government, with its active social and health agenda, had made archival legislation an immediate priority, Tommy Douglas replied that he and his colleagues were appalled when they discovered that the offices recently occupied by Liberal ministers were devoid of any records. In Douglas's view, the previous government's actions were reprehensible and a violation of the public trust, eliminating records fundamental to the public accountability of government in a democracy. The history of the Patterson government has been written, and because of the deliberate destruction of its own records, historical research on the period has relied on newspapers and on the extensive records of its political opponents. The Patterson government has not fared well as a result.

Every government that is elected eventually resigns. In coming to terms with electoral defeat or retirement, individual politicians have to make a number of decisions – some small, some large – before they can move on with their lives. One critical concern, although it may not seem so at the time, is the fate of the records that they and their staff have created in the feverish daily activity of public life. When the record of an outgoing government is discussed or publicly debated, most Canadians undoubtedly have in mind a "scorecard" of some kind, listing a series of legislative achievements and failures.[1] To some members of the public service, however, the "record" of the last government is not only a concept (or a scorecard), but the very real physical contents of filing cabinets and computers – briefing books, subject and correspondence files, minutes of meetings, petitions, press releases, speeches, promotional films, e-mail correspondence, and databases – all launched in the information wars of modern politics. While departmental records are generally maintained in a systematic and organized fashion, a minister, together with his or her staff, has also created and stored information. This record of their actions, decisions, and contributions affecting public policy are, very largely, public property; such records are generally significant, unique, and often at high risk in the transition phase from one government to the next.

In due course, Tommy Douglas's own extensive files as premier were transferred to the Saskatchewan Archives. In 1984, when all restrictions on research use expired, Douglas recalled that when he left office in 1961, he had asked that all records created during his premiership be kept. He admitted too that all governments make mistakes, and that his was no exception, but he hoped only that in light of the full authoritative record future historians would assess that his party's achievements outweighed its errors. No government can ask for more.

The federal government, as well as every province save British Columbia, currently has archival legislation similar to that introduced by Douglas in Saskatchewan. In spite of various legal requirements, the protection of the record has not been uniformly respected by departing ministers. However, with the adoption of access to information legislation at the federal level and in many provinces, information commissioners, auditors, and lawyers are reinforcing archival considerations and pressing for a more systematic approach to protection of the official records. As the Honourable E.M. Culliton observed in his report on freedom of information in Saskatchewan: "There is an essential link between freedom of information and the archival function of preservation of information. Unless a government makes effective provision for the selection and preservation of official records, there is little point in talking about freedom of information for the information will not be there to be studied. Selection must be done by an official dedicated to the integrity of the historical record and free from partisan influences."[2]

With the enactment of appropriate legislation in the past twenty years, there is no longer any reason why records created at the ministerial level should be wantonly destroyed by their creators, especially in the process of transition from one government to another. This is clearly the time of greatest risk to the records, but now, with legal safeguards in place, these records are protected against unauthorized access, personal information and privacy concerns are addressed, and the records can be preserved for future research use. While the Saskatchewan example from 1944 may be an extreme case of obliterating the record, it is not unique; over the past several decades, in all jurisdictions, persons leaving public office have deliberately destroyed valuable documents. Preservation of these records, however, is essential to our democratic way of life; it allows the smooth functioning and continuity of government and, more importantly, it ensures that our elected officials and the senior bureaucracy are accountable for their actions and that the legal rights of the citizenry are protected and documented.

The role of government archivists in a time of transition is to convince ministers and their staff that perhaps the end is not as final as it may seem. As the new government's transition team is "cycling into Saigon," others are already moving precious cargo to a safer haven. A period of transition can provide opportunities that would otherwise be impossible when the daily concerns of governing weigh heavily upon the minds of ministers and their staff. Along with other players in the transition, archival staff make quiet preparations, enter the scene during that period of post-election uncertainty, accomplish their mission, and return to their institutions before the window of opportunity closes, the new cabinet is sworn in, and the main show of governing begins once more. The archivist argues for the preservation of all archival information to ensure the long-term maintenance of the public record and to offer an alternative resting place (other than the shredder) for political records. In a period of transition, it is the archivist's primary responsibility to advise ministers and their staff on how to provide for their place in history.

Archival institutions are perhaps the oldest member of the transition team – practising the transition game long before it was formally named – and they bring unique expertise, facilities, and increasingly powerful tools onto the field. This article makes some general observations on issues surrounding preservation of records based on recent experiences in provincial archives in Saskatchewan and Ontario, and in the National Archives. Regardless of the changes in scenery, politics is all about winning office and losing it, and many of the fundamental issues surrounding creation and disposition of records remain the same, whether in Regina, Toronto, or Ottawa.

Government records archivists and records managers often refer to the life cycle of a record. From the initial creation of a memo written by some toiling executive assistant, a document enjoys a brief but active life circulating among political colleagues and senior civil servants. It then proceeds to a semi-active phase in the minister's office file, during which from time to time it may be examined for reference purposes. Subsequently the document slips into a dormant period at the back of the file room where it is all but forgotten until, one day (perhaps on election day plus one), a decision will be made on its ultimate disposition. The life cycle of a record can take years, sometime decades, to be completed. But in the world of modern politics, where a week can be a long time, the lifespan of a document can also be surprisingly short. For example, consider a briefing note on the short-term objectives of the new mandate that is created in the late afternoon of election day by an executive assistant and saved on the network drive at 6:00 p.m. It is active until 8:00 p.m. that night when the election coverage starts, is semi-active by 8:35 p.m. as the first surprising results are announced, is dormant by 9:15 p.m. as the voting trend becomes clear, and reaches its final stage as the television networks make their predictions about a new majority government in time for the 10:00 p.m. news. Even for those records with the shortest of life cycles, key decisions about preservation need to be made.

In the aftermath of an election, cleanup begins. Offices need to be vacated for the new regime; condolences are given and received; résumés are prepared as a first step in job searches, personal belongings are boxed and sent home, and severance packages are investigated. But what is the fate of that briefing note, which is no longer relevant, a reminder of what might have been, prepared for a government that no longer exists? Recycle or shred? Click "yes" on the "delete all?" query, or reformat that hard drive? What is to be done with all of those other records, some of which remain in the ministry office, some of which have been taken to the legislative office, some of which have been sent to the deputy minister for review, comment, and action? Can all of these inner secrets of government be left behind?

In these matters, it is helpful to have a clear understanding of the evolution of private and public records relating to parliamentary government, to be familiar with records management principles and the legislative framework that shapes the modern public record, and to keep in mind the physical realities of records and the inherent dangers to those records in a time of transition. The importance of archives cannot be understood outside of the public purpose that preserving records supports, both in terms of the operations of government and protection of the rights of citizens and within a broader historical and cultural context. It is one aspect of cabinet government in which the old traditions and understandings are rapidly giving way to legal requirements and regulatory review. In examining each of these themes briefly, it should become clearer why the fate of a government's records reflects some of the larger issues connected with the transition from one government to another.

Documenting the decisions of government is a critical factor in ensuring the accountability of government in a democratic society. The ultimate test of that accountability is the election. For a government just defeated, it is clear that the public no longer has confidence in its ability to make decisions that reflect the popular will and to operate effectively the machinery of government. Parliamentary tradition, however, allows the members of that government (the premier and his or her cabinet ministers) the right to consider and to debate policy choices in secret before making a public decision. This permits members of the government to disagree, to take different points of views, and to debate an issue before a decision is made. Cabinet solidarity insists that once the decision is made, all members of the cabinet must support that decision. The tradition of cabinet secrecy also protects the documents created during policy debate within government, including documents prepared as advice to cabinet by civil servants and documents circulated between ministers and their staff. This tradition, and protection of documents related to this activity, remains in force after the fall of a government, a tradition now guaranteed by legislation in most jurisdictions for a period of twenty or thirty years following the creation of the records. All modern access to information legislation protects such confidences and requires absolute closure unless an authorized representative (often the former premier) of the government that created the records approves access to those records. This protection is non-discretionary and is often reinforced by a formal agreement between the incoming and outgoing premiers to respect the confidentiality of the proceedings of the former government. With the tradition of cabinet confidentiality now enshrined in legislation, the tendency in the past to destroy cabinet or ministerial records to protect a former government is no longer necessary.

In Canada, the recording of cabinet discussions and decisions is a surprisingly recent development. Arnold Heeney, who was appointed clerk of the Privy Council and secretary to the cabinet in March 1940, soon discovered that the decision-making process employed by Mackenzie King and his colleagues was "incredibly haphazard." "I found it shattering," he later reminisced, "to discover that the highest committee in the land conducted its business in such a disorderly fashion that it employed no agenda and no minutes were taken."[3] Before Heeney's appointment, the clerk of the Privy Council was not present during cabinet discussions and was only informed about government decisions by checking a deep wooden box set on the table before the prime minister: documents in the right-hand compartment had been initialled and approved and were to be sent to the governor general for signature; documents in the left-hand compartment had been rejected or postponed. This informal approach to documentation reflected the long-held view that cabinet business was, in effect, private business, where little or no distinction was made between politics and government.

The pressure of wartime demands eliminated the informality of federal government decision making and led to an incredible growth of documentation for the highest (and most secret) decisions. This trend continued in the post-war period when government activities expanded rapidly, as did the role of cabinet and the Privy Council Office. In 1957, the newly elected government of John Diefenbaker established a precedent with its decision on the disposition of cabinet records created by the previous Liberal governments. John Diefenbaker and outgoing Liberal Prime Minister Louis St. Laurent agreed to follow the British practice that dated from the 1920s, deciding that the clerk of the Privy Council Office should become the custodian of cabinet documents and be responsible for determining which documents succeeding administrations should be allowed to examine.[4] A similar approach has been instituted in several provinces.

Since the creation of public records derives from the much longer parliamentary tradition of cabinet secrecy, those who are interested in documenting or studying a modern parliamentary democracy must understand and accept that the preservation of both public and private records is necessary. Issues of ownership, physical control, and public access, however, must be viewed from a very different perspective. According to parliamentary tradition, some records under the control of the Prime Minister's Office or the Premier's Office are considered to be private records, as are the records of ministers relating to discussions with other members of cabinet and those dealing with party business and strategy, election planning, and constituency matters. Public records relate directly to the legislative responsibilities of the cabinet and to its discharge of public duties as individuals or collectively as the government. This distinction is often a fine one, and has become increasingly so in recent years.

Building on this increasing interest in the nature of the public record, the National Archives of Canada Act, passed in 1987, attempted to refine the past practice of handling records created in a minister's office by introducing the concept of "ministerial records." In addition to recognizing the traditional institutional records under the control of the deputy minister and the personal and constituency records under the control of the minister, the act establishes the category of "ministerial records," defined as public records created by the minister relating to his or her portfolio that are not under the control of the department. Such ministerial records are to be transferred directly to the National Archives when the minister leaves the cabinet, thereby avoiding having to leave these sensitive ministerial documents under the direct control of the department.[5] This initiative was undertaken in the hope that it would further expand the definition and meaning of the public record, while protecting cabinet confidences. The experience of the last ten years, however, indicates that this legislation has not had a significant impact on record-keeping practices in federal ministerial offices. The National Archives subsequently refined its approach to the care of institutional records by developing a generic disposition authority for records in a minister's office, in effect recommending the transfer of significant departmental records to the National Archives five years after the minister leaves office.

In Ontario, the past fifteen years have witnessed a progressive clarification and definition of what constitutes "official" records. In the months prior to the June 1999 election, the Archives of Ontario and Cabinet Office worked together to develop and refine a new general schedule for the retention and disposal of records in ministers' offices, including documentation of all kinds, such as correspondence, subject files, notebooks, and electronic records created by members of the ministers' staff in the course of their duties. The schedule, approved by the cabinet secretary and the archivist, required that all such records be transferred to the custody of the provincial archives when a minister resigned his or her portfolio. Only records relating directly to internal party matters and to the minister's constituency responsibilities as an MPP are excluded. Premier Mike Harris issued this policy to all ministers on 5 May 1999, and it represents a significant step forward for the protection and retention of ministerial records in the province.

The protection of public records created at the highest level, in the office of the premier or his or her ministers, must be a key duty of civil servants, particularly government archivists, during a period of transition. There should be a clear understanding between political staff members and civil servants on what constitutes a public record in a minister's office. As in the case of Ontario, procedures and rules are best developed well in advance of an election and should include the participation of the cabinet secretary, legal counsel, and the premier. Following the defeat of a government, it is critical in any discussion on the disposition of the records that a single individual, sometimes the minister himself or herself, be responsible for all decisions affecting records; the alternative – having individual staff members decide the fate of records – is a recipe for disaster. In addition, the appropriate deputy minister is often responsible for advising on the proper management of records, for the protection of information stored in computers, and for monitoring improper or illegal destruction or removal of records. When the ministers and their staff, the deputy ministers, and archivists work together, the uncertainty associated with transition from one government does not unnecessarily threaten the public record.

The integrity of the official record is a matter of public concern; clarification of the public and private roles of political leaders is essential. Ideally, the distinction between official and private records should be determined when ministers first assume office. In establishing records procedures and file classification systems for incoming ministers – perhaps considered by politicians to be a very low priority in the early days of a new government – civil servants are setting clear boundaries to mark the distinction between public and private records and creating a framework for their proper care and eventual preservation. The National Archives of Canada and several provincial archives have developed guidelines to assist ministers' staff in establishing filing systems and retention schedules. With the increasing use of electronic records, planning the control of information in the first instance becomes more important – both to protect the confidentiality of government discussions and to ensure a retrievable record while in office and after a government's defeat and resignation.

This definition of the public record, and questions concerning the control of information, have been thoroughly debated in recent years in conjunction with access to information and privacy legislation. More than any archival or historical interest in records, access to information requests have reinforced the public nature of government discussions and decisions; in addition, access to information legislation has introduced a new discipline and reality to discussions of information management in most jurisdictions. At the federal level and in almost every province, access to information legislation has defined, and in some cases redefined, the nature of public records. Subsequent decisions by information commissioners at the federal and provincial levels and by the courts have provided additional precedents in this matter. Just as a concern for the efficiency of cabinet in the 1940s led to the creation of a better public record of government decisions, legislative changes in the 1980s and 1990s have focused attention on the need to and the value of making records publicly available. This general concern about access to public records applies, of course, to both politicians and civil servants. Recent federal legislation that establishes a fine of $10,000 for the unauthorized destruction of records when done to frustrate an access request is a clear indication of growing public demand that the rules be enforced and, ultimately, that a full and complete record be preserved.[6]

While playing a strong role in preserving the public record, government archivists also need to act as defenders of the politician's right to determine the fate of his or her personal and constituency records.[7] In the short term – and during a transition there is only the short term to consider – this role may appear to be in conflict with the archivist's primary role as defender of the public record. In protecting the public record, the national archivist and his provincial counterparts need to exercise their legislative authority over the public record, but in dealing with purely private records they need to exercise their power of persuasion. An archivist suspected of aiding an outgoing government in its effort to hide a full and complete record of its administration would understand the delicacy of this role. In the Saskatchewan provincial election held on 26 April 1982, the Conservatives, led by Grant Devine, unexpectedly defeated the NDP government. On the day after the election, the provincial archivist wrote to all outgoing ministers and asked that any destruction of records be suspended until after a full discussion of the issue could be had at the final meeting of the NDP cabinet. Premier Allan Blakeney directed that all of his files – personal files, those at his constituency office, and those created as president of the Executive Council – be transferred to the Saskatchewan Archives immediately. Following the final cabinet meeting, most other ministers did the same. When members of the news media observed trucks leaving the Legislative Building, stories were published that the records of the NDP administration were going to the dump. The archivist immediately called a press conference and, surrounded by about thirty-seven cubic metres of cabinet records and the records of various ministers, refuted any such claims. In the heated partisan atmosphere of the time, some saw this as the archivist defending the defeated government. The archivist's new minister, however, recognized that this was the proper and professional role of the provincial archives.

Those interested in preserving the political records of a government need to understand that outgoing politicians have the right, under parliamentary tradition, to dispose of as they wish all of their personal and constituency records, if they choose to do so. From time to time, this has happened. Over the years, members of outgoing governments have sent their most trusted staff into the basements of legislative buildings in the dead of night to consign confidential files and records to the furnace or, in more recent years, to have office shredders work overtime. It is helpful – to say the least – to persuade politicians that such wholesale destruction of their personal files is probably their third-best option. Their second-best option is simply to find a safe and secure storage location for their records until they have had a chance to give more reasoned consideration to the disposition question. Their best option would be to plan ahead, but within the confines of modern political reality such an initiative might be seen by some to be a political death wish. Ministers who have decided not to run for office again may have time to plan for this best option, and archival staff can use the time available during an election campaign to complete these arrangements.[8] After the election, archivists need to concentrate on the second-best option, the physical protection of private records.

Given the nature of modern government, there can be little dispute that the volume of private records generated by a prime minister or a premier can be substantial. The entire papers of Sir John A. Macdonald, which document the birth and growth of the nation, measure only 38 metres in linear extent. One hundred years later, Lester B. Pearson left more than ten times this amount (437 metres) with the National Archives in Ottawa, while Pierre Elliott Trudeau created more than 700 metres of textual records. Canadian prime ministers since Trudeau have continued to generate increasing amounts of paper, photographic, audiovisual, and electronic records. The National Archives has approached the issue of preserving private records created by ministers of the crown by divorcing the question of physical preservation from that of research access or final disposition. This has been accomplished by a very simple process – offering to the prime minister and members of his or her cabinet free storage for their political records.[9] By establishing contact with ministers' offices early in the life of a government, national archivists hope to create an atmosphere of trust among political staff by handling smaller and less sensitive transfers of records during cabinet shuffles. They rely on this "trust" relationship and hope that it will carry over into the post-election period of panic and uncertainty, especially when the party in power has been ousted by the electorate, which is when records are most at risk.

Once the physical preservation of public and private records is secure, careful consideration of related and more sensitive issues can take place. The use of and continued access to public records under the control of deputy ministers, or clerk of the Privy Council or Cabinet Office, allows for appropriate continuity in government. Management of information, as much as the management of public finances or policy agendas, is a key component to effective modern government. Public information protects the rights of citizens, establishes the obligations between levels of government, and provides a collective knowledge upon which a modern state operates. Whether it is a question of native land claims, the treatment of children in residential schools, or the location of forgotten toxic waste sites, the proper management of government records and archives is critical to defining, responding to, and resolving these issues. As the responsibility for such matters continues long after a specific government is gone, so the records documenting these issues must be retained and made available, under suitable control, for the greater public good.

Within this larger principle, however, it is important to respect the parliamentary rights accorded a former government. Although the day-to-day administration of cabinet records, for instance, is clearly the responsibility of the clerk of the Privy Council or Cabinet Office, the former prime minister or premier continues to play a role in granting access to cabinet confidences of his or her day where access to such records is required for public purposes. While access to information legislation has brought a new spirit of openness to government operations, the confidential nature of cabinet discussions remains sacrosanct and is protected in this legislation.

In the case of constituency and private records, however, each minister is individually responsible for the decisions on public access for research purposes. As part of the donation process, archival institutions usually negotiate a general policy governing access, which usually reflects the conditions of access one might expect for similar government records. Since most citizens who correspond with their elected representatives have no idea that their personal problems or opinions might eventually form part of the archival record, it is also important that access policies incorporate protection for personal information. In most cases, agreements between donors and archivists provide that private political records be made available in twenty or thirty years. In some instances, private political records have been closed for much longer; those created by former Ontario Premier George Drew, for instance, were only opened in 1998 as spelled out in the terms of donation to the National Archives. This was a full twenty-five years after Drew's death and fifty years after he had served as premier. In other cases, former premiers or ministers have allowed researchers early access to their records to assist with biographical projects or to allow the study of some aspect of public policy.

Since the 1970s, the retention and preservation of private records relating to public life has had another consequence for politicians – the federal tax credit. The introduction of the Cultural Property Export and Import Act in 1974 recognized those who donate cultural property to heritage institutions across the country. In addition to providing compensation by granting a receipt for tax purposes for donations of works of art and other cultural items, this legislation has resulted in archival collections of Canadians in all walks of life being turned over to archives, museums, and libraries, greatly enriching the historical record available in public repositories. Among these many donors are politicians from federal, provincial, and even municipal levels. In all instances, a tax receipt is allowed for the appraised fair market value of the private records donated, with the appraisal made by professional third-party appraisers and certified by the Cultural Property Export Review Board. This practice has generated some public debate and criticism about the personal financial benefit accruing to former politicians who created the records while in public life; in 1995, a private member's bill was introduced in the House of Commons that would have eliminated tax credits for politicians.[10] On the other hand, some former ministers and politicians have refused any receipt for tax purposes. In spite of the criticism, this practice is widely used and has been a popular option for politicians for many years. In the days immediately following an electoral defeat, the possibility of a future tax benefit for outgoing ministers adds compelling weight to the more esoteric issues of history and legacy and perhaps, on a few occasions, has tipped the scale towards the preservation of records. It also serves to confirm that it is in the public interest to have such records saved for posterity and to supplement the official record.

As the civil service, in general, waits anxiously for new policy direction from the incoming government, provincial and national archivists appear to be looking in the wrong direction. When John Diefenbaker's government was steering a new course for Canada, the dominion archivist at the time was closely connected to the official biography project of Mackenzie King. During the Trudeau years, the National Archives and the University of Saskatchewan were collaborating on the Diefenbaker Project. And if Brian Mulroney had had time to notice, he would have seen the National Archives' Trudeau Project in full swing, just as Jean Chrétien might have been mildly puzzled at all the interest shown by archival staff in Brian Mulroney and his cabinet following the change of government in 1993.

The role that archival institutions play in providing a focus for research, analysis, and commentary on public figures, former governments, and their policies is perhaps the final stage in the transition process. While some historical research and analysis based on archival sources never finds its way off of the university campus, political history is popular with the public, the press, and political commentators. The memoirs of former prime ministers and premiers vie for space on the library book shelf with those of their former cabinet colleagues and political opponents. The constitutional discussions of the past several decades result in conflicting and competing accounts of positions taken and credit gained. Journalists join in the debate, as do political scientists, historians, and ordinary Canadians. Records of the past are essential for informed debate on issues of this nature, issues that engage Canadians, issues that help to define who we are as a nation, issues that mark our place in the global community. Records that once were fuel for bonfires now mark the road to a greater understanding of our past and our identity as Canadians.

By coincidence, National Archives staff completed work on the organization and arrangement of the Trudeau papers in 1993, about the same time that Pierre Trudeau completed his memoirs. In late fall, the National Archives hosted a ceremony to mark the final donation of Trudeau's records and to launch his book. A very respectful Ottawa audience included most of the recently sworn-in members of Jean Chrétien's new government. Reflecting on his initial experience as a cabinet minister in 1967, Trudeau remarked that at the time he gave little thought to the final chapter of his life in politics, or to archival matters. His advice to incoming cabinet members was characteristically blunt: "You should."

Notes

The authors wish to acknowledge the assistance of colleague Glenn Wright in the preparation of this paper.

1   The "scorecard" approach to history is currently very topical, as the recent book of J.L. Granatstein and Norman Hillmer, *Prime Ministers: Ranking Canada's Leaders* (Toronto: HarperCollins, 1999), on Canadian prime ministers attests. It is interesting that among Canadian historians William Lyon Mackenzie King ranks the highest, since he also created and preserved for future generations the most complete and candid historical record ever assembled by a modern politician over the course of his long political career. Perhaps this is not a mere coincidence.

2   Saskatchewan, *Commission on Freedom of Information and Individual Privacy,* Report of the Honourable E.M. Culliton, former Chief Justice of Saskatchewan, on the Matter of

Freedom of Information and Protection of Privacy in the Province of Saskatchewan (Regina, 1983), 49.
3 Arnold Heeney, *The Things That Are Caesar's: The Memoirs of a Canadian Public Servant* (Toronto: University of Toronto Press, 1972), 74-5.
4 The issue of access to cabinet documents, especially to minutes of cabinet discussions, created by the St. Laurent government apparently caught Diefenbaker by surprise, but putting the clerk of the Privy Council in control of access to records was approved by the first Progressive Conservative cabinet meeting. However, Diefenbaker himself indicated that he wanted to confirm this practice with the British government during an upcoming trip to the United Kingdom; see Denis Smith, *Rogue Tory: The Life and Legend of John G. Diefenbaker* (Toronto: Macfarlane Walter and Ross, 1995), 246. The "tradition" of cabinet secrecy was soon tested, and became an issue during the 1966 Munsinger affair. When Liberal members later questioned Diefenbaker's handling of questionable conduct by some of his ministers and their contact with Gerda Munsinger, it became clear that they had obtained access to information that could only have been cabinet confidences.
5 National Archives of Canada, *Guidelines for Managing Recorded Information in a Minister's Office* (Ottawa: Ministry of Supply and Services, 1992).
6 House of Commons Bill C-208, *An Act to Amend the Access to Information Act*, which received Royal Assent on 25 March 1999, states that no person shall destroy, mutilate, or alter a record, falsify a record, make a false record, conceal a record, or direct, propose, or counsel any person to do so, and sets penalties of imprisonment of up to two years or a fine of $10,000 for an indictable offence, or imprisonment of up to six months or a fine not exceeding $5,000 for summary conviction.
7 Note that in Quebec, the *Loi sur les archives* defines the records of all members of the National Assembly as public records, subject to the requirements of the archives and access to information legislation. All other provinces regard such records as private.
8 In the United States, where fixed terms for presidential and senatorial elections are established, it is common practice to commence work on a presidential library during the incumbent president's final term in office. Funds for building presidential libraries are raised privately, but once built, funds for the continued operation of the libraries are provided through the National Archives and Records Administration. Some American senators employee an archivist to sort political records and to make arrangements with a university in their state to preserve their records years before leaving office. Members of parliamentary governments have not followed this practice.
9 The National Archives of Canada deposit service, first introduced in 1957, has been very successful in physically preserving private political records. At recent count there are on deposit 10,000 boxes of material from former ministers in the Trudeau governments and 5,000 boxes from the Mulroney governments, thus ensuring years of work for archival staff – completing donation agreements, organizing the collections, and arranging for public access.
10 *The Hill Times* (Ottawa), 26 January 1995, 2. John Harvard, Liberal Member of Parliament, planned to introduce a private member's bill to prohibit federal politicians from receiving tax credits for donation of historical records; "These documents were signed when the members were working for Canadians; it is really the property of all Canadians."

Notes

Chapter 1: Transitions

1 Evert Lindquist, "Transition Teams and Government Succession: Focusing on the Essentials," in *Taking Power: Managing Government Transitions*, ed. Donald J. Savoie (Toronto: Institute of Public Administration of Canada and Canadian Centre for Management Development, 1993), 33-5, 42-4.
2 This is evident in the references to the American literature and the limited references to Canadian, British, and Australian literature in the Lindquist and Campbell chapters in Savoie's *Taking Power*.
3 Leaving aside the early non-partisan or coalition eras in some provinces, as of the beginning of 2000, transitions from one governing party to another have occurred fourteen times in Ottawa, eighty-three times in the provinces, and four times in the Yukon (Nunavut and the NWT operate without political parties).
4 Hans J. Michelmann and Jeffrey S. Steeves, "The 1982 Transition in Power in Saskatchewan: The Progressive Conservatives and the Public Service," *Canadian Public Administration* 28, 1 (1985): 1-23.
5 Allan Blakeney and Sandford Borins, *Political Management in Canada*, 2nd ed. (Toronto: University of Toronto Press, 1998), chapter 18.
6 Micheline Plasse, "Les chefs de cabinet ministériel au Québec: la transition du gouvernement liberal au gouvernement péquiste (1976-1977)," *Canadian Journal of Political Science* 14 (June 1981): 309-35.
7 Jacques Bourgault and Stéphane Dion, "Governments Come and Go but What of Senior Public Servants? Canadian Deputy Ministers and Transitions in Power (1867-1987)," *Governance* 2 (1989): 125-51; Bourgault and Dion, "Managing Conflict in a Context of Government Change: Lessons from the Federal Government of Canada, 1984-1988," *International Journal of Conflict Management* 1 (October 1990): 375-95; Bourgault and Dion, "Canadian Senior Civil Servants and Transitions in Government: The Whitehall Model Seen from Ottawa," *International Journal of Administrative Science* 56 (Fall 1990): 149-69; Bourgault and Dion, "Haute fonction publique et changement de gouvernement au Quebec: le cas des sous-ministres en titre (1976-1989)," *Revue québécoise de science politique* 19 (1991): 81-106; Bourgault and Dion, "Etude d'une transition gouvernementale: Le cas du Quebec en 1985," in *Taking Power*, ed. Savoie, 145-62; Jacques Bourgault and Patrick Nugent, "Les transitions de gouvernement et la théorie des conflits: Le cas de la transition de 1984 au gouvernement du Canada," *Canadian Journal of Administrative Sciences* 12 (March 1995): 15-26.
8 Bourgault and Dion, "Managing Conflict."
9 Donald J. Savoie, "Introduction," in *Taking Power*, ed. Savoie, 2.
10 Ibid.
11 Desmond Morton, "*Sic Permanet*: Ontario People and Their Politics," in *The Government and Politics of Ontario*, 5th ed., ed. Graham White (Toronto: University of Toronto Press, 1997), 7.

12 Sean Conway, John Reynolds, Lorne Nystrom, and Jacques Baril, "Interview," *Canadian Parliamentary Review* 21 (Summer 1998): 35.
13 See Rosemary Speirs, *Out of the Blue: The Fall of the Tory Dynasty in Ontario* (Toronto: Macmillan, 1986), chapter 5; Graham White, "Ontario," in *Canadian Annual Review of Politics and Public Affairs 1985*, ed. R.B. Byers (Toronto: University of Toronto Press, 1988), 259-80.
14 Georgette Gagnon and Dan Rath, *Not without Cause: David Peterson's Fall from Grace* (Toronto: HarperCollins, 1991), 85.
15 For data on Ontario's economic performance in these years, see Thomas J. Courchene with Colin R. Telmer, *From Heartland to North American Region State: The Social, Fiscal and Federal Evolution of Ontario* (Toronto: University of Toronto Centre for Public Management, 1997), 71.
16 See Gagnon and Rath, *Not without Cause*, chapter 4.
17 For an account of the 1990 election, see Gagnon and Rath, *Not without Cause* and George Ehring and Wayne Roberts, *Giving Away a Miracle: Lost Dreams, Broken Promises and the Ontario NDP* (Oakville: Mosaic Press, 1993), chapter 6.
18 The NDP years in government generated extensive – and highly diverse – commentary; see Ehring and Roberts, *Giving Away a Miracle*; Thomas Walkom, *Rae Days: The Rise and Follies of the NDP* (Toronto: Key Porter, 1994); Patrick Monahan, *Storming the Pink Palace: The NDP in Power – A Cautionary Tale* (Toronto: Lester Publishing, 1995); Bob Rae, *From Protest to Power: Personal Reflections of a Life in Politics* (Toronto: Viking, 1996); Chuck Rachlis and David Wolfe, "An Insiders' View of the NDP Government of Ontario: The Politics of Permanent Opposition Meets the Economics of Permanent Recession," in *The Government and Politics of Ontario*, ed. White, 331-64.
19 John Ibbitson, *Promised Land: Inside the Mike Harris Revolution* (Toronto: Prentice-Hall, 1997), 82. This was in line with Ontario experience; in 1985 after each had led his party for three years (and with Peterson shortly to become premier), fewer than 30 percent of Ontarians could identify David Peterson or Bob Rae.
20 Ibid.
21 Quoted in Ibbitson, *Promised Land*, 90.
22 The account of the Conservative revival and the election in the following paragraphs draws heavily on Ibbitson, *Promised Land*, chapters 3-4; Robert Drummond and Robert MacDermid, "Elections and Campaigning: 'They Blew Our Doors Off on the Buy,'" in *The Government and Politics of Ontario*, ed. White, 216-35; and Peter Woolstencroft, "Reclaiming the 'Pink Palace': The Progressive Conservative Party Comes in from the Cold," in *The Government and Politics of Ontario*, ed. White, 365-401.

Chapter 2: The 1985 and 1990 Transitions

1 This chapter is a shortened and revised version of Graham White, "Traffic Pile-ups at Queen's Park: Recent Ontario Transitions," in *Taking Power: Managing Government Transitions*, ed. Donald J. Savoie (Toronto: Institute of Public Administration of Canada and Canadian Centre for Management Development, 1993), 115-43.
2 See Rosemary Speirs, *Out of the Blue: The Fall of the Tory Dynasty in Ontario* (Toronto: Macmillan, 1986), chapters 4-5; Georgette Gagnon and Dan Rath, *Not without Cause: David Peterson's Fall from Grace* (Toronto: HarperCollins, 1991), passim.
3 MacGregor Dawson taught Canadian politics at the University of Toronto for decades; his *The Government of Canada* introduced generations of students to Canadian politics (including the notion of the cabinet as a representative institution).
4 This enumeration does not take into account the three deputies from the disbanded policy secretariats. All three were reassigned to deputy minister-level positions.
5 See Richard A. Loreto, "Ontario," in *Getting the Pink Slip: Severances and Firings in the Senior Public Service*, ed. William A.W. Neilson (Toronto: Institute of Public Administration of Canada, 1990), 49.
6 Thomas Walkom, *Rae Days: The Rise and Follies of the NDP* (Toronto: Key Porter, 1994), 57.
7 Quoted in Jamie Swift, "New Democrats in Power, Part II: The Transition," *Kingston Whig-Standard Magazine*, 9 March 1991, 10.

8 Quoted in Walkom, *Rae Days*, 49.
9 Quoted in Gene Allen, "Ontario NDP Takes over October 1," *Globe and Mail*, 11 September 1990, A1.
10 *A Very British Coup* was a television drama about a decidedly leftist British government that was destroyed by the establishment through illegal and underhanded means with the connivance of the civil service.
11 Quoted in Swift, "New Democrats in Power," 8.
12 This tabulation includes all line deputies plus the secretary and deputy secretary to cabinet, but excludes various special advisors, heads of agencies, and others with deputy minister status.
13 The one, Hydro head Marc Eliesen, had served in senior political-bureaucratic positions in NDP governments in Manitoba and British Columbia as well as in Ottawa. Nonetheless, he had been appointed deputy minister of energy under the Liberals.
14 Walkom, *Rae Days*, 54.

Chapter 3: Transition Building Blocks
1 Andrew Heard, *Canadian Constitutional Conventions* (Toronto: Oxford University Press, 1991), 59.
2 Sharon Sutherland, "The Al-Mashat Affair: Administrative Accountability in Parliamentary Institutions," *Canadian Public Administration* 34, 4 (1991): 579.
3 There is some discussion about the extent to which the spoils system actually prevailed in Canada after Confederation. See J.E. Hodgetts, William McCloskey, Reginald Whitaker, and V. Seymour Wilson, *The Biography of an Institution: The Civil Service Commission of Canada, 1908-1967* (Montreal: McGill-Queen's University Press, 1972), 12-14.
4 Quoted ibid., 9.
5 Ibid., 8.
6 For a discussion of the emergence of the merit principle in Ontario, see J.E. Hodgetts, *From Arm's Length to Hands-on: The Formative Years of Ontario's Public Service 1867-1940* (Toronto: University of Toronto Press, 1995), 176-88, 209-13.
7 For a wide-ranging review of the political functions of patronage, both positive and negative, see the special issue (volume 22, Summer 1987) of the *Journal of Canadian Studies* on the subject.
8 See Allan Blakeney and Sandford Borins, *Political Management in Canada*, 2nd ed. (Toronto: University of Toronto Press, 1998), 99; and Howard Pawley and Lloyd Brown-John, "Transitions: The New Democrats in Manitoba," in *Taking Power: Managing Government Transitions*, ed. Donald J. Savoie (Toronto: Institute of Public Administration of Canada and Canadian Centre for Management Development, 1993), 169-71, 179. Blakeney notes that this may entail moving senior civil servants to other equally senior posts, rather than dismissing them.
9 Hugh Segal, "The Accountability of Public Servants," *Policy Options* (November/December 1981): 11-12.
10 See Reeves Haggan, "Patronage Observed," *Journal of Canadian Studies* 22 (Summer 1987): 184-91.
11 Quoted in David Zussman, "Walking the Tightrope: The Mulroney Government and the Public Service," in *How Ottawa Spends 1986-87: Tracking the Tories*, ed. Michael J. Prince (Toronto: Methuen, 1986), 255.
12 Thomas Walkom, "Harris Revolution Looking More Like a Restoration," *Toronto Star*, 15 June 1995, A29.
13 Thomas Walkom, *Rae Days: The Rise and Follies of the NDP* (Toronto: Key Porter, 1994), 68.
14 David Wolfe, "Queen's Park Policy-Making Systems," in *Revolution at Queen's Park: Essays on Governing Ontario*, ed. S.J.R. Noel (Halifax: Lorimer, 1997), 154.
15 Sutherland, "The Al-Mashat Affair."
16 The route by which events set precedents that may – or may not – be transformed into binding customs and conventions is illuminated in a small way in the diaries of André Laurendeau, kept during the time he was co-chair of the Royal Commission on Bilingualism and Biculturalism. At the beginning of the commission's work, Laurendeau travelled

across the country to meet all of the premiers to determine, among other things, whether they would present briefs to the commission. In Toronto he met Premier John Robarts, who stated clearly that the Ontario Government would not. Robarts's stated reason for this astonished Laurendeau: a sovereign government does not make submissions to the creature of another sovereign government. When Laurendeau met Premier Jean Lesage of Quebec, Lesage stated that he would not present a brief to the commission unless Ontario did, too. (André Laurendeau, *Journal tenu pendant la Commission royale d'enquête sur le bilinguisme et le biculturalisme* [Montreal: VLB Éditeur, 1990], 55, 59.) Twenty-five years later, when the Charest Committee of Parliament was holding hearings on the Meech Lake Accord, Quebec officials unwittingly offered Robarts's exact reason in explaining why Quebec would not appear before the federal body, while Premier David Peterson of Ontario went happily off to Ottawa to testify. (Personal communication.)

17 Edward E. Stewart, *Cabinet Government in Ontario: A View from Inside* (Halifax: Institute for Research in Public Policy, 1989), 49.
18 Joel D. Aberbach, Robert D. Putnam, and Bert A. Rockman, *Bureaucrats and Politicians in Western Democracies* (Cambridge: Harvard University Press, 1981), 5.
19 Donald Savoie, *Thatcher, Reagan, Mulroney: In Search of a New Bureaucracy* (Toronto: University of Toronto Press, 1994), 23.
20 Aberbach, Putnam, and Rockman, *Bureaucrats and Politicians*, 9, 241.
21 Ibid., 254
22 Ibid., 4.
23 Ibid., 6.
24 Stewart, *Cabinet Government in Ontario*, 49.
25 Aberbach, Putnam, and Rockman, *Bureaucrats and Politicians*, 242.
26 Ibid., 17-20.
27 Colin Campbell, "The Political Roles of Senior Government Officials in Advanced Democracies," *British Journal of Political Science* 18 (April 1988): 243.
28 John L. Manion and Cynthia Williams, "Transition Planning at the Federal Level in Canada," in *Taking Power*, ed. Savoie, 105.
29 Ibid., 100.
30 See, for example, Harold D. Clarke, Jane Jenson, Lawrence LeDuc, and Jon H. Pammett, *Absent Mandate: The Politics of Discontent in Canada* (Toronto: Gage, 1984, and subsequent editions); Richard Johnston, André Blais, Henry E. Brody, and Jean Crête, *Letting the People Decide: Dynamics of a Canadian Election* (Montreal: McGill-Queen's University Press, 1992).
31 Ontario Conservative Party, *The Common Sense Revolution* (May 1994), 5, 17.

Chapter 4: Bureaucratic Preparations

1 Bob Rae, *From Protest to Power: Personal Reflections of a Life in Politics* (Toronto: Viking, 1996), 129.
2 The volumes and the offices responsible for their preparation were: "Post Election Decisions and Procedures" (Cabinet Office); "Personal Information for the Premier Designate" (Cabinet Office); "Organization of Government and Ministries" (Cabinet Office/ministries); "Ontario's Finances" (Ministry of Finance); "Public Appointments" (Public Appointments Secretariat); "Critical Issues" (Cabinet Office/ministries); "Draft Ministers' Handbook" (Cabinet Office); "Cabinet Office and the Decision-Making System" (Cabinet Office).

Chapter 5: The Parties Prepare for Power

1 The winner was decided not on straight vote totals, but through a system in which votes were totalled by constituency and transformed into a certain number of "points." For a full discussion of the leadership selection process, see Peter Woolstencroft, "'Tories Kick Machine to Bits': Leadership Selection and the Ontario Progressive Conservative Party," in *Leaders and Parties in Canadian Politics: Experiences of the Provinces*, ed. Kenneth Carty, Lynda Erickson, and Donald E. Blake (Toronto: Harcourt Brace Jovanovich, 1992), 203-25.
2 David Lindsay, who became principal secretary to the premier, described the change in this way in a speech he made to the Public Affairs Association of Canada on 7 September 1995: "Not brokerage politics among the political elites at a convention, but genuine

grassroots democracy. On that Saturday afternoon the housewife from Peterborough had the same ballot as the bank president in Rosedale. The school teacher in Dryden had the same vote as the former premier from Brampton who cast the same ballot as the university student in Kingston and the farmer in Tillsonburg."
3 See, for example, David Lindsay's PAAC speech, ibid.
4 Morley Kells, "New Revolution, Old Imperialism," *Toronto Star*, 21 July 1995, A19.
5 See Christina Blizzard, *Right Turn: How the Tories Took Ontario* (Toronto: Dundurn Press, 1995), 10; and Peter Woolstencroft, "Reclaiming the 'Pink Palace': The Progressive Conservative Party Comes in from the Cold," in *The Government and Politics of Ontario*, 5th ed., ed. Graham White (Toronto: University of Toronto Press, 1997), 370-2.
6 The following account draws heavily on Woolstencroft, "Reclaiming the 'Pink Palace,'" 368-81, and John Ibbitson, *Promised Land: Inside the Mike Harris Revolution* (Toronto: Prentice-Hall, 1997), chapters 3-4.
7 Woolstencroft, "Reclaiming the 'Pink Palace,'" 373.
8 There is some confusion in the statement. Sometimes it speaks of there being three elements, sometimes four. When it refers to four, "building a safe and prosperous Ontario" appears both as the overarching commitment and as one of the elements.
9 Ibbitson, *Promised Land*, 63.
10 In the 30 January 1995 issue of *The Common Sense Revolution Update*, an occasional newsletter aimed at the party faithful but available to the public, a column profiling members of "Team Harris" noted that David Lindsay was co-chairing the "transition committee" with William Farlinger.
11 Interview with Lyn McLeod, 7 May 1997. Subsequent quotations in this chapter are taken from this interview. Our thanks to Ms. McLeod for agreeing to be interviewed on the record for this project.
12 McLeod interview.
13 A few minor elements of the briefing binder had not been finalized before the inevitability of the Tory win led to the shutdown of the transition process, and thus were never completed.
14 "The Liberal Approach to Organization, Management, and Decision-Making in the Government of Ontario," June 1995, 2 (reprinted as Appendix C, pp. 169-79).
15 "Generic Piece for Mandate Letter for Deputy Ministers" (draft), June 1995.
16 The following paragraphs are based in part on "The Liberal Approach to Organization, Management, and Decision-Making in the Government of Ontario" (June 1995) and on an undated draft memo to Lyn McLeod from members of the transition team on organizational and decision-making issues.
17 Curiously, the proposed starting point for enhancing the role of the government caucus in the legislative process was to be election of the speaker by secret ballot, despite the fact that towards the end of the Peterson government, the Assembly's *Standing Orders* had been amended to provide exactly that.

Chapter 6: Cycling into Saigon
1 Quoted in Christina Blizzard, *Right Turn: How the Tories Took Ontario* (Toronto: Dundurn Press, 1995), 131.
2 We recognize that the distinction between politics and policy, on the one hand, and management and organization, on the other hand, ultimately breaks down, but it remains a useful distinction in describing the transition process, and it is faithful to the way in which the participants defined their roles.
3 Of the dozen members of the official transition team, five remained in government, though only two left the private sector to join government (Eves, of course, had been an MPP, while Lindsay and Cowieson had worked for Harris in opposition). Mitch Patten, who had worked in Tory ministers' offices in the Davis-Miller years, was hired on as deputy principal secretary in the Premier's Office; soon after the Conservatives took office, Farlinger became chair of Ontario Hydro.
4 John Ibbitson, *Promised Land: Inside the Mike Harris Revolution* (Toronto: Prentice-Hall, 1997), 107.

5 MacNeil was a Davis-era political staffer; Ashworth was a key aide to David Peterson.
6 Ibbitson argues that many of the numerous political errors in the Tories' controversial Bill 26 in the fall and winter of 1995 and 1996 were attributable to inexperience and lack of capacity in the Premier's Office; *Promised Land*, 145-7.
7 Twenty of the Conservative MPPs had sat in the previous legislature; one, Morley Kells, had been an MPP in the Davis years but had lost his seat in the 1985 election.
8 Interview with Brenda Elliott, 18 June 1998.
9 Letter from David Lindsay to authors, 29 November 1996.
10 Within two years, three of those interviewed at the Park Plaza had left the government: Dicerni, Mottershead, and Taman; a fourth, Wolfson, followed suit a few months later.
11 Martin Mittelstaedt and James Rusk, "Harris Targets Top Mandarins," *Globe and Mail*, 13 June 1995, A1.
12 James Rusk, "Harris Sweeps Out NDP-aligned Bureaucrats," *Globe and Mail*, 28 June 1995.
13 David A. Wolfe, "Queen's Park Policy-Making Systems," in *Revolution at Queen's Park: Essays on Governing Ontario*, ed. S.J.R. Noel (Toronto: James Lorimer and Co., 1997), 153-4.
14 Two important pieces of evidence support the former interpretation: the early decision by the government to award a healthy salary increase to the Senior Management Group (the top 3 percent of the OPS) and nothing to those at lower levels, and the strong case to be made for the proposition that the government deliberately sought the massive (and first ever) strike by the Ontario Public Service Employees Union in the spring of 1996 (see Ibbitson, *Promised Land*, chapter 7).
15 Letter from George Boddington to Graham White, 26 June 1996.
16 Letter from Tom Clark, Acting Director, Minister's Staffing Unit, to job seeker, 18 July 1995.
17 Elliott interview.
18 Gordon Osbaldeston, "Dear Minister: An Open Letter to an Old Friend Who Has Just Been Appointed to the Federal Cabinet," *Policy Options* (June/July 1988): 3-11.
19 Interview with Bob Runciman, 18 June 1998.
20 We were told that the estimates tabled by the Conservatives were precisely those that had been prepared for the NDP during the previous spring.

Chapter 7: Not Politics but Good Government
1 This excludes a small number of deputy-level positions at large agencies and the deputy-level officials in the offices reporting to the legislature, such as the clerk of the House. The principal documentary sources for the data in this and the following paragraph are those most valuable research tools, the Ontario Government telephone directories. The fall/winter 1996-7 directory had a closing date of 27 August 1996 (fourteen months after the swearing-in); the 1998 directory had a closing date of 17 October 1997 (twenty-eight months after the swearing-in).
2 By this point only one of the original ministers had been dropped from cabinet and two others had been given new assignments. Other ministers had been added but, as non-originals, they and their staff are not included in these calculations. In terms of staff, "original" doesn't necessarily imply that they were in place at the very beginning, but that they were the first to hold their positions. The number of political staff varies because, at the baseline we chose in the fall of 1995, not all ministers had both policy advisors and communications assistants (though one minister had four policy staff).
3 For early analyses see the special issue of *Canada Watch* 7, 6 (1999), available on-line at www.robarts.yorku.ca, as well as Stephen Dale, *Lost in the Suburbs: A Political Travelogue* (Toronto: Stoddart, 1999).
4 Letter from David Lindsay to authors, 11 December 1996.
5 Letter from William Farlinger to David Cameron, 15 October 1996.
6 Chuck Rachlis, former director of policy and issues and coordinator of economic policy, Office of the Premier, speaking at a seminar on "The NDP in Power," University of Toronto Department of Political Science, 8 December 1995.
7 Leslie A. Pal, "'Thanks for the memories ...': Political Memoirs, Public Policy and the Political Imagination," *Canadian Public Policy* 14 (Winter 1988): 96.

Bibliography

Aberbach, Joel D., Robert D. Putnam, and Bert A. Rockman. *Bureaucrats and Politicians in Western Democracies.* Cambridge: Harvard University Press, 1981.
Allen, Gene. "Ontario NDP Takes Over October 1." *Globe and Mail,* 11 September 1990, A1.
Blakeney, Allan, and Sandford Borins. *Political Management in Canada,* 2nd ed. Toronto: University of Toronto Press, 1998.
Blizzard, Christina. *Right Turn: How the Tories Took Ontario.* Toronto: Dundurn Press, 1995.
Bourgault, Jacques, and Stéphane Dion. "Canadian Senior Civil Servants and Transitions in Government: The Whitehall Model Seen from Ottawa." *International Journal of Administrative Science* 56 (Fall 1990): 149-69.
–. "Governments Come and Go but What of Senior Public Servants? Canadian Deputy Ministers and Transitions in Power (1867-1987)." *Governance* 2 (1989): 125-51.
–. "Haute fonction publique et changement de gouvernement au Quebec: le cas des sous-ministres en titre (1976-1989)." *Revue québécoise de science politique* 19 (1991): 81-106.
–. "Managing Conflict in a Context of Government Change: Lessons from the Federal Government of Canada, 1984-1988." *International Journal of Conflict Management* 1 (October 1990): 375-95.
Bourgault, Jacques, and Patrick Nugent. "Les transitions de gouvernement et la théorie des conflits: Le cas de la transition de 1984 au gouvernement du Canada." *Canadian Journal of Administrative Sciences* 12 (March 1995): 15-26.
Campbell, Colin. "The Political Roles of Senior Government Officials in Advanced Democracies." *British Journal of Political Science* 18 (April 1988): 243-72.
Clarke, Harold D., Jane Jenson, Lawrence LeDuc, and Jon H. Pammett. *Absent Mandate: The Politics of Discontent in Canada.* Toronto: Gage, 1984.
Conway, Sean, John Reynolds, Lorne Nystrom, and Jacques Baril. "Interview." *Canadian Parliamentary Review* 21 (Summer 1998): 33-43.
Courchene, Thomas J., with Colin R. Telmer. *From Heartland to North American Region State: The Social, Fiscal and Federal Evolution of Ontario.* Toronto: University of Toronto Centre for Public Management, 1997.
Dale, Stephen. *Lost in the Suburbs: A Political Travelogue.* Toronto: Stoddart, 1999.
Ehring, George, and Wayne Roberts. *Giving Away a Miracle: Lost Dreams, Broken Promises and the Ontario NDP.* Oakville: Mosaic Press, 1993.
Gagnon, Georgette, and Dan Rath. *Not without Cause: David Peterson's Fall from Grace.* Toronto: HarperCollins, 1991.
Haggan, Reeves. "Patronage Observed." *Journal of Canadian Studies* 22 (Summer 1987): 184-91.
Heard, Andrew. *Canadian Constitutional Conventions.* Toronto: Oxford University Press, 1991.
Hodgetts, J.E. *From Arm's Length to Hands-on: The Formative Years of Ontario's Public Service 1867-1940.* Toronto: University of Toronto Press, 1995.

Hodgetts, J.E., William McCloskey, Reginald Whitaker, and V. Seymour Wilson. *The Biography of an Institution: The Civil Service Commission of Canada, 1908-1967.* Montreal: McGill-Queen's University Press, 1972.
Ibbitson, John. *Promised Land: Inside the Mike Harris Revolution.* Toronto: Prentice-Hall, 1997.
Johnston, Richard, André Blais, Henry E. Brody, and Jean Crête. *Letting the People Decide: Dynamics of a Canadian Election.* Montreal: McGill-Queen's University Press, 1992.
Kells, Morley. "New Revolution, Old Imperialism." *Toronto Star,* 21 July 1995, A19.
Laurendeau, André. *Journal tenu pendant la Commission royale d'enquête sur le bilinguisme et le biculturalisme.* Montreal: VLB Éditeur, 1990.
Loreto, Richard A. "Ontario." In *Getting the Pink Slip: Severances and Firings in the Senior Public Service,* ed. William A.W. Neilson, 45-65. Toronto: Institute of Public Administration of Canada, 1990.
Michelmann, Hans J., and Jeffrey S. Steeves. "The 1982 Transition in Power in Saskatchewan: The Progressive Conservatives and the Public Service." *Canadian Public Administration* 28, 1 (1985): 1-23.
Mittelstaedt, Martin, and James Rusk. "Harris Targets Top Mandarins." *Globe and Mail,* 13 June 1995, A1.
Monahan, Patrick. *Storming the Pink Palace: The NDP in Power – A Cautionary Tale.* Toronto: Lester Publishing, 1995.
Ontario Conservative Party. *The Common Sense Revolution.* May 1994.
Osbaldeston, Gordon. "Dear Minister: An Open Letter to an Old Friend Who Has Just Been Appointed to the Federal Cabinet." *Policy Options* (June-July 1988): 3-11.
Pal, Leslie A. "'Thanks for the memories ... ': Political Memoirs, Public Policy and the Political Imagination." *Canadian Public Policy* 14 (Winter 1988): 92-103.
Plasse, Micheline. "Les chefs de cabinet ministériel au Québec: la transition du gouvernement liberal au gouvernement péquiste (1976-1977)." *Canadian Journal of Political Science* 14 (June 1981): 309-35.
Rae, Bob. *From Protest to Power: Personal Reflections of a Life in Politics.* Toronto: Viking, 1996.
Rusk, James. "Harris Sweeps Out NDP-aligned Bureaucrats." *Globe and Mail,* 28 June 1995.
Savoie, Donald. *Thatcher, Reagan, Mulroney: In Search of a New Bureaucracy.* Toronto: University of Toronto Press, 1994.
Savoie, Donald J., ed. *Taking Power: Managing Government Transitions.* Toronto: Institute of Public Administration of Canada and Canadian Centre for Management Development, 1993.
Segal, Hugh. "The Accountability of Public Servants." *Policy Options* (November/December 1981): 11-12.
Speirs, Rosemary. *Out of the Blue: The Fall of the Tory Dynasty in Ontario.* Toronto: Macmillan, 1986.
Stewart, Edward E. *Cabinet Government in Ontario: A View from Inside.* Halifax: Institute for Research in Public Policy, 1989.
Sutherland, Sharon. "The Al-Mashat Affair: Administrative Accountability in Parliamentary Institutions." *Canadian Public Administration* 34, 4 (1991): 573-603.
Swift, Jamie. "New Democrats in Power, Part II: The Transition." *Kingston Whig-Standard Magazine,* 9 March 1991, 4-13.
Walkom, Thomas. "Harris Revolution Looking More Like a Restoration." *Toronto Star,* 15 June 1995, A29.
–. *Rae Days: The Rise and Follies of the NDP.* Toronto: Key Porter, 1994.
White, Graham. "Ontario." In *Canadian Annual Review of Politics and Public Affairs 1985,* ed. R.B. Byers, 259-304. Toronto: University of Toronto Press, 1988.
–, ed. *The Government and Politics of Ontario,* 5th ed. Toronto: University of Toronto Press, 1997.
Wolfe, David A. "Queen's Park Policy-Making Systems." In *Revolution at Queen's Park: Essays on Governing Ontario,* ed. S.J.R. Noel, 151-64. Toronto: James Lorimer and Co., 1997.

Woolstencroft, Peter. "'Tories Kick Machine to Bits': Leadership Selection and the Ontario Progressive Conservative Party." In *Leaders and Parties in Canadian Politics: Experiences of the Provinces,* ed. Kenneth Carty, Lynda Erickson, and Donald E. Blake, 203-25. Toronto: Harcourt Brace Jovanovich, 1992.

Zussman, David. "Walking the Tightrope: The Mulroney Government and the Public Service." In *How Ottawa Spends 1986-87: Tracking the Tories,* ed. Michael J. Prince, 250-82. Toronto: Methuen, 1986.

Index

Aboriginal Affairs Committee, 111
"Accord" (Liberal-NDP, 1985-7), 12, 19, 20, 89
"Agenda for People" (NDP, 1990), 19, 35
Agnew, David: attitude of public service towards, 63, 86; as cabinet secretary, 48; as member of NDP transition team, 27, 104; and organization of Cabinet Office, 38; post at Massey College, 104-5; praise for professionalism of, 86, 97; on priority of policy implementation, 74-5; replacement of, by Liberals, 64, 96-7, 105, 115; and study methodology, ix, xi; and transition planning, 1995, 60-2, 67, 146, 147
"Al-Mashat Affair," 49
Ashworth, Gordon, 20, 21, 26
Audit Committee, 111
Auto insurance, and NDP platform, 38

Bailey, Jim, 114
Bill 26, "omnibus bill," 141
Blakeney, Allan, 8, 28
Boddington, George, 83-4
Borins, Sandford, 8
Bradgate Group, 82
Britain, speed of government transition, 19
British Columbia, government transitions in, 8
Brzustowski, Thomas, 116
Burak, Rita, 104; appointment as cabinet secretary by Conservatives, 1995, 105; bureaucratic transition planning for 1999, 144; Cabinet Office appointments by, 110; and depoliticization of ministries, 118; expansion of deputy minister committees, 111; initial meeting with Conservative transition team, 104; as member of Conservative transition team, 105; and orientation of potential ministers, 114-15; as replacement for David Agnew, 115
Bureaucracy. *See* Public servants; Public service
Bureaucrats and Politicians in Western Democracies, 52
Business Climate Committee, 111

Cabinet: appointments, under Harris Conservative government, 108-9; collective responsibility, as parliamentary government principle, 41; committees, reduction under Harris government, 109, 110; committees, under Peterson Liberal government, 26; committees, under Rae NDP government, 38-9; consisting of small businessmen, under Harris government, 109; cuts to, under Harris government, 108; in Liberal restructuring plan for, 1995, 99; relationship with civil service, according to Harris, 118; secretary, importance of, 152; selection, as act of patronage, 45; structure and formation, Conservative anticipatory scenarios, 87; swearing in, of Harris government ministers, 124
Cabinet Office: appointments by Rita Burak, 110; bureaucratic transition planning for 1999, 66, 144-5; calendar of key events, for 1995 government transition, 66; communication with, under Harris government, 135-6; cuts

to, under Harris government, 110; first day after Conservative win, like "cycling into Saigon," 102; under Harris Conservative government, 118; in Liberal restructuring plan, 1995, 99; link with Premier's Office, 113; NDP memo to bureaucracy on caretaker nature of governance, during 1995 election, 68; under Peterson Liberal government, 26; under Rae NDP government, 26, 34, 37-9; restructuring of, by Harris Conservative government, 116
Campbell, Alistair, 82
Campbell, Colin, 53
Campbell, Tom, 82, 83, 84, 117
Caplan, Gerry, 37
Carman, Robert, 24
Charter of Rights and Freedoms, and public servants' political activities, 49
Chrétien, Jean, 14, 105
Civil service. *See* Public service
Civil Service Act, 43, 44
The Common Sense Revolution: and briefing documents for Conservative ministers, 115; contents, 82; development of, 81-2; as election platform, 82; not approved at party policy convention, 78; as plan for Conservative policy implementation, 82, 147; scrutiny by public, 76
Connell, Martin, 20, 84
Conservative Party: *See* Harris, Mike; Miller, Frank; Mulroney, Brian; Progressive Conservative government (Ontario) transition, 1995; Progressive Conservative Party (federal); Progressive Conservative Party (Ontario), pre-1990; Progressive Conservative Party (Ontario), under Harris
Constitutional negotiations, and opposition party briefings, 155
Conway, Sean, 22, 90
Cowieson, Barbara, 114

Decter, Michael, 28
DeLottinville, Peter, xi, 187-95
Deputy ministers: appointment of, by cabinet, 44; committees, expansion under Harris government, 111; importance of cabinet secretary position for, 152; management responsibilities of, according to William Farlinger, 116; meeting with opposition parties at Public Policy Forum, 102; and policymaking process, 51, 53; politicization of, by Rae NDP government, 44-9; relations with Harris Conservative government, 104, 141; relations with Rae NDP government, 120; role of, 44-5; speech by Harris on roles of public service and politicians, 118-19, 183-6; study of opposition election platforms, 1999, 146; transition planning, 1995, 68-73; turnover, under Harris government, 116, 141. *See also* Ministries; Public Policy Forum
Dicerni, Richard, xi, 96, 104, 127
Drew, George, 108

Economic conditions, during Rae NDP government, 13
Ehrenworth, Shelly, xi
Elections: and changes in government, in democratic countries, 6; platforms, and policy implementation, 56-9; and preparation for transition, 7. *See also* names of political parties
Elliott, Brenda: briefing by bureaucrats, 126, 127; as Environment and Energy minister, 109, 122; experience as proprietor of environmental products store, 109, 126; lack of large organization management experience, 126; ministry cuts by, 127; relationship with bureaucracy, 126-7; staff appointments by, 122
Elston, Murray, 14
Eves, Ernie: cabinet experience, 124; on efficiency of Conservative transition, 103-4; as member of Conservative transition team, 106; and orientation of MPPs, 113-14; presentation of "1995 Fiscal and Economic Statement," 134
Executive Development Committee, 111
Ezrin, Hershell, 21, 26

Family Responsibility Office, 128
Farlinger, William: briefing of Mike Harris during 1995 election campaign, 85; as chair of Ontario Hydro, 83, 84-5; as Conservative transition co-chair, 83, 106, 147; on effective transitions, 150; on importance of cabinet secretary, 152; on management responsibilities of deputy ministers, 116; and vetting of potential ministers, 114
Free trade, 57
Freedom House, 4
From Protest to Power, 60

Gourley, Michael: as deputy minister of Finance, 96, 105, 135; replacement of Jay Kaufman, 115
Government: and authority, 5; definition, 4; as distinct from the state, 5. *See also* Elections; Government transitions; Public servants; Public service; names of political parties
Government transitions: benefits of understanding, 10-11; and boundaries between politics and administration, 152; comparison of Canadian and US systems, 7-8; in constitutional systems, 3-6; depoliticization of, as key to improvement, 149; effective, attributes of, 73-4; effective, recommendations for, 153-9; exercises, and appearance of defeatism, 55-6; importance of clear platform and policies for, 150-1; literature on, 8; low interest in, among academics, 148; low priority of, in Canadian provincial political system, 148-9; party in power, effect on bureaucratic transition exercise, 151; and policy implementation, 38-9, 56-9; preparation for, 10, 38, 60-75; as problematic, 5, 159; and public service, 38, 139, 149; stages, 6-7; study methodology, ix-xi; successful, and subsequent term of office, 159; in unconstitutional systems, 5-7. *See also* Liberal government (Ontario) transition, 1985; Ministries; New Democratic government (Ontario) transition, 1990; Progressive Conservative government (Ontario) transition, 1995; Public service

Hampton, Howard, 143
Harnick, Charles, 128, 129
Harris, Mike: cabinet experience, 113, 124; election as leader of Ontario Conservatives, 77; importance of effective transition to, 146; meeting with Jean Chrétien, 105; meeting with Public Policy Forum representatives, 88; and *Mission '97*, 79-81; opponents' view of, 14; post-election meeting with Agnew regarding transition, 104; response to questions of feasibility and implementation, 85; riding of, Ministry of Solicitor General cuts in, 134; on roles of public service and politicians, 118-19, 183-6; self-portrayal as "tax fighter" in 1990 election, 79. *See also* Progressive Conservative government (Ontario) transition, 1995; Progressive Conservative Party (Ontario), under Harris
Hartt, Stanley, 84, 106
Herman, Thea, 116

Ibbitson, John, 14, 82, 109

Justice Committee, 111

Kaufman, Jay, 64, 105, 115
Kells, Morley, 78-9
Kirby, Michael, 21, 91
Kroeger, Arthur, 73-4

Lacey, Veronica, 96
Laughren, Floyd, 134
Legislation and Regulations Committee (of Cabinet), 110
Lewis, Stephen, 27, 28, 37
"The Liberal Approach to Organization, Management, and Decision-Making in the Government of Ontario," 94, 169-79
Liberal government (federal): election victory, 1993, 14; "Red Book" policy platform, 1994 and 1997, 15, 57-8; relationship with civil service, 46; transition exercises, under Trudeau in 1984, 55; transition style, after 1993 election, 92
Liberal government (Ontario) transition, 1985: and "Accord" with NDP, 12, 19, 20, 89; briefing material, 21, 23; cabinet, factors in selection, 22; cabinet Office, restructuring of, 26; compared with NDP 1990 transition, 17-20; conflict of interest, checking for, 20, 22; contact with outgoing Tories, 22; deputy ministers, reshuffling of, 25; economic conditions favouring, 19; effective, reasons for, 17-20; election victory, 1985, 12, 17, 19; lack of preparation for, 18; and legislature resumption, 21; Premier's Office, 26-7; and public service, establishing relations with, 23-5; restructuring of government departments, 25-7; staff recruiting, 20-2; swearing in ceremony, 21, 22-3; transition teams, and roles, 20-3
Liberal Party. *See* Liberal government (federal); Liberal government (Ontario) transition, 1985; Liberal Party (Ontario), under McGuinty; Liberal Party (Ontario), under McLeod; Liberal

Party (Ontario), under Peterson; McLeod, Lyn; Peterson, David
Liberal Party (Ontario), under McGuinty: recruiting and screening political staff, 1999, 143; transition planning in 1999, 143
Liberal Party (Ontario), under McLeod: as anticipated winner of 1995 election, 77; election loss to Tories, 1995, 14; as exhibiting "governing mindset," 150; lack of planning for minority government, 99-100; "The Liberal Approach to Organization, Management and Decision-Making in the Government of Ontario," 94, 169-79; and *The Liberal Plan for Canada* ("Red Book"), 15, 89; public service, plans for restructuring, 1995, 88-9, 95-7; staffing process, for potential positions, 97-8; transition planning, 1995, 90-9; transition planning, compared with Conservatives, 100-1
Liberal Party (Ontario), under Peterson: election loss to NDP, 1990, 12-13, 17; policies, lack of clear agenda, 1987-90, 12; style of government, compared with NDP and Tories, 18
The Liberal Plan for Canada ("Red Book"), 15, 89
Lieutenant governor, and preparation for government transition, 1995, 68
Lindsay, David: as Conservative transition co-chair, 83, 84-5, 106; interview with, xi; meeting with Agnew regarding transition, 104; as member of Bradgate Group, 82; and political staff orientation, 124; as principal secretary, 83, 112
Long, Tom: as Conservative campaign chair, 1995, 83; liaison with transition team, 84; as member of Bradgate Group, 82

McGuinty, Dalton, 143
McKeough, Darcy, 114
McLeod, Lyn: briefing papers of, xi; delegation of transition team to meet with Public Policy Forum, 88; interview with, xi; non-confrontational political philosophy, 14; as Ontario Liberal Party leader, 14; plan for restructuring government, 94-5; and transition planning, 1995, 89-90, 91. *See also* Liberal Party (Ontario), under McLeod
Major Transfers Committee, 111

Management Board, 38, 111
Management Board Committee (of Cabinet), 109, 110, 111
Management Board Secretariat, 116
Manitoba, government transitions in, 8
Meech Lake Accord, 13
Mendelson, Michael, 38, 64, 116
Miller, Frank, 12, 108, 113, 124
Ministers: briefing of, under Harris Conservative government, 69-71; briefing of, under Peterson Liberal government, 23; briefing of, under Rae NDP government, 31; cuts to, under Harris government, 127-8; dependency on relationship with civil service, 74; isolation of, under Harris government, 128; lack of contact with departing NDP ministers, 115; staff selection by, 122-3. *See also* Cabinet; Ministries
Ministries: briefing of new ministers, planning for, 69-71; fiscal and staff cuts to, 127-8, 134-5, 136; internal transition teams, 69; lack of planning for minority government, 73; lack of preparation for Conservative government, 124; Liberal restructuring plan, 1995, 98-9; transition preparations, 68-73. *See also* Deputy ministers; Ministers; Public service
Ministry of Community and Social Services, 116
Ministry of Culture, Tourism and Recreation, 110
Ministry of Economic Development and Trade, 110-11
Ministry of Education and Training, 136
Ministry of Finance, 67, 111
Ministry of Intergovernmental Affairs, 116, 128
Ministry of Labour, 116
Ministry of Natural Resources, 125, 136
Ministry of the Attorney General (MAG): briefings for new minister, 129-31; loss of revenue, due to removal of photo radar, 129; political staff, 130; responsibilities of, 128; transition activity, 128; transition difficulties, 131
Ministry of the Environment and Energy (MOEE): cuts by Harris government, 127-8; full-scale review, in anticipation of cuts, 72; Interim Waste Authority, 126, 127; lack of knowledgeable deputy minister, as problem, 127; Ontario Hydro, 125, 126, 127; political staff, 127; responsibilities of,

125; staff reductions, 136; transition period, 125. *See also* Elliott, Brenda
Ministry of the Solicitor General and Correctional Services (SolGen): appointment of Bob Runciman as minister, 131; appointment of new deputy minister, 132; briefings of minister and deputy minister, 132; cuts to, 133-4; implementation of policy agency, 133; relations with bureaucrats, 133; responsibilities, 131
Mission '97, 79-81, 167-8
Mogford, Mary, 88
Monitor (management consulting firm), 84-5
Morton, Desmond, 33
Mottershead, Margaret, 104
Mulroney, Brian, 46, 57. *See also* Progressive Conservative Party (federal)

Native Affairs Secretariat, 116
NDP. *See* New Democratic government (Ontario) transition, 1990; New Democratic Party (Ontario), under Hampton; New Democratic Party (Ontario), under Rae; Rae, Bob
New Brunswick, government transition planning, 10
New Democratic government (Ontario) transition, 1990: advisors, 28; and "Agenda for People," 19, 35; briefing, by civil servants, 34-5; cabinet committees, 38; Cabinet Office, role in policy and planning, 37, 38; cabinet selection, 30-1; campaign team as transition team, 27; comparison with Miller Conservative transition, 17-20; contact with outgoing Liberals, as limited, 27, 32; division of labour, and lack of delegation, 27-8; economic decline, as negative effect on, 19-20; lack of experience with large bureaucratic organizations, 28; lack of planning for, 17, 18, 150; legislature, resumption of, 33; ministers, seminar for, 31; MPPs, inexperience of, 19, 31-2; policies, as priority, 29, 31, 58; Premier's Office, 32-3, 37; and public service, politicization of, 44-9, 86; and public service, relations with, 17, 18, 31, 33-7, 120, 149; staff recruiting, 29-30; swearing in ceremony, 31; Throne Speech, 38; transition style, compared with Liberals, 17-20; tribalism of, 27
New Democratic Party. *See* New Democratic government (Ontario) transition, 1990; New Democratic Party (Ontario), under Hampton; New Democratic Party (Ontario) under Rae; Rae, Bob
New Democratic Party (Ontario), under Hampton, 142-3
New Democratic Party (Ontario), under Rae: "Accord" with Liberals (1985-87), 12, 19, 20, 89; "Agenda for People" (1990), 19, 35; cabinet committees, 109; election loss to Conservatives, 1995, 13-14, 15; election victory, 1990, 13-14, 17, 19, 79; ideology, and interventionist style of government, 18; management, neglect of, 30, 33; "The Ontario Budget Plan," as unapproved 1995 budget, 134; poll ratings in 1995, 77; style of government, compared with Liberals, 18; transition planning, before 1995 election, 60-2, 76 *See also* New Democratic government (Ontario) transition, 1990; Rae, Bob
Nixon, Robert, 90, 92
Noble, Leslie, 82, 83, 84
Noble, Michelle, 104
Non-profit housing, moratorium on, 137

Olympics (1996), Toronto bid for, 31, 66
Ontario: government transition, planning, 10; government transition, studies of, 8; Liberal election victory, 1985, 12; New Democratic election victory, 1990, 12-13; Progressive Conservative government, 1943-85, 11, 17; Tory election victory, 1995, 11, 16
Ontario Hydro: rate freeze, as Conservative policy, 126; as responsibility of Ministry of the Environment and Energy, 125
Opposition parties: adversarial role, and Question Period, 53; briefing documents given to, at Public Policy Forum, 161-6; and bureaucracy, recommendation for open relationship, 154-6; "governing mindset," importance of, 150; ignorance of government operations, 55; inclusion in transition planning process, 56; meeting with bureaucrats at Public Policy Forum, 102; meeting with Cabinet Office staff, and transition planning for 1999, 14; view of public service as allied with government, 54
OPS. *See* Public service
Osbaldeston, Gordon, 129

Pal, Leslie, 159
Parasiuk, Wilson, 28
Parliamentary system: and cabinet, collective responsibility of, 41; and ministerial responsibility, 42; public service, obligation to refrain from political involvement, 42; Question Period, as adversarial, 53
Pascal, Charles, 116, 127
Patronage: critique of Conservatives by Liberals, 18; elimination of, 43-4
Pawley, Howard, 28
Peterson, David: calling of 1990 election, 79; idea for transition teams, 20; preoccupation with constitutional matters, 12
Photo radar, removal of, 129, 136, 137, 140
Pitre, Karen: argument against inclusion of legislative commitments in "Red Book," 90-1; interview with, xi; as Liberal transition team coordinator, 90-2, 94; and transition planning in 1999, 143
Policy and Priorities Committee (of Cabinet), 109, 110, 136-7
Policy making: policy implementation, by incoming governments, 56-9; process, as collaboration between politicians and public service, 51-3; and public administration, 50, 51
Political Management in Canada, 8
Political parties: as governing agents, 139-40; ideology, and government transitions, 9; opposition, lack of contact with public service, 53-5; party discipline, 41; platforms, and policy implementation, 56-9; and transition planning, 156-7; underestimation of gulf between politics and public service, 51-2. *See also* Liberal Party; New Democratic Party; Politicians; Progressive Conservative Party
Politicians: compared with bureaucrats, 50-3; difference between political office and officeholder, in constitutional governments, 4, 5; importance of good relationship with civil service, 73-4, 159-60. *See also* Political parties
Politics. *See* Political parties; Politicians
Porter, Michael, 85
Power: and authority, 3; legitimacy of, 3; transfer, under constitutional governments, 3-4; transfer of, 3-4
Premier's Councils, 116

Premier's Office: under Harris Conservative government, 106, 110, 111-13, 123, 136-8; Liberal restructuring plan for, 1995, 99; under Peterson Liberal government, 26-7; under Rae New Democrat government, 32
Prichard, Rob, 114
Proctor, Rosemary, 116
Progressive Conservative government (Ontario) transition, 1995: Bill 26, "omnibus bill," 141; briefing material, 62-7, 115, 181-2; centralization of decision making, 137-8; conflict of interest issues, vetting MPPs for, 114; economic statements, in lieu of budget, 134-5; first day in Cabinet Office, like "cycling into Saigon," 102; fiscal cuts, 134-5, 137, 140-1; "governing mindset," 58-9; on government transitions, 150-1; lack of government experience, 151; legislature recall, timing of, 134; orientation programs for MPPs and ministers, 113-15; policies, underestimation of opposition to, 141; policy implementation, according to *The Common Sense Revolution*, 85, 134, 136; political staff, high turnover of, 141-2; political staff, hiring of, 121-3; Premier's Office, 106, 110, 111-13, 123, 136-8; and Public Policy Forum, 86, 87-8, 102, 161-6; and public service, relations with, 85-7, 104-5, 107-8, 120, 137, 147-8, 149; public service restructuring by, 110-11, 116; success of, vii, 16, 101, 146-7, 180; transition planning, compared with Liberals, 100-1; transition team, 83-8, 106-8, 180. *See also* Harris, Mike; Progressive Conservative Party (Ontario), under Harris
Progressive Conservative Party (federal), 79-81; "chiefs of staff" appointments, 9; election victory, 1984, 21, 84. *See also* Mulroney, Brian
Progressive Conservative Party (Ontario), pre-1990: cabinet size, 108; election loss to Liberals in 1985, 12, 17, 18; as governing party, 1943-85, 11; as government, 1943-85, 17; and public service, relations with, 46
Progressive Conservative Party (Ontario), under Harris: abolition of central office and paid staff, 78; and *The Common Sense Revolution* policy commitments, 15, 58-9, 81-2; corporate planning exercise, to correct party deficits, 79-81; election campaign, 1990, 79;

election victory, 1995, vii, 11, 16, 77, 102; election victory, 1999, 142; emphasis on policy implementation, 74-5; fundraising by, 80; leadership of Mike Harris, 14; and *Mission '97* statement, 79-81; and *New Directions* policy papers, 80; policy development process, 79-82; populism, and leader accountability to rank and file, 77-8; volunteers, increase in influence of Harris loyalists, 78. *See also* Harris, Mike; Progressive Conservative government (Ontario) transition, 1995

Public administration: and policy making, 50, 51. *See also* Public service

Public Guardian Trustee, 128

Public Policy Forum: on Agnew appointment as cabinet secretary, 86; briefing documents for opposition parties, xi, 161-6; meetings with Liberal and Conservative transition teams, 88, 144, 156; members' discussions with opposition parties, 86; on principles of public service, as content for Harris' speech to deputy ministers, 118

Public servants: appointments, and patronage issue, 43-4; Charter of Rights and Freedoms, and political activities of, 49; compared with politicians, 52-3; lack of job security, 49; loyalty to government, 54, 151-2; political activities of, 42, 47, 49; politicization of, 44-9; and preservation of status quo, 46-7; and "whistleblowing," 49. *See also* Deputy ministers; Public service

Public service: administrative professionalism of, 42; briefing documents, in anticipation of change of government, 62-8, 161-6; and change of governments, 1985 and 1990, 18; communication with Cabinet Office and Premier's Office, 135-6; "critical" issues, and presentation of personal projects, 66-7; decentralization, tradition of, 117; displacement fears, with new government, 9, 64; and elections, issues during, 55-6, 151-2; and government, relationship with, 50, 53-4; and implementation of government's political agenda, 42, 56-9, 89, 135-6; interests and constituencies among, 48-9; legislation concerning, 43, 44, 49; loyalty to government, 54, 62-8, 151-2; and merit principle, 42-4; non-partisan nature of, 43-4, 46, 147-8; and

opposition parties, lack of contact with, 53-5; and policy-making process, role in, 51-3; and politicians, importance of good relationship with, 118-19, 159-60; politicization of, 44-9, 86, 95; relations with Harris Conservative government, 85-7, 104-5, 107-8, 110-11, 116, 120, 137, 147-8, 149; relations with Peterson Liberal government, 23-5; relations with Rae NDP government, 17, 18, 31, 33-7, 44-9, 86, 117, 120, 149; restructuring of, under Conservatives, 116-20; as state's core of memory, 42, 70; transition planning, subversion of, 63, 65; transition planning by, 68-73, 144-7, 157-9; values and interests of, 152. *See also* Deputy ministers; Public administration; Public Policy Forum; Public servants

Public Service Act, 49

"Public Service Reform in Ontario: Key Messages for Party Leaders," 87-8

Quebec, 8, 10
Question Period, 53

Rae, Bob: and 1990 election, 12-13; on 1990 NDP transition, 60; appointment of NDP sympathizers to civil service, 47-8; Cabinet Office, and policy planning, 38; calling of 1995 election, 76; on professionalism of civil servants, 33; social skills, and negative relations with civil service, 120; support for transition planning, 1995, 60-1, 146, 147, 151

Rae Days, 48

"Red Book," 1994 and 1997, 15, 57-8, 89, 90-1

Richardson, Bob, 90

Robarts, John, 142

Rose, Jeff, 48, 64, 105, 116

Sanderson, Bill, 109

Saskatchewan, 8

"Saskatchewan Model" (NDP) of decision making, 37-8

Savoie, Donald, 8

Scott, Graham, 117

Scott, Ian, 114

Segal, Hugh, 45, 48

Smith, Brock, 117

Social Policy Committee, 111

State, as distinct from government of the day, 5

Sterling, Norm, 113, 128
Stewart, Ed, 24, 51, 53
Sutherland, Sharon, 42
Sweeney, John, 90, 91, 92

Taking Power: Managing Government Transitions, 8, 61, 84, 93
Taman, Larry, 104, 128
Thomas, Jim, 64, 116
"Tomorrow Project," 34
Tories: *See* Progressive Conservative Party
Transitions. *See* Government transitions
Treasury Board, 38, 111
Treasury Board Committee (of Cabinet), 109
Trudeau, Pierre, 57

Wage and price controls, 57
Walkom, Thomas, 48
Wedge, Grant, 116
Welfare rates, cuts in, 137, 140
Westminster "responsible government" model, and transitions, 7, 8, 41
Wilson, Ian, xi, 187-95
Wolfe, David, 117
Wolfson, Judith, 104
Women, in Harris cabinet, 109

Young, Bill, 82

Zizys, Tom, 91